Phil Tufnell: What Now?

Peter Hayter, who also collaborated with Phil Tufnell on his 1997/98 West Indies tour diary, *Postcards from the Beach*, has been cricket correspondent of the *Mail on Sunday* for the past ten years. Formerly football correspondent of *Sportsweek* magazine, Peter has written for the *Independent* and *Observer*. His other books include two bestselling collaborations with Ian Botham, the great all-rounder's autobiography and the more recent *Botham Report*, as well as *England's Cricket Heroes* and *Great Tests Recalled*. His lives with his wife and two children in Shropshire.

Phil Tufnell: What Now?

WITH PETER HAYTER

CollinsWillow
An Imprint of HarperCollinsPublishers

First published in 1999
by CollinsWillow
an imprint of HarperCollins*Publishers*
London

First published in paperback in 2000

© Phil Tufnell 1999

1 3 5 7 9 8 6 4 2

A CIP catalogue record for this book
is available from the British Library.

ISBN 0 00 218817 1

Printed and bound in Great Britain by Clays Ltd, St Ives plc.

The HarperCollins website address is www.**fire**and**water**.com

PICTURE CREDITS

All photographs supplied by Phil Tufnell
with the exception of the following:
P A News picture nos. 4, 30, 44; **Allsport** 5, 6, 10, 13, 14, 19, 20, 25,
27, 28, 29, 37 (photo), 41, 43, 45; **David Munden Photography** 7;
Graham Morris 8, 12, 18, 24, 26, 31, 34 (photo of Atherton), 38, 39,
46; **Patrick Eagar** 11, 17, 21, 22, 23, 40, 42; **News of the World** 15, 34
(cuttings); **National Pics** 16 (photo of Tufnell); **Stephen Lock** 16
(photo of McEvoy); **The Sun Newspaper** 35, 36 (cuttings);
© **Times Newspapers Limited**, 1997 37 (cutting).

Every effort has been made by the Publishers to contact the
copyright holders of the photographs used in this book.
We apologize for any omissions in this respect.

Career statistics courtesy of Wendy Wimbush

Contents

Acknowledgements

My thanks and love to Mum and Dad for everything; to my brother, Greg, for keeping an eye on me when he could; to Lisa and Poppy for helping me to extinguish the hellfire; to my colleagues, coaches, managers and minders in the England and Middlesex dressing rooms, and to Don Bennett, in particular, for trying to show me the right way even when I couldn't see it; and to Peter Hayter for his efforts in attempting to tie the ends together.

Phil Tufnell

To Mary, Max and Sophie, thanks for your support and patience; to Tom Whiting, Chris Stone and Christine Forrest, thanks for your industry. Many people helped in ways they don't know, but thanks specifically to Greg Tufnell, Linda Hurcombe, Angus Fraser and Samantha Richards. Finally, thanks to Phil Tufnell, whoever he is.

Peter Hayter

Introduction

You all know or have heard of those rare individuals who are supposed to make things happen. I'm one of those common or garden types that things happen to.

I've done a bit of the inspirational stuff in my time, I suppose. Wickets taken, Test matches won here and there with the ball and, for those who like their cricket laced with a sprinkling of comedy, cowardliness below and beneath the call of duty with the bat. And I like to think that in my scrapes with authority I have done my bit in standing up for the people who do not like being bossed about.

But so far, in the main, my life has been about dealing with whatever tomorrow brings, rather than planning it in advance.

Such a way of life has caused me plenty of strife over the years, and plenty of fun. They call me The Cat for an entirely different reason, namely being able to curl up for a nap any time, any place, anywhere, but curiosity has got the better of me sometimes – and we all know what curiosity killed.

In my time I've been arrested, spent a night in the cells on three separate occasions I can remember, and been hit over the head with a half brick by a man I sincerely believe wanted to kill me for my treatment of his daughter. I've been married twice, divorced once from a girl whose subsequent choice of employment was prostitution, and I've been accused of all sorts of antisocial activities with all sorts of materials, some of which I didn't even do. I've been fined by my cricketing bosses at England and Middlesex for a variety of real and supposed misdemeanours that ranged from kicking my England cap all over Vishakhapatnam to suffering an emotional breakdown that had me nutting the walls of my Perth hotel room and sent for observation in the local psychiatric hospital.

Some of you may think that these are not the activities normally associated with a gentleman cricketer and you may be right. I do know, however, that had it not been for the game of cricket I might well by now be six feet under.

The book you are about to read deals with the experiences that have shaped my life. I have tried not to draw many firm conclusions or employ deep analysis, although on occasions such unpleasantness has been unavoidable and I do crave your indulgence for that. I would also ask that should you come across any clues you think may be useful in explaining my story so far, please feel free to discuss them among yourselves, but try and keep them from my ears. I'm afraid I'm far too busy living my life to try and make sense of it.

Phil Tufnell

ONE

Waste the Roses

It would be difficult to imagine a more idyllic early childhood. A mum and dad who loved me, big brother Greg – very sensible, good at everything – to look up to and to look out for me. And sport, always sport. Dad, Alan, a third-generation silversmith who ran his own business round the corner from the tube station at the Angel, Islington, and Mum, Sylvia, were both mad about sport. Dad played a lot of football and I later learned that he and Mum used to cut rather a dash together down at Alexandra Palace as ice skaters. In the forties and fifties this was *the* thing to be doing, apparently, and they once competed in the equivalent of the British Championships. Must be where I get my unique ability to execute evasive manoeuvres against high-velocity projectiles aimed at my head. Tufnell skating on thin ice? I won't even go there.

Anyway, they were typical, driven, middle-of-the-twentieth-century Londoners. Deprived of most things during the Second World War, afterwards they fought like mad to get whatever and wherever they could. Dad banging out molten silver in sweatshop conditions and exceedingly good at it and Mum, the rock for me and the family, doing what mums did.

By the time I arrived on 29 April 1966, a lovely sunny spring day by all accounts, they had dragged themselves to the middle-class comfort of Hadley Wood, northern suburbs. Posh neighbourhood, very leafy, nice big house and good-size garden capable of being transformed into Lord's or Wembley, depending on the mood or the season.

Greg was four years older than me and also sports crazy. There were no such things as videos or playstations so, from the time I was able to run about, we seemed to spend our entire lives in the garden. Our parents were much more into a kickabout than those of Greg's mates, so a whole gang of them used to come round to our place all the time as well. The result was that, whereas all our neighbours had beautifully manicured lawns with lines that could cut paper and a reflection you could comb your hair in, the Tufnells were famous for having cultivated a patch of land that was a desert in summer and a swamp in winter. Which, of course, for us and our mates, was totally brilliant. To be honest, there were no complaints from Mum and Dad because they were out there with us most of the time, kicking or throwing balls. When the inevitable choice had to be made between the footballs that were damaging the roses or the roses whose thorns were puncturing the footballs, there was only one winner. The roses didn't stand a chance. There were about sixty bushes and Dad got rid of the lot. The Hadley Wood chainsaw rose massacre. I can still hear the whirring of the blades.

Football was the kiddy at first and Dad remains convinced that my earliest sporting influence was Rivelino of the great Brazilian side, led by Pele, that won the 1970 World Cup. As I would have been just over four at the time, I find this somewhat difficult to believe. But he insists that, having watched these gods at work on the telly, we would then go out and practise for hours, bending and swerving balls with both feet around imaginary defensive walls.

Then came cricket and an example of my old man's Heath Robinson tendencies. Although a good size, the garden was not quite long enough to accommodate my tearaway fast-bowler's run-up and a full-length pitch. In fact the run-up was rather a complicated affair. For some reason known only to myself, I would begin by doing a complete circuit of the summer house, then leap out through the leaves of a weeping willow tree, shouting some kind of war cry and, with an almost perfect action, would fling the ball as fast as I possibly could towards my intended victim. It was *Commando* magazine (*Hände hoch, Fritz!*) meets *The Ladybird Book of Cricket*. The problem was that the majority of deliveries arrived at their destination around head height. Fortunately the casualties were still light by the time Dad realized what was to do and stepped in.

He built this contraption that consisted of a free-standing frame, from the top of which he hung a recently past-it crêpe Suzette pan. Nothing if not thorough, he had worked out the correct trajectory for a good-length delivery and placed the pan in the centre of the target area. If I hit the pan, the ball was a good one – straight and on a length – and I'm sure that the kitchen utensil of uncertainty helped me in the long term.

There wasn't much evidence then of any sign of rebellion, although I think it was bubbling just beneath the surface. Greg is sure that, almost from day one, I had

11

a strange streak: defiant, but for no obvious reason – or should that be deviant? Undoubtedly Dad used to let us, and me in particular, get away with murder, and as time went on, Mum was the one putting her foot down. It was probably always in me to be contrary, though. Why do what you were told to, or even asked to, when you could do something else? You know the sort of thing. Mum says, 'Don't put your hand in the grill.' You say, 'Why not?' She says, 'It's hot and you will burn yourself,' and you just do it anyway. Competing with Greg for attention? I don't think so. Just naturally twisted, I guess. All that sort of business really began to emerge once I started school.

I never have got to the bottom of the three initials – Philip Clive Roderick. Perhaps my folks had read a book on etiquette, or something. As for the schooling, theirs had been interrupted by the war and they were always very strong on their children having the best available. Greg was a Highgate boy, and an outstanding pupil, so it made sense that they should try and get me in there as well. Sadly for our parents, that is where the similarity ended. Academically speaking I stood out all right, but rather in the way a third buttock would, as a useless appendage.

By the time I had moved to pre-prep school age a pattern had begun to emerge. If there was trouble, my gang would be in it, and I would be the mug at the front. I have absolutely no idea why; that was just the way I was. None of it was particularly serious, but Mum used to have to deal with quite a few irate parents during that period.

Even after I joined the junior school at Highgate, things didn't really improve. In fact, quite early in the piece I had my first taste of juvenile delinquency. The story of how I ended up in court at the ripe old age of eight is suitably bizarre. I had been selected to swim for the school at an away fixture, and when I got there I decided off the top of my head to swap events. I was good at the crawl, if I say so myself, and was expected to win that event. But I had always liked the look of the butterfly – all that splashing about looked the business – and chose this moment to inform the swimming master that this was the stroke I would be specializing in from now on.

When Dad picked me up from school he asked me how I had done, fully expecting to hear that I had won the crawl event. When I told him that my first attempt at a new stroke had ended with me very nearly drowning, he went spare. I stood my ground; he got angrier; and by the time we had reached the tube station at East Finchley we were in a full-scale shouting match. Dad stopped the car, ordered me out and marched me to the station where he bought me a ticket to High Barnet, a couple of stops down the Northern Line on the way home to Hadley Wood. He reasoned that by the time he picked me up from there a few minutes later, we would both have calmed down. He certainly had done and was ready to make peace, but unfortunately the mood did not last. When he arrived at the station he discovered I had been taken into custody for travelling without a valid ticket.

I did have a ticket, but I had mutilated it beyond recognition. The ticket collector would not listen to reason and we had to go to court the following Monday. At least the court appearance did teach me one thing – a measure of sceptisism regarding the law. Here was the choice: eight-year-old Highgate Prep Schoolboy Philip Tufnell, accused of not paying his tube fare, pleads 'not guilty'. The school is informed (disgrace and humiliation), the local paper tells the story and the defence of the case costs a bomb. Or eight-year-old Philip Tufnell pleads 'guilty', is delivered a lecture and a thick ear, a small fine is paid and no one is any the wiser. We cut a deal.

Throughout my life cricket has been the thing that has kept me together. Even at this early age that was the case. I was lucky in that I was at a school where people took the time and trouble, doubly lucky in as much as my achievements on the cricket field tended to overshadow my total lack of effort and interest in academic affairs. I was good at the game, and even now I was aware that there was more to it than bowling, batting and fielding. First rule of schoolboy bowling – get yourself put on to bowl at the end from which your teacher is umpiring. When it comes to close lbws and catches behind the wicket, a little helping finger here and there works wonders. And being captain of the side meant I had choice of ends. The umpire in question, Mr Kelland, was top drawer. A Henry Cooper look-alike, he had a unique way of expressing dissatisfaction if he felt you had sent down a particularly naff over, namely chucking the sweater and cap at you. It was Mr Kelland who recommended me for a trial with Middlesex. I didn't really know what this meant, to be honest. In fact the first time it was mentioned to me I broke down in tears. The fine had already been paid, for God's sake. What more did that ticket collector want from me?

But it was becoming clear to me now that cricket might be the ticket to greater things. After one school match in particular, Dad drove us home in a huge state of excitement. During the tea interval he had apparently had a conversation with the headmaster and a mate of his, who was an Oxford don. This bloke told my old man that he had seen me play before. He then intimated that even with the most moderate of results he could get me into the university. As things turned out, the city of dreaming spires is probably breathing a sigh of relief. But with three initials, Highgate, Oxford and Middlesex, how could I not have been captain of England?

The roller-coaster nature of my existence was also becoming more evident. Academically even now I was a complete waste of space. I was the kind of pupil that makes teachers become bus drivers. It was not that I was thick; in fact I was considered bright. I was just lazy and uninterested, and I'm afraid that as far as I was concerned teachers fell into two categories: those who could play sport, like Mr Kelland, and were therefore worthy of respect, and those who couldn't and were therefore tossers. There was nothing in between. Really, when I think back and look back to what I was then, I do get a slight cringing feeling.

Greg must have been doing his nut. He was all set up to be captain of the senior school, so I'm led to believe – good at games, good academically and a top bloke – then along came his oikish younger brother to put paid to all that. There were scrapes a-plenty, but the funny thing was that, so long as the cricket was going well, they were largely put down to high spirits. The trial with Middlesex was duly arranged and I won a place in the county Under-11s. Jack Robertson, a former county and Test player, and Gordon Jenkins, who ran the coaching at the Finchley indoor school, were suitably impressed and I was off and running.

Of the players selected I was the youngest by a year, now aged nine. The coaches told me they liked the fact that I hated giving my wicket away. During the intervening years, when my walk to the crease has been the signal for the groundsman to start up the heavy roller, I have often recalled those kind but misplaced words.

Apart from increasing tension between myself and the teachers at Highgate, mainly stemming from the fact that by now I was starting to become quite bolshie, things went pretty swimmingly. The next season Jack Robertson and Gordon Jenkins gave me the choice of going along in the same stream and captaining the Under-12s, or staying down with my age group and captaining them. I chose the latter as I didn't fancy the prospect of telling older boys what to do.

Then came the moment that changed my cricket forever. Jack and Gordon took me to one side and gently explained that, although I had plenty of pace, fast bowlers were ten a penny. A change of bowling, from quick to slow left-arm, they suggested, might be good for the team and for myself. At first I didn't fancy the idea at all. I loved charging in and trying to frighten the batsman out of his wits, and taking advice from people in positions of authority has never been one of my strong points, but they must have hit the right nerve somehow. I tried it. It worked. The ball landed and went boom and, of course, batsmen used to the usual medium-pace stuff didn't really have a clue how to play it. From then on, spinning was my game – and I found I was very successful at it, too.

The next momentous event to occur around this time was my first meeting with Jamie Sykes, a fellow Middlesex schoolboy cricketer who had recently moved from his East End roots and with whom I was to share a chequered future. Jamie was the star batsman in the 1979 Middlesex Under-13 side and I was the star bowler. He averaged around 200 while I took 30 wickets at 8.6. But we were partners off the field as well and I do not think it coincidental that after our second tour together – to the Midlands during which the odd curfew might have been ignored – my parents were told: 'Philip bowled very well, but that is the last time he comes on tour with us.' In fact they were right, but for reasons no one at this stage could possibly imagine.

It's hard for me to unravel the next period of my life with any certainty. The fact is that from this point on, until very nearly the present day, there were no two days alike and no two days of sanity. How did I come out the other side? The truth is I really don't know.

TWO

Pointless

By the time I was thirteen, I was a full-blown rebel without a clue. Punk rock was at the centre of the yoof culture and its creed – no future, no point, never mind the bollocks etc. – suited me fine. Granted, I had only just stopped talking like Aled Jones, but for a teenager naturally predisposed to sticking up two fingers to the world, nihilism seemed the perfect conduit for self-expression. School could naff off. Latin? Do me a favour. And cricket, what was that all about? I wanted a motorbike, not a Gray-Nicolls. I think my attitude towards school upset my parents most. After all, though it was never rammed down anyone's throat, it was quite clear that my old man had worked a million hours a week to earn the money to give me and Greg a proper education. Then when I got there, to the senior school at Highgate, I was intent on doing everything and anything I could to get out as quickly as possible. The bottom line was that I started to realize what fun you could have buggering about. I liked misbehaving. It was far more interesting than behaving. Sod off coppers, sod off teachers, sod off Mum, sod off Dad, sod the lot of you. What a lad I was!

I remember my state of mind quite vividly. It was as if I was testing the system, just seeing how far I had to go before I got a reaction. And that put my folks in a terrible position. Dad would probably say now that he should have been tougher, but he and Mum were both conscious of the possibility of pushing me further away. Given the mood I was in, had they taken a more confrontational stance, I might just have used that to justify fighting against them even harder. Punk in attitude, I started dressing the part too. Five rings in one ear, Mohican style haircut, Dad's dress-suit jacket several sizes too big for me, winkle-pickers or brothel-creepers depending on the mood, and up yours everybody. And what were the accompaniments to this lifestyle? Booze, fags, and whatever else me and my mates could lay our hands on. Was this fun, or what? Well, actually, my first experience of drink was anything but. It ended up with me arriving on the doorstep, ringing the bell and passing out, only to wake up in the middle of having my stomach pumped.

Anyway, I learned another lesson in the process. The birds loved it. I'm sorry, but in those days if you gave a teenage girl, especially the precious well-brought-up ones with loads of Daddy's lolly to spare, the choice between Tom Cruise and Johnny Rotten, it would be praise the Lord and pass the Antichrist. I started to get a reputation as a wild boy and I did my level best to live up to it. I realized I was the centre of attention and, what is more, I realized I loved it. I seemed to carry a lot more clout with people this way. Before, there had been a bit of respect because of the cricket and the football, but now this was big time.

I was your actual complete adolescent nightmare. And the more I acted the part the more I got carried away with it. What started off as just general larking about became much more serious. I took to bunking off at lunchtime to go drinking with a few of my mates. In those days we knew we could get served at a load of local pubs – and so we did. We had money. They served us. We got smashed on Pomagne and Woodpecker cider, and if we did finally get back to school in the afternoon, we spent the whole time taking the piss out of the teachers and being generally obnoxious. I revelled in it, but I was getting out of control. And inevitably, being a curious sort of cat, I went along with the dabbling in other substances. Nothing too hard at first, maybe the odd puff. But it didn't take long for some bright spark to imagine what fun it would be to introduce me to the joys of glue. Yum, yum. It was cheap, easily available and easy to use.

Looking back now, I shudder to think of what I was doing. It was nothing at all to be proud of, and thank God my parents never had a clue. But at the time the consequences of what I was doing never entered my head. It was a laugh, that was all. Greg reckons this was the time I really fell among the wrong crowd. Sure, I was hanging around with a gang of blokes and birds who were slightly older than me, riding motorbikes and getting up to all sorts, so there was a certain amount of peer pressure at work. But I'm not saying I was goaded into it. I just did it. Quite often, actually. Sometimes for a day at a time. I liked getting out of my head and going to a place where no one could touch me.

With things going from bad to worse at school, matters came to a head when I had a fight with an English teacher in class. Don't even remember his name. I walked into his class, late I presume, wearing the usual gear – the creepers on, one pink sock, one green sock, tartan bondage trousers, a shoestring tie and a spiky haircut. As I walked through the door, the teacher said to me: 'Turn the light on, please.' And I just looked at him as though he was shit on my shoe. He asked me again, I ignored him and eventually his patience snapped. He came over to my desk and booted me in the leg. As he turned to walk away, I picked up my sports bag, swung it and belted him around the head. I knocked him out. So I had what they called a 'misdemeanour with a teacher' against my name. And this was in my first term at senior school!

I started to become a bit paranoid as well. I could see through them; I could see their game. They wanted to keep me under control. They wanted to keep me under their tyranny. So I got stuck into it and decided that I was going to rebel against the establishment, against the teachers and everyone else in authority. I just abandoned the idea of getting an education. Had it not been so serious it would have been hilarious, and this time even my sporting prowess couldn't save me. I'd more or less given up cricket, and although I starred as a tricky left-winger for the same senior house football team as my brother, the school thought it was all over – and it very soon was.

As far as the story about me burning down the gym is concerned, I have no idea where that came from, but it stuck, and over the years I've seen no reason to deny it. Of course I didn't burn down the bloody gym. I may be a nutter but I'm not crazy. No, it was nothing so dramatic as that. I was kicked out because I was considered by the school to be unteachable, untouchable, unreachable. Just a bad lot. Can't say I blame them. I didn't give them too much to work with. They gave up the challenge and were probably right to do so. I remember the headmaster coming to the house to inform my folks that perhaps it would be in the best interests of Philip and the school if I did not return for the following term. Asked to leave, they called it. And what if I'd said no, I wonder? Who gave a rat's arse, anyway? Southgate Comprehensive was far more my current style.

In fact, by this time I couldn't give a toss about anything. I was completely into the lunacy and was so busy destroying myself that I barely noticed the change that had come over Mum. Looking back now I realize that she was becoming paler and losing weight, but at the time all I could think of was what I could get up to next.

Mum was ill for about three years, but I don't think I ever really understood what was going on until it was too late. She started to get ill almost as soon as I went to the senior school at Highgate. I did notice that this strong, vibrant, powerful woman was becoming a little less strong, vibrant and powerful but I didn't think too much of it at the time. For how long Mum and Dad shared the secret that she was dying I never knew, but she put a terrifically brave face on it. The way the information reached me was that Dad would tell Greg, who was seventeen or eighteen, and then Greg would pass on the news to me. Greg is still not sure how much we were actually told. Dad and Mum would have wanted to protect us from the worst news for as long as they could, I'm sure. So muggins just carried on as if nothing was wrong. My way of dealing with it, I suppose, was just to pretend it wasn't happening. So I went about my crusade against everything and everyone, happy to be in the dark.

It wasn't all totally grim, either. For long periods Mum was, well, pretty close to how Mum had always been. Very together, very much aware of how she wanted things to be. Increasingly pissed off with the behaviour of her younger son, I'm sure, but inclined to believe that this hairy layabout rebel would sort himself out in the end. My old man reacted a bit like me, although in a totally different way. He also refused to accept what he didn't want to, but his means of escape was his work. Instead of six days a week, now it was seven. Slowly the structure of our home life had started to become a bit more haphazard. But this suited me fine as I was rarely home anyway.

The first sign that Mum's condition was more than just tiredness came when she started to have some tests at the local hospital. These became more and more regular over a period of around six to twelve months and then one day she was due to have what we were told was a sort of routine operation. The next thing we knew, Greg and I were told that she had been taken from there to Bart's – something about the blood not clotting properly during the surgery. And that is when I remember Greg and I both sort of thinking that there was something not right about all this. We never communicated our fears to each other, nor did we talk to Mum and Dad about what was going on. None of us had ever been very expressive when it came to emotions. From the start our lives were about sport, football, cricket, training, achieve and get on with it. From an early age, if ever Greg or I was hurt playing, it was a matter of belt up, don't be a cry-baby. So when it came to dealing with something like this, I don't think either of us had the slightest idea how.

In any case, immediately after the scare at the hospital, Mum seemed to improve. But then she got worse and eventually Dad told us what was going on. Greg and I had come back from football one Sunday lunchtime and he sat us down at the dining room table. The words didn't come easy to him. He said he had something to tell us, that Mum was not well and that there was no real cure for what she had wrong with her. He mentioned the word leukaemia. I just sat there, either not comprehending or not wanting to. Greg seemed to understand better than me. Then Mum came in and told us that it was a case of fighting the disease and she was going to fight it, come what may.

I was stunned, really. I just sat there thinking to myself, what is this all about? Here's this woman, my mum, a kind, strong, lovely lady and she is dying and there is nothing anyone can do about it.

It took perhaps another eighteen months for my mother to die. As her condition became progressively worse, she first had to be moved around in a wheelchair, was in and out of hospital for blood transfusions, and then became completely bedridden, meanwhile getting obviously sicker and sicker and thinner to the point where she was almost like a skeleton. We watched her waste to nothing in front of our eyes, watched her slowly being eaten away. As far as normal life was concerned I blanked most of it out. Even if I had wanted to, I couldn't concentrate at school. I didn't see the point. I was just bumping from place to place. What are you lot to me? Nothing. My mum is everything to me and she is dying. Dad was just working and looking after her. He was up at the hospital twice a day, taking my mum in for complete blood transfusions – eight and a half pints in and eight and a half pints out. The house was empty and cold. On the odd occasion when she was able to come home, it was a case of you boys look after yourselves with a couple of steaks. What time did he have left to keep an eye on me?

And then one November day Mum's fight was over. Dad had gone to work and I was at home with her. I remember she called me into her room. I took her to the loo and back, but when I tried to lift her from the wheelchair back on to the bed, I couldn't lift her; I couldn't get her out of the wheelchair. So she said: 'It's all right, darling.' You know, 'Just leave me, leave me.' So I went and sat in my room and time passed and I remember watching Tottenham on the box. Later I heard my old man come home and the next thing I knew it was dark and there were lights flashing outside our house. I looked out of the window and saw an ambulance, with Mum being taken into it. I went to bed and didn't see Dad again until the next day, when I came back after Sunday football. He was there in the house and he just said: 'Your mum's dead now.' And that was that.

Looking back now, I suppose I was her blue-eyed boy. She was a very strong woman in as much as she always knew what she wanted. I know it pained her that I used to get into trouble so often, but I think also she appreciated and maybe admired the fact that I had enough spirit in me to be a bit of a rebel. She had a huge, kind heart. She was my rock, and the rock of the family. Apart from when I was totally out of order, she would always support me in everything I did.

I never really got over it, I don't think. You never do. What is certain is that my mum's death hardened my attitude. I hated the world and everything in it. No matter what anyone tried to tell me, my experience of life was that it was just not fair. So the concept of fairness or unfairness, of right or wrong, went out of the window. Whereas before I think I might have been sort of just playing at being a wild boy, now it was serious. Now I was the real deal. And I was determined to be it all the way.

THREE

Rebel

How did I react to Mum's death? I just gave it all away, I suppose. Decided to completely turn my back on everyone and everything.

I didn't have a clue what I was doing. All I was interested in was having a laugh with my mates, because the moment I stopped having a laugh with my mates, the thoughts of Mum became too much. I remember more or less the last chat I had with her; it was just a couple of days before she died and she sat me down and said to me that whatever happened I should be my own man. She said, 'Don't believe what all these other people say about you and tell you. They can judge you and put their rules on you, but they are nothing and they have no bearing on your life.' So when she died, I decided that no one was going to tell me what to do or how to live. And if that meant they were going to judge me, to say to me that I was a bad person or say my life was terrible, at least it would be my life – at least it would be a life. Because nothing was worse than being dead.

I had long since turned my back on school and had left the summer before she died. It had become a farce. I would sit there and listen to the teachers having a go at me, thinking to myself, 'I don't give a shit what you say about me or my results. I couldn't give a monkey's, because my mum is dying.'

Then I would start spoiling for fights. I would come into school for exams wearing a pair of tatty old jeans, knowing full well what the reaction would be. And I would be sent home or called in to see the headmaster. Again and again, until finally everyone realized that the whole thing had become pointless. So I went – with an O-level in Art and a head full of nothing but having a good time with my mates.

Girls, girls, girls. And motorbikes. And booze. And girls. If anyone had asked me to name my list of interests around this time, that would have been it. Cricket? No thanks. Who's got time for cricket, with girls, motorbikes and booze to deal with? And nipping down the kebab shop with your mates for an hour or two on the Galactic Invader?

Mum's death had left a great big hole in our family life. With Dad trying to find a new life for himself, and eventually a new companion, as it happened, he would be off and away at weekends, leaving Greg and myself the run of the house, the fridge and the drinks cabinet. From then on the Tufnell residence was the venue for some of the greatest parties Hadley Wood has ever seen.

Although the first version of the Mohican had gone, its replacement seemed to be equally popular with the ladies. The change had come about in dramatic circumstances, when, after a particularly hard day at work, Dad decided that enough was enough. Mumbling something indecipherable save for the words 'no son of mine', he came at me with eyes blazing. I turned and legged it up the stairs, but he kept on coming and caught me easily. Those who have tried to run upstairs wearing bondage trousers will appreciate why. My cries for help were studiously ignored by Greg, as was my being dragged collar first into the car for what turned out to be a short trip to the local barber. 'Shave off the bloody lot,' was the instruction, which was followed to the letter, leaving me as bald as a tub of lard.

This caused even more titillation for the opposite persuasion. Not that many of them needed that much persuading, as a matter of fact. Don't ask me why. Maybe it was the rebel tendency, maybe it was the four-bedroomed, largely unoccupied house (with the aforementioned fridge and drinks cabinet). Maybe it was the odd twenty quid here and there that my old man used to bung my way. Maybe it was the motorbike. Maybe it was the fact that the motorbike seemed to attract the boys in blue like bluebottles – on one occasion two of them appeared at our front door wanting to know if I was the young man fitting the description of the fiend who had been spotted churning up the grass courts at Hadley Wood Tennis Club (with my reputation?) – maybe it was my natural charm. Whatever the cause, the result was a comprehensive and challenging sex education programme. This was my kind of schooling and I couldn't get enough of the homework.

Then one day the snogging stopped and the other stuff began in earnest. Sandra was her name. The best-looking bird in my former school. I didn't have a clue, as it happens. One of my mates told me that she fancied me and I thought he was having a laugh. Turned out he was right. She did, we did and I was up and running.

It was about this time, I think, that I became aware of,

or possibly invented, the voices in my head. Nothing too sinister, no 'Son of Sam' stuff here. Rather that whenever a choice had to be made between doing the right thing and doing the thing I wanted to do because it would be fun and knickers to the rest of the world, the voices would start up. It was almost as if I had on my shoulders an angel and a devil. 'Philip, think about what you are doing. You know you shouldn't,' would be the advice in one ear, and in the other, 'Philip, think about what you are doing. You know you shouldn't. Go on my suuuun…'

It is my shameful duty to report that the angel had a pretty poor strike-rate. And so my attitude changed from hating the world and all its ways to exploring new ways of having the most fun I could. Inevitably, away from the gymnasia of lust, this spirit of free enterprise led to shady scenes and more uncomfortable moments with the law, mainly regarding the subject of motorbikes.

The group I was knocking about with were all a few years my senior and, strictly speaking, I was not actually old enough to drive myself. After playing around on other people's machines, I finally managed to acquire a set of wheels of which I was inordinately proud. Chatting to some bloke in the Kentucky Fried Chicken in Southgate one night, I was presented with an offer I couldn't refuse. He was willing to sell me his CZ50, plus helmet, for the princely sum of £10. What a mug; he must have been born yesterday. Anyway me and my mate tinkered around with it for a while and actually managed to get it working. The helmet didn't appear to be in great nick, it has to be said, but I couldn't see the helmet for looking, having been blinded by the light emanating from this cross between a Harley-Davidson and Triumph Bonneville.

I invited a mate out for a maiden voyage, down to

Barnet. Within a very few moments, I realized we had company. When the policeman pulled us over, the smirk on his face suggested he was about to take a great deal of pleasure from his work. After establishing that I was driving under-age, he then asked a few questions about the machine, such as 'Are you aware that this bike has no suspension?' and 'Why do the bolts have no nuts?' Just for good measure he gave it a kick, an action that led to a reaction we had not expected. The bike quite literally fell to pieces before our eyes.

Ah yes, the helmet. Well, he didn't kick the helmet, just sort of gave it a tap, really. It shattered into little pieces like an Easter egg. This might have been natural wear and tear, of course, but on closer inspection was more probably due to the fact that the bloke who sold it to me had painted over the cracks with black emulsion.

Once that dream machine had died, I renewed my efforts to persuade my old man that what I really, really needed to sort myself out was a proper bike. In pursuit of a machine to call my own, I made his life a complete misery. Blinkered by the selfish desire to get what I wanted at all costs, I behaved like a total prat at home and Dad, unsure of how to deal with my obsession and my unruliness, and still reeling from Mum's death, finally gave in to my demands. Needless to say, within months of my being bought a brand new Suzuki, the obsession was out of my system, for good. The Suzuki was swapped for someone else's Kawasaki, and then, for reasons I cannot recall, for another heap of junk that ended its life rotting in our garage.

Greg says that my problem at this stage was not that I was streetwise, but that I was the complete opposite. If the gun was loaded and some sucker was required to fire it, I would be the sucker. That didn't quite extend to the weekend punch-ups against rival gangs, chiefly because although I was always right behind the lads, it was a case of as far behind as I could get.

Until this point, the odd brush with the rozzers notwithstanding, most of my misdemeanours had been pretty trivial. But as the initial buzz of mucking about began to wear off, the part played by the booze started to grow. Still under age, I spent far too much time draining my old man's Scotch or pestering people in pubs until they bought me drinks. Then the parties started to get a little out of hand. As I've said, I had always hung about with a slightly older crowd, and now an even older and more sinister group started turning up. And they brought a rather more exotic brand of materials with them. Being an inquisitive sort, of course, I had my share.

I always felt that I was going to be okay. I never thought I would end up being one of those wrecks you find lying in the gutter jacking up, or dead. I saw some of my mates who I felt might struggle, that's for sure, and of course I enjoyed being bad to the full. But I always felt I would be the one who would get through. Then again, I suppose the cemeteries are full of those who have said exactly the same thing. I thought I was immortal. Don't they all?

Greg has a slightly different perspective on things. He told me recently that, had I kept going the way I had been, he personally believes I wouldn't have survived. He believes I would have been trapped in a downward spiral, progressively doing worse things. Banged up or bashed up, is how he puts it. Greg is generally right about most things.

It couldn't last, of course, and it didn't.

The big problem facing me now was what I should do for a living. I wasn't too overjoyed at the prospect of going to work for my old man in the silversmith trade, but to be honest I wasn't exactly fighting off the captains of industry either, and – not that it had ever seriously been thought of as a career – cricket had long been forgotten.

So I went down with Dad to his place at the Angel one morning and he set me to work. I had a rough idea of what to do from having watched him. Banging out, soldering, silver plating, polishing. I was a good hammerer, as a matter of fact, but it didn't take a genius to work out that I wouldn't hack it in the profession. It was only while working in this place that I fully realized what my old man had gone through all those years. It was hot, the fumes were pretty filthy and it was bloody hard work. Needless to say, not the life for me.

We thought again. A string of odd jobs were tried and I was found hopelessly wanting. Perhaps the most glamorous was working as a film extra. Job description: wander about a bit and don't look at the camera, and, let's be honest, how can you fail? I was fine at the wandering about bit, but it was when I decided to put my acting skills to use in another way that my fast train to Hollywood left the rails. The method of payment was straightforward. During the day's filming you were given a voucher which you later exchanged for your pay packet. One day I happened to chance upon a book containing three unused vouchers. Man of a thousand faces, I do not think. The first two disguises worked – i.e. sunglasses on, jacket collar turned up, then sunglasses off, jacket collar turned down – but the third signalled the final curtain, when I became hopelessly confused and forgot whether the sunglasses should be on or off and the collar up or down and walked in looking exactly the same as I had some ten minutes previously.

So there I was, looking for gainful employment with a curriculum vitae which read something like this: Philip Clive Roderick Tufnell. Education: Highgate School – expelled. Southgate Comprehensive – all but expelled. Qualifications: one O-level, Art. Work experience: a few weeks banging and hammering in old man's silversmith's workshop (not cut out for it) and former film extra (asked to leave following the rumbling of a pathetically amateurish attempt at criminal fraud). Hobbies: drinking, running around with my mates, the opposite sex, and getting into strife. Used to play cricket and football. Second prize school swimming gala, aged nine.

By this time Dad was all set to sell up the house and the business and move to his new life in Gloucestershire. He bought me a flat in Barnet near to where Greg was now living. As for my future, there seemed nothing for it but to have a crack at cricket. Looking back now, getting involved with the game again was almost certainly my salvation. There were scrapes a-plenty and from time to time my career has hung by the thinnest of threads. But where would I be now without it? In the considered opinion of many, either an institutionalized 'victim of society' or six feet under.

It was all down to my old man. After having persuaded me to have another go, he phoned up my old club, Finchley, explained the situation and asked them to give me a game in order to try and rekindle my interest. They did, selecting me for their fifth eleven for a match on some horrible park pitch at the back of beyond. I spent all afternoon stuck on the boundary, watching an assortment of odds and sods serve up cafeteria bowling while the opposition racked up around 300 for two. This was a good idea. Finally I was thrown the ball to send down the last couple of overs of the innings. Dad, who had been there pacing up and down in increasing frustration, wrote a letter to the club that night, thanking them for their help but announcing my official resignation. He explained: 'I do not want my son playing for a team whose bowling attack is decided on weight.' A couple of phone calls later, I was set up to join Southgate instead.

The next step – and this I only took after more cajoling from my old man – was to take part as a playing guinea pig in a clinic for local cricket coaches, to be run by Les Lenham, the former Sussex player who was now one of the foremost coaches in the country. I knew most of the boys there from my days with the Under-11s and so forth, and I also knew only too well one of the coaches in particular – the man whose bad report over that tour of the Midlands four years earlier had scuppered my chances of receiving an age group county cap. As the day wore on, it became clear that Les was not impressed by the standard of the coaching that the boys had been exposed to. Some of the bowling actions were extraordinary, like watching a reflection in one of those fairground mirrors, and the results were pretty shocking. The batting was not much better. Then at the end of the evening, in order to prove his point to the coaches, he selected five bowlers and asked us to bowl to his instructions. I was the last to go. 'Now, son,' he said, 'I want you to bowl the first ball on middle stump, the second between middle and off, and the third on off stump. We are trying to lure the batsman across his crease without him knowing it.' I duly completed the job, to order. Lenham turned to the other coaches and said, 'Thank goodness there is someone here who seems to have learnt something from somewhere. And he hasn't played for three years!'

Encouraged by this, soon afterwards I signed up for some coaching at the MCC indoor nets at Lord's and, after this seemed to go okay, it was decided that I should take the trials for the next year's induction into the Lord's groundstaff. Luckily, my old ally from the Middlesex colts, Gordon Jenkins, was now on the MCC coaching staff, and there was hope, too, in the fact that the head coach, Don Wilson, was a former left-arm spinner with Yorkshire and England. What also spurred me on was a meeting with my old partner in crime, Jamie Sykes. Jamie was no less lary than he had ever been in the old days, but while I had been busy disappearing down the plughole, he had managed to do well enough to be taken on to the groundstaff. The thought of renewing our dangerous liaison was a massive incentive to try to impress.

Things progressed reasonably smoothly when I won an MCC Young Taverners' award. John Hampshire, another ex-Yorkshire and England player and now a Test umpire, was the adjudicator and apparently, at one stage during the competition, he turned to one of the coaches and said: 'This boy will play for England one day.' Good job I didn't hear him. I might have freaked completely.

When the day of the final groundstaff trials arrived, however, I woke up with a stinking headache, nose running like a jammed tap, and flu. I felt like death, I bowled even worse and within days the letter arrived from Lord's telling me that they would not be taking me on. They had plumped instead for a lad named Keith Medlycott.

Now, had that rejection occurred at the time when I was busy saying f*** off to the world, it might well have been the end of the matter. As it was, I was genuinely disappointed that, for the first time in my life, people in cricket had decided I was not good enough. That was a shock. I may have been an identikit adolescent basket-case, but no one was going to tell me I couldn't play cricket.

A challenge had been presented, and for the first time in a good few years, I was in the right frame of mind to take it on. Perversely, I had decided that my way back into the reckoning was the abandonment of left-arm spin. If they didn't want one of those, I reasoned, I was going back to bowling fast and knocking a few heads. The results, as anyone who witnessed my efforts in the nets at Southgate CC around this time would testify, were distinctly ordinary. Finally, just prior to the start of the summer of 1984 and in sheer desperation, Dad rang up Gordon Jenkins and asked if they could meet for a chat.

Dad has always had nearly as much of a problem with figures in authority as I have, but Gordon was different. Both of us felt that he had always been on my side. Dad went to Lord's and apprised him of certain facts. I was becoming a bit of a rascal, he told him, running around with the wrong sort, getting into trouble. Dad was worried that I would end up completing the mission of self-destruction I seemed to have identified as an achievable ambition. Advice was all my old man was after, I'm sure, but it just so happened that luck was about to play its part.

That very day, Surrey had decided they wanted to sign Medlycott on a full-time contract. So MCC had a vacancy on their groundstaff for a left-arm spinner. Gordon suggested that if I could come down the following day, he would try and persuade Don to give me another trial. As they parted, Gordon urged Dad, 'Make sure Phil gets his mop trimmed and looks smart. Don hates scruffy buggers.'

Dad tried his best, he really did. Yet another haircut was arranged. Farewell Adam Ant, welcome David Bloody Niven. Up at the crack next morning, he stood over me while I attempted to squeeze myself into the uniform of the school I had only recently been asked to leave. Then it was, 'Now listen, Philip, get down there and mind your ps and qs and for God's sake don't upset anyone....'

Of course, as soon as he left for work off came the jacket and tie and back on with the gear; ripped jeans, winkle-pickers, the lot. I turned up a little nervous but the first bloke I clapped eyes on was Phil DeFreitas with his great big Afro hair looking like Jimi Hendrix, also wearing jeans and a T-shirt and I thought he'll do for me. We got chatting, before we knew it time had drifted by and suddenly I realized we were late for clocking on.

Sprinting through the Long Room and up the stairs we arrived at the meeting point, the visitors' dressing room, about twenty minutes later than we were supposed to have done, barged open the doors, crashed into the room and collapsed in a heap. We got up to see all these blokes with their Middlesex Under-19 blazers, ties, grey flannels and shiny black shoes you could eat your dinner off. Don Wilson took one look at us and enquired politely, 'Who the fookin' 'ell are you?'

It was the spring of 1984 and I had arrived.

FOUR

Headbanger

Life on the groundstaff was a real hoot. Aside from Jamie, there were other good lads in the mix and £60 a week in the pocket. For the first time in my life I actually looked forward to the prospect of getting up and going to work. If you could call it work, that is.

The deal was that you would play club cricket at the weekends, in my case for Southgate in the Middlesex League, then during the week it was practising, bowling at the members, or playing for the groundstaff against clubs or county second elevens and the like. And, after that initial fracas with Wilson, I soon discovered how fortunate I was to have him as a coach.

Having been away from playing the game for so long, my all-round game had gone to the dogs. My batting was a joke and, despite all the efforts of the coaches, destined to be a long-running one, while my fielding was a little, shall we say, rusty. In fact the only thing I could do was run up and bowl the ball. Then again, I knew how to bowl the ball but I hadn't a clue how to bowl an over. In terms of the skills, techniques and instincts required to actually play a game of cricket, I was about as 'match-fit' as a saveloy. And this is where Don came in.

From the outside it must have been like watching one of those corny American sports films. After having accidentally killed a spectator with the home run hit to win the World Series, the hero, played by Kevin Costner or Charlie Sheen or someone, gives up the game and hits the bottle. Ten years on, he is persuaded out of retirement by a fan who remembers him at his peak and cannot bear to see what he is doing to himself. 'You gotta be kidding,' says the hero. 'I haven't hit a ball for ten years. I'm washed up. It's over. Over. Leave me alone, godammit.' But the fan won't take no for an answer. Cue Tufnell and Wilson. And the recommencement of my cricketing education.

I think he and I both understood that my ability to bowl a ball that landed in the correct area and spun away from the right-handed batsman was the least of our worries. It was the rest of the package that needed to be addressed.

For instance, I was and always have been hopeless at dealing with the prospect, possibility or fact of failure. It was always someone else's fault: the batsman was lucky or a cheat, the fielders were not trying, the umpire was blind, deaf, mad or all three. And because I hadn't been brought up in the cricketing environment that teaches you certain things about how the game is played, my etiquette was non-existent. If some bastard came down the track and hit me for four, it was all I could do to stop myself walking down the track and chinning him. To be honest, I never really lost that sort of innate hatred of batsmen. To me they were the over protected poncy poufs who had everything their own way. Benefit of the doubt to the sodding batsman? Why? Why not give the benefit of the doubt to the poor bloody bowler, for a change?

I was possessed also of a natural fast bowler's aggression. But whereas a fast bowler could let some of it loose by bowling a bouncer or just faster, us twirlymen are forced to keep it bottled up. Failure to do so caused me an awful lot of problems in the years to come.

While Don understood that my time away from the game meant that I was nowhere near as cricket-wise as the rest of my colleagues, he recognized some semblance of talent still in there somewhere and resolved to help drag it out. It must have been in my favour that he was a fellow slow left-armer as we are all, of course, by definition, stark staring mad. As for the specifics, what Don taught me was that to win the battle on the field you had to win it in the mind. Words like patience, stealth and subtlety started to creep into the conversation. Words I was about as accustomed to as Sunday School, rambling and flower-pressing. Slowly it dawned on me that he might have a point. If anyone else but Don had tried to teach me, it probably wouldn't have worked. My irrational but heartfelt hatred of figures in authority would have seen to that. But he got through to me and, slowly but surely, the learning started to pay off.

I was still living it up away from the cricket, of course, and by this time I had progressed from beaten up old piles of junk to an ancient and rather unique Volvo saloon. What made it so special was that it housed on the back seat the two biggest speakers in the known universe. Monsters, they were, each as big as a fridge. I might have been wearing my MCC blazer at work, but after hours the hits just kept on coming, as did the birds. Then, quite unexpectedly and out of the blue, I met the girl who was to become the first Mrs Phil Tufnell.

One of the jobs we groundstaff boys were detailed to do

was running the scoreboxes on match days, putting up the numbers, making sure they added up. On the fateful day, I was working in scorebox No 2 during a Test match at Lord's. Don't ask me who England were playing, but during my lunch break I was strolling around the back of the stands when I caught sight of this rather splendid-looking blonde. The next thing I knew I was asking her if she wanted to come up and see my scorings. She duly paid a visit and the rest started to become history quite soon afterwards. More of which anon.

First, there was the 1984–85 England Young Cricketers' tour to West Indies to contend with. Talk about keys to the candy store. Me and Jamie and Daffy DeFreitas and the rest of the boys, flown out to the Caribbean for an all-expenses paid junket. With our reputation? How I was ever again selected to represent any team on an overseas tour remains one of the great unsolved mysteries.

We were still in the days of the anti-apartheid sporting boycott and the itinerary was buggered about after three of the proposed venues – Antigua, Trinidad and Guyana – refused to admit four of the players – Jonathan Addison, Steve Andrew, Neil Burns and Gary Palmer – who had played cricket in South Africa. So the cricket was restricted to games in Barbados, St Lucia and Jamaica, and most of the St Lucian leg of the tour was washed out. Oh dear, oh dear, oh dear.

Wisden's rather gentle description was as follows: 'The tourists ... found it difficult to gain any real momentum and this, allied to the fact that West Indies Young Cricketers were particularly strong, especially in fast bowling, meant that in cricketing terms the tour was not a great success. However, the English players returned as wiser cricketers.'

That was one way of looking at it. My recollection is that, from the moment we arrived, it was more or less a full-scale riot. It must have been a nightmare for Bob Willis and Bob Cottam, the management team. On the day we touched down, we trolled up to this guest house in Barbados, put our bags down in the room, then hacked off to a bar called the Carlisle Club (now known as the Harbour Lights) and it was all on. For three days I didn't see the right side of seven o'clock in the morning, and even if I had done I wouldn't have recognized it. As a result, the management enforced the quickest curfew in touring history and, as it turned out, the least effective. If the management fined a player for being out at midnight, we fined each other for being in by then.

As for the cricket, I was in one of my most grown-up moods. I simply wasn't interested in practice, or nets, or fielding, or batting or any of that malarkey. It was bowling in the middle or nothing at all, and it wasn't long before I was hauled in to see Willis and told that I wasn't concentrating enough. Well, that depends on what I was supposed to have been concentrating on. Among the misdemeanours were such heinous crimes as sunbathing while we were batting and generally being a nuisance. Fair cop, I suppose, and although I played in one of the 'Test' matches against guys like Jimmy Adams and Cool Carl Hooper, I soon found that my opportunities were becoming fewer and farther between.

Years later, I spoke to Cottam about the tour. 'From the point of view of discipline, you and a few others were the worst group of layabouts I have ever had the misfortune to work with. Bloody headbangers,' was his assessment. Get off the fence, Bob.

'You could bowl all right', he told me, 'but we should

have sent you home within the first week. If we had done, maybe you wouldn't have had all those problems later on.' In hindsight, Bob might well have had a point. But there and then, all I was interested in was having the time of my life. In other circumstances my performance on tour might have been the beginning and end of the whole matter. It is certainly true that players have been cast adrift for less. But, quite unbeknown to me, fate and Philippe Edmonds were about to intervene on my behalf.

For the best part of the previous decade, Middlesex had been pre-eminent in county cricket. Their dominance had begun in 1976, when they won their first outright Championship since 1947. They shared the title the following season, but won it outright again in 1980 and 1982 and were about to win it again in 1985. They had also, by the way, won the NatWest Trophy/Gillette Cup in 1977, 1980 and 1984 and the Benson and Hedges Cup in 1983.

One of the secrets of their continued success was that they knew when individual players needed to be eased out, and they tried to make sure they had ready-made replacements when the time came. The spin partnership between John Emburey (off-spin) and Edmonds (slow left-arm) had been a vital part of the club's success, but things were changing. Edmonds was nearing the time when his outside commitments – work in the city and in the media – began to drag him away from first-class cricket. Middlesex recognized this and started looking around. During that 1985 summer, on the advice of Don Wilson, they started looking around at me. As things turned out, they did well to spot me.

You were never exactly told when one of the county clubs was going to be watching you but word soon got round. And it was *en route* for an MCC match against Surrey that word reached me that I was about to be watched.

This was my chance. A good performance here, and who knew what might happen? The dreaming started: Tufnell takes all ten, is offered contract with Middlesex, bowls them to the Championship, plays for England, follows Yellow Brick Road … So when we won the toss and opted to bowl first, I was itching to get at it. But it all went horribly awry.

By the time Wilson, who was captaining the side, put me on to bowl, Bennett had not yet arrived at the ground. For some quite unfathomable reason I started arguing with Wilson about a field placing. Inevitably, thinking I knew it all, I wouldn't take no for an answer. Then I lost my rag. The next thing I knew, Wilson took me off and banished me to field at fine leg both ends. So when Bennett turned up, he was somewhat surprised to find that the slow left-arm bowler Don Wilson had invited him to come and run the rule over was none other than Don Wilson himself. As a result of our falling out, Don kept himself on all day, while I didn't bowl another ball.

I took it brilliantly as you can imagine. My big chance was being wasted and there was absolutely nothing I could do about it. I couldn't see Wilson's action as justifiable discipline to an unruly gobshite, i.e. me. All I could think of was that he was deliberately trying to ruin my career.

Don Bennett must have been highly impressed by what happened later, when a ball from Wilson was hit towards me on the deep square-leg boundary. This was my opportunity to make my protest and I didn't waste it. Instead of picking the ball up and throwing it in towards the wicket-keeper, I trapped it with my foot, controlled it and gave it an almighty boot back where it came from. And I sent after it a tirade of what you might describe as colourful language. Wilson stood there for several seconds in text-book double-teapot pose, both arms on hips, staring in disbelief. Bennett decided he had seen enough, got into his car and buggered off. Well done, Philip.

Thank God Bennett was not put off permanently. He was now quite determined, I think, that his journey should not have been a wasted one but, possibly realizing that Wilson and I could just as easily fall out again, he decided to take matters into his own hands. I was duly invited to play for Middlesex seconds against Hampshire at Southampton. This time, surely this time, in a two innings per side match, I was bound to get a chance to bowl.

We won the toss and bowled first on a green seaming wicket. Our pace bowlers bowled them out for nothing much. I didn't bowl. Having racked up a sizeable lead against seam bowling that was not in the same class as ours had been, it was out in the field for a second time to bowl them out and win the game. Thus far not a single delivery had been bowled by a spinner in the match, and once again our quicks duly did the job. In no time Hampshire were very few for four, with all wickets taken by seamers and Tufnell unused. It was at this point that Bennett intervened. He took the captain, Keith Tomlins, to one side and explained: 'You have got to put this lad Tufnell on to bowl. I've got to make a decision about whether to offer him a contract, and in two matches I've never yet seen him bowl a ball.'

So Tomlins ushered me to the crease and, of course, by this time I was having kittens. But once I had the ball in my hand, everything seemed to fall into place. I took six for 36 and we won the game in a canter. On such detailed examination was Middlesex's offer of a two-year contract made. It *is* a funny old game.

Off the field, and my raving exploits with Jamie notwithstanding, I was by now happily ensconced with Alison Squires of scorebox No 2 fame, and the notion and the fact of the relationship were both very cosy. We moved in together to a place in South London and it was fine.

Prior to our coming together, my bachelor life was like the episode of *Men Behaving Badly* that the BBC would not screen because it was too far-fetched. For instance, my flat in Barnet was furnished, if that is the correct term, with furniture straight out of a Dali nightmare. The sofa was made from pizza boxes glued together. I never had any clean whites to play cricket in. I hardly ever ate. Then Alison came on the scene and it was Sunday lunch, clothes in the washing machine, and I thought, well, very nice, I'll have some of this. Domesticity beckoned.

FIVE

Muppet

When I turned up for the following season – 1986, my first full year on the staff – I walked into a dressing room full of international cricketers, including players like Mike Gatting, John Emburey, Phil Edmonds, Paul Downton, Graham Barlow, Clive Radley and Wayne Daniel. Although it was intended that, along with other young players like Sykes, Mike Roseberry, Angus and Alastair Fraser and Keith Brown, I should only be eased into the mainstream through second eleven cricket, we would still mix with the first-team squad in the nets, and there was always the possibility that one of us would be called up in case of injury. So this was the real thing. And when we were not required for Middlesex duty at weekends, we would be expected to play for our club sides.

I don't think Alison really got any of this, at all. I tried to explain the situation to her, but as far as she was concerned weekends were weekends – and they were supposed to be spent together. So when the first weekend of the season came around and she informed me that I had better be free on Saturday because we were going to buy a fridge, I was forced to try subterfuge.

This was what I was supposed to do, according to Middlesex: as there was no second-team match over the weekend and the first team were playing at Lord's, I was expected to turn up on Saturday morning for nets, then go off in the afternoon to play for my club, Southgate.

This was the plan: on the Friday evening I would ring up a chap named Micky Dunn, the Southgate skipper, and tell him I was, unfortunately, not well enough to be considered for their match the following day. Then I would go to the Middlesex first-team nets in the morning, leave at around 11.30 a.m. when their match started, ostensibly to play for Southgate but actually to bugger off and buy the sodding fridge.

This is what actually happened: immediately after receiving my call to cry off, as a courtesy Micky Dunn rang up Don Bennett. So when I turned up for the nets bright, chirpy and obviously fit as a fiddle the next day, he knew something was up. 'Hello, Tuffers,' he said. 'Have you got a game for Southgate today?'

'Oh, yes, Don,' I lied. 'Big match, big match. Top of the table. Really up for it.'

'Good luck, then. See you next week.'

Net duties duly completed, I changed into my civvies, climbed into the Volvo and made for the North Gate exit. I was about fifty yards from the gate and thinking to myself how clever I was to have pulled the wool over the club's eyes when I noticed a strangely familiar figure running towards the same exit. It couldn't be. It bloody was. It was Bennett, now absolutely legging it. Realizing I had been rumbled, I booted the accelerator. In a state of terror and panic, all I could think of was escape. The question was whether I could make it through the gate without running him down.

The answer was no. With scant disregard for his personal safety, Don threw himself across the bonnet, shouting, 'Stop the f***ing car! Stop the f***ing car!' Just in time I slammed on the anchors and the car came to a skidding halt.

'Right. Get out of that car. Now!' he said.

So I got out of the car, shaking like a leaf. Don was bright red in the face. 'Would you like to tell me exactly what the f*** you think you're doing?' he enquired.

'Er, I'm off to play for Southgate,' I whimpered.

'Really?' he replied. 'In that case, who was that ringing me up last night and impersonating Micky Dunn, telling me that you'd cried off? Let's start again. Where the f*** do you think you're going?'

'Er … er. Well, Don I didn't feel very well, er, yesterday, you see, and er, and now I feel a bit better. No. No, that's not right. Er, well, Don, look, you see, my missus, well, she, er, she says, er, I've got to go with her to buy a fridge.'

It took Don a few seconds to recover from that one.

'Look here, son,' he continued. 'I don't give a f*** about your fridge. Park that car. You are coming with me, now.'

So he dragged me back to the pavilion by my ear, informing me that I could forget about the fridge because I was now the Middlesex twelfth man for the day.

'If you ever do that again,' he told me, 'if you ever lie to me again, you little bastard, your feet will not touch the floor. Understand? Now sit here and watch. You might learn something.'

Needless to say that when I finally arrived home I then received the full earful from Alison. Two bollockings for the price of one.

I suppose if the penny was going to drop at this stage,

this would have been the moment. But it didn't and it wasn't. The fact is that, although I sort of realized that this was my job, my profession, it never really felt like that to me. Cricket was not and never had been my vocation, as it was and had been for almost everyone else with whom I came into contact. It was more than just a last resort, but not much more. A job was something you did from nine to five, either in a stuffy office, a silversmith's factory or on a building site. Running around with your mates, bowling a bit, taking a few wickets, then buggering off home the moment a drop of rain fell out of the sky – that wasn't work. That was having a laugh.

To a greater or lesser degree, I was in trouble with Middlesex almost from the day I signed on, and mostly because I just couldn't take the petty rules and regulations seriously. There was always something. If it wasn't the hairstyle or the leopardskin G-string or some other fashion accessory from the night before, it was lying down in the outfield, or kicking the turf, or a spot of backchat or, well, you name it, every minor offence in the book, and some rather major ones along the way as well. I lost count of the number of times I was hauled in front of this senior player or that committee man, and the result was invariably the same. A stern warning to 'buck up your ideas', and a threat of what would happen if I didn't.

In years to come, some of my team-mates might have been wondering exactly what I would have to do to get thrown out, and the thought did occur to me once or twice. I was playing for the seconds and winning games. What's yer problem? You don't like my snakeskin shoes? Big deal.

I did get the slight feeling that the club was prepared to bend over backwards to accommodate me and I suppose

I took advantage. The fact was that I could bowl. The club knew it and I knew it. Whether in second-team cricket, or in the nets against the senior batsmen, it was fairly obvious that I was talented and Edmonds was not going to be around for ever.

To be fair, I was learning some things on the pitch as well, like when and who to sledge and when and who not to. I learned this in a match against the guys from Haringey Cricket College. Set up to provide under-privileged kids in the Haringey and Tottenham area with a cricketing outlet for their dreams and their frustrations, the college produced a number of fine players, including the Gloucestershire captain, Mark Alleyne, who made his full international debut for England in the one-day tournament in Australia at the start of 1999. And, bearing in mind the extremely rough and hazardous conditions in which most of these lads grew up, it also dealt with a number of blokes who knew how to look after themselves physically.

My lesson came when one bloke I had been having a go at marched into our dressing room at the close of play, brandishing his bat and enquiring: '*Now* which one of you thinks I'm a f***ing clown?' From then on I decided that two categories of opponent no longer qualified for sledging under any circumstances: a) anyone who was bigger than me and b) anyone who bowled fast. But in the main, the education I was receiving had as much to do with how to get away with murder as with how to get people out.

One bloke I couldn't pull too many strokes with was Bennett. From very early on it was clear that you had to fight to get even a pat on the back from Don, which was something I respected a lot, strangely. It meant that when he did give you a nod, you knew you had earned it. 'Well bowled, Tuffers,' was the equivalent of winning the Nobel prize for cricket.

We still managed to enjoy ourselves rather too much on away trips, but although Don was strict when he felt he needed to be, he also respected the fact that, as long as we were performing, as long as you woke up in the morning and did the job on the pitch, a certain amount of, shall we say, high jinks was acceptable. When he travelled with us, he also had a way of letting you know he knew what you were up to. Don was everywhere and nowhere. Like a ghost.

The other man who was to have an enormous bearing on my progress was John Emburey. Of all the faces I was confronted with when I came on to the staff full time, Ernie's was the friendliest. He could see that, behind all the bravado, I was quietly shitting myself in the company of the senior players, and whenever he could he had a quiet word to see how I was. It made a big difference to me that at least one of these blokes seemed to be aware of my existence, and I'll never forget his kindness towards me after my big moment – my first-class debut for Middlesex in the County Championship – very nearly signalled the end of a promising career.

John wasn't actually playing in the match, against Worcestershire at New Road between 4 and 6 June 1986, when the new star of English spin bowling soared across the firmament. Both he and Edmonds were on international duty, along with Mike Gatting, playing for England in the first Test against India at Lord's. I had been told to report for the first-team trip the previous day. There was no song and dance about it. There never was at Middlesex. When you came into the side the message was that you wouldn't be picked if you weren't good enough to play, so just get out there and get on with it.

We batted first, and weren't getting many. Cometh the hour, cometh the mouse. Not even Neal Radford's mum would ever have described him as quick, but for some reason, from my hiding place in the corner of the dressing room, his bowling now appeared to me to be faster than anything I had ever seen in my life. And when the time came for Middlesex's latest No 11 to enter the arena, my attempts to conceal from the Worcestershire players the sheer panic that engulfed me failed miserably.

My walk to the wicket must have been a dead give-away. It took absolutely ages. It was as though I felt that if I delayed the innings as long as possible, either the skipper would declare or the umpires might decide the light was too bad for play to continue. When I did finally reach my destination, my attempt to ask for the guard of 'Middle, please' came out as a high-pitched squeak. By this time, the Worcestershire players were fully aware that I might be about to provide them with some entertaining sport. My teeth were almost literally chattering with fear, and my colleagues told me later that, as Radford ran in to bowl, they could see the helmet shaking on top of my head.

My first delivery in county cricket remains a mystery to me, even now. I didn't see it at the time and I have no idea where it pitched, or what happened to it thereafter. In fact, it was only because I didn't hear the sound of ball on stumps that I knew it had not bowled me. Then I realized I had become paralysed. I was stuck in the shot I had just attempted and simply couldn't move. I only emerged from this trance-like state what seemed like several hours later, thanks to a warm welcome from David Smith, standing at short leg. The tall and burly left-handed opening bat had a reputation for fisticuffs that was as impressive as it was well earned. This time he rendered me all but unconscious with five words. 'Who is this f***ing muppet?' he asked.

I recovered sufficiently to scratch out a glorious eight to help us reach 244, but if I thought the worst was over, I was sadly mistaken. When it was our turn to bowl, Worcestershire racked up 421 for six. My first experience of bowling in county cricket was to be beaten up by Graeme Hick (70), Dipak Patel (108) and Phil Neale (118 not out) and my figures did not lie: thirteen overs, three maidens, nought for 76. I thought I was doing okay, as a matter of fact, but Hick and Neale, in particular, kept driving to the offside boundary what I considered reasonable balls – bowled at off stump or just outside and turning away a fraction – and for the life of me I couldn't understand how. It didn't get any better. We were bowled out again for next to nothing in the second dig, with me making nine out of 176 to leave us beaten by an innings. There were those among my team-mates who believed they might well have been witnessing a moment of genuine historical importance, something to tell their grand-children: the shortest first-class career on record.

I have to say I was pretty depressed by the whole business. This had been my big chance, and for all the 'who gives a monkey's?' nonsense with which I tried to console myself afterwards, the truth was that I was angry that I had not made more of it. It was abundantly clear now that I was nowhere near as good as I had allowed myself to believe. A week or so later, I was still in a state of sulk about it when, out of the blue, Embers pulled me over and asked if he could have a chat.

'I heard you had a spot of trouble up at Worcester,' he

began. 'A word of advice, take it or leave it. The lads tell me that Hick and Neale kept driving you through the covers. Well, learn from that. You might have thought that by bowling in that area you would be challenging them to drive and possibly get an edge. The fact is that while that is perfectly good bowling, no two batsmen are alike. You have to alter and adapt your bowling for individual batsmen. You must learn to use your brain like a library, indexing and storing information about every batsman you have played against or are going to play against, so that you can take it out and use it again when necessary. Now, Hick and Neale are very good off-side players, excellent drivers and cutters. Next time you bowl at them, bowl a little bit straighter and make sure your leg-side field is set so that if they try and milk you that side of the wicket, you are well covered.'

I was completely taken aback. Not that the points John was discussing constituted what you might call earth-shattering revelations. It was just that this was almost the first time anyone had actually thought to pass this kind of information on to me. Don Wilson had helped me with the theory, but until this point I had no experience of the fact of different batsmen playing me in different ways and me needing to adapt accordingly. The idea of actually 'thinking' people out hadn't really dawned on me. I had a lot to learn. From then on I began to lean more and more heavily on Embers for help and advice. Whenever I played alongside him in the first team – and I had a few more opportunities in the remainder of that season – I would always ask Ernie to set the field for me, and I would pick his brains over how to bowl at individual batsmen. I must have driven him round the bend. In fact, I know I did.

In the meantime, my first wicket in first-class cricket was just an absolute shocker. It came a month after my debut débâcle in my second match, against Surrey at Uxbridge, and it did so as a result of a rank long hop which their wicket-keeper Jack Richards obligingly slapped straight to Roland Butcher in the covers. So much for science. Two more in the second innings and two in my next match against Warwickshire on the same ground a few days later, and that was the sum total of my Championship wickets for the season. Five for 479, since you ask, at a cost of 95.80. It is fair to say that cricket's grapevine was not exactly buzzing.

It was about this time that Alison and I were making plans to tie the knot. Everyone was against it, needless to say. When I first passed on the good news to my old man, he very nearly had a thrombie. 'Don't do it. Don't do it,' he pleaded. 'I'm sure Alison is a nice girl, but you are only nineteen years old, for God's sake. You've got your whole life ahead of you, you prat'. 'No, no, Dad. It's all right,' I assured him. 'We know what we are doing.' Of course we did.

The first problem was deciding on a date. By this time I was playing regularly for the seconds and so summer Saturdays were out of the question. Or at least, I thought they were. Alison had other ideas.

Now Alison was a powerful woman, with a mind of her own and physical strength to match. If she wanted to get married on a Saturday in the summer, that was when she was going to get married and it was not advisable to argue. 'Listen, love,' I said, 'you know this is the cricket season and this is what I'm supposed to be doing now. I've only just been signed on to the staff and I don't think they would take very kindly to me having a Saturday off in the season to get married.'

Light blue touchpaper and retire.

'I don't give a toss what Middlesex think,' she insisted. 'I can't get married on a Saturday? You f***ing what?'

She went completely mental.

'Come on Phil, we're going down to the Middlesex office to sort this out. Now.'

And so we did. The club secretary at the time was Tim Lamb, now the chief executive of the England and Wales Cricket Board. A former player, he was always willing to try and see the player's point of view, but, having been born the Honourable Timothy and educated at Shrewsbury School and Oxford University, he was also fully cognizant of the proper way of doing things.

Poor bloke didn't know what hit him. First, she barged through the door of the office with me in tow, banged her fist down on Lamb's desk and demanded: 'What's all this about I can't get married on a Saturday?' Lamb was speechless. Then she leaned across the desk, grabbed him by the old school tie and pulled him towards her. 'I said, what's all this about I can't get married on a Saturday?' she repeated.

Considering the fact that he was turning purple at the time, I'm not sure he could have answered even if he had wanted to. It was as much as he could do to emit a low gurgling sound. After I had wrestled Alison off the Middlesex club secretary and we had all recovered our decorum, Tim managed to explain that he was terribly sorry and all that but, as I might be required to play on a Saturday, marriage on that day of the week during the season was out of the question. But what about the first Saturday straight after the end of the season? I closed my eyes, covered my ears, and waited for the end of the world. Amazingly, Alison agreed.

Looking back now, I suppose we did well to stay together for as long as we did. I'm not sure she sees it that way, but when you consider that our marriage coincided not only with the full resumption of my lunatic relationship with Jamie Sykes, but also my early years running around all over the country with the Middlesex second eleven and all that that entailed, three months might have been par for the course, rather than the three years we actually managed.

From start to finish, ours was not what you might call normal married life. We did get on well, no question, and we enjoyed each other's company a lot. This was mainly, I suppose, because in many respects we were just as barking as each other. Take the honeymoon, for instance. Once the season was over, and with a few bob knocking about, we could pretty much have gone anywhere we liked. I left the arrangements to Alison, all the while thinking along the lines of the Caribbean, or Mauritius, somewhere nice and hot with a beach, a bar and a beer. She chose Sweden. It was freezing.

As the rumpus with Tim Lamb over the arrangements for the wedding indicated, Alison had no real concept of what I did for a living, nor could she have cared less.

And so to Australia, in the winter of 1986–87, and my first Ashes series. Well, not precisely. My part in the Aussies' downfall? A trip to Brisbane to play a season's club cricket for Queensland University and, through my expert batting, to lull Allan Border and company into a false sense of security.

Alison came too, and created quite an impression among the wives and girlfriends of my new team-mates when, during our first match, she announced that it was her ambition to sleep with the lead singer of Def Leppard.

I gather she was not joking, but whether she achieved her aim, I cannot say.

Lively. That was the word most observers used of our marriage at this stage. I soon discovered just how charming some of those young Aussie birds can be, and already, surprise, surprise, was finding it rather tricky keeping myself to myself. Not particularly proud of this; just the way it was. The devil getting the upper hand over the angel again, although there were rumours that the angel took a dive.

The cricket was top hole, too, tough stuff against very committed players. I soon found out that club cricket meant something completely different in Australia than it did back home, although some of the facilities were rather spartan to say the least. My first match was to be played on what turned out to be a rugby field in the middle of nowhere. When all the lads started walking out towards the square I went with them, thinking we were all going out to take a look at the wicket. When we got there, however, I was slightly taken aback by the fact that they all began taking off their clothes. Aye, aye, I thought to myself, what sort of cricket is this then? It turned out that, as there was no pavilion, the done thing here was to change in the middle, that being the furthest point from the prying eyes of the spectators on the far side of the boundary.

Next lesson: Australian umpires have a physical aversion to giving batsmen out when hit on the front pad by a spinner. Forget it. It just doesn't happen. I wish one of my team-mates had warned me in advance, because it would have saved me a lot of wasted appeals and a lot of wasted time. On reflection, though, I think the reason no one bothered was that they quite enjoyed my regular spats with the officials. There was one umpire I remember in particular, Neville somebody or other. The first time I came up against him, I got rather carried away. After about the twelfth lbw shout had been dismissed I turned to him and said: 'Not out? Not f***ing out? Who the f*** are you anyway?' And he stared straight ahead and said: 'I'm the bloke who decides if it's out or not. Not out, you pommie bastard.' That seemed to crack the ice and from then on we got on well. He had red hair and big sticking-out ears. Wingnut, I called him. He was a good bloke and didn't mind me taking the piss, but he never gave me spit and as the season progressed our sparring became big box office among the players. I gave up appealing in the end. Instead, when I hit someone on the front leg, I'd just turn around and say: 'That's not out, is it, Wingnut?' And he would say: ''Fraid not, ya pommie f***er.'

The overall experience was made even more pleasurable by the fact that the real poms – the touring England team under Gatt, and including Embers and Edmonds, as well as Ian Botham, David Gower and Allan Lamb – were busy murdering the Aussies for months on end. Funnily enough, the bloke who inspired me most that winter was none of the above. It was the kid who had walked through the Grace Gates at Lord's wearing jeans and an Afro on my first day as a professional cricketer – Phil DeFreitas.

While I had been bumbling along at Middlesex, Daffy had gone on to great things. Picked up by Leicestershire and identified as an outstanding all-round talent, he was taken on this tour as a sort of understudy to Beefy. On the field, it hadn't been expected that he would play in the first-choice eleven in the state games, let alone the Test matches, but by the time the first Test came around, at the

Gabba in Brisbane, there he was making his England debut, at the age of twenty.

That started me thinking. There I was, walking into the Gabba with my tatty old jeans and my plastic carrier bag, watching my mate Daffy playing Test cricket against Australia. Suddenly you could see the progression. You could see that all that larking about and playing for a laugh could actually lead somewhere. And what rewards might be in store! This was the real thing, and Daffy who, on that morning we both joined the Lord's groundstaff, was clearly as clueless as me, was part of it. Bugger me if he wasn't out there with those gigantic figures, making 40 in the first innings at No 9, sharing the new ball with Graham Dilley and getting out David Boon and Dean Jones, catching Border off Edmonds, bowling out Geoff Marsh and Greg Ritchie and Merv Hughes in the second innings, and helping win the Test match, with all the Brits in the crowd going berserk and me jumping up and down with my tatty jeans and my plastic carrier bag.

For the first time I could see what might be possible. Not that this was a road to Damascus job or anything. I didn't immediately commit myself to a life of nets and push-ups and clean living by any stretch of the imagination. It was just that, maybe, some time in the future, there could be more to cricket than having a laugh. In the meantime, though, having a laugh would do nicely.

SIX

Cat

From the club's perspective, 1987 was the season when they needed me to start proving to them that I was worth the trouble. Although he had played a successful part in England's Ashes triumph – the last time in the twentieth century that England would win a Test series against the old enemy – it was clear that the off-field pursuits of Philippe Henri Edmonds were becoming more interesting to him than cricket. Meanwhile Gatt, for his part, as captain of a side that appeared to be in decline following years of undiluted success, became increasingly irritated that one of his senior players so obviously had other things on his mind.

At thirty-six, Edmonds was still young enough and good enough to have carried on for a while, and he did try to persuade the club that he could continue to operate as an amateur. Gatt wouldn't have it. As far as he was concerned, the days of gentlemen and players were long dead. You either played full time or not at all. And his patience snapped during a match against Somerset at Bath in June. As they were both what you might call stubborn characters, it was something of a surprise that it took this long.

In the middle of a bowling spell, Edmonds came up with rather an unusual request: 'Can I go off? I've got a very important phone call to make.' Gatt was not amused. 'You are not going anywhere,' he replied. 'I forbid you to leave the field under any circumstances.' A couple of overs later, Edmonds told the umpire that he needed to change his boots, and walked off. Gatt went a very dark colour.

Twenty minutes later Edmonds came back on, but something about the phone call had annoyed him and he was clearly distracted. Fielding at third man, he went to pick the ball up one-handed, made a complete bollocks of it, then slowly chugged after it. When the batsmen stole another run from the misfield, Gatt looked as though he was on the verge of spontaneous combustion. It was not a pretty sight and it didn't sound great either. 'Get that ball in, Henri,' he bellowed in his best Henry VIII off-with-her-head voice. But Henri was riled as well. He took aim and winged it fast and straight as a bullet, not at the wicket-keeper, but at Gatt, standing at slip. When the ball then flew beyond the stumps and the batsmen ran two further overthrows, Gatt was spinning like a Catherine wheel. Play was held up for several minutes while the two men came together for a magnificent slanging match.

Edmonds did play for England again that summer, but at the end of it the committee made sure he would play no more for Middlesex. And from approximately the point where they fell out, I became the first-team first-choice left-arm spinner.

Although that should have been the signal for me to take my career and my responsibilities more seriously, it wasn't. If anything I probably went the other way. Jamie and I were now both playing a lot of first-team cricket, and that meant trips away from home, and that meant ... I think we all know what that meant. Alison was well enough hacked off already with the fact of what I was doing, but now I think she also started to realize that we might be going around in ever decreasing circles. Not employed by the club during the winter of 1987–88 and with time on my hands, I did involve myself in a few odds and sods jobs, but the main features of my life were going down to the pub, getting lashed and chasing poon-tang.

The beginning of the end for Alison and me and, not very coincidentally, for Jamie and me as well, came in somewhat peculiar circumstances midway through the 1988 season.

In between home matches, James and I had decided on a big night out in his neck of the woods. It may not actually be possible to drink in every one of the pubs in the Mile End Road in one lifetime. We tried to do it in an evening. Finally giving up well after midnight, and having found ourselves with a couple of lively ladies in the back of the Volvo, we set off for the journey back to civilization.

Now my co-pilot, being from the area, claimed he knew it like the back of his hand. Unfortunately he didn't seem to know the bit we were actually driving round in. And round and round and round. Tired, emotional, confused and now lost, we started guessing, so that by the time we had completed the tenth lap of the same stretch of road, not surprisingly we had aroused the suspicions of the local constabulary.

It was about 3 a.m. and I was at the wheel. When I spotted the cop car coming towards us, my first instinct was to slow down and act natural. But I was a bit too eager on the brakes, so that what I had intended should be a smooth cruising motion through the gears turned into virtually an emergency stop. Jamie, having been otherwise engaged with one of the girls, flew forward. The car passed by and it was obvious that the occupants were taking a long hard look. For a few moments I thought we might have got away with it, but then I looked in the wing mirror and saw the police vehicle making the manoeuvre that made my heart sink – a U-turn.

'Oh f***,' was about the most sensible thing anyone could think of to say. Then Jamie had a bright idea. 'Put your foot down,' he said. 'We're going to lose them.'

In hindsight I'd rank it about third on the list of the most stupid remarks ever uttered in the whole history of mankind. Certainly, 'Put your foot down. We're going to lose them,' has to be up there near the very top of the list.

It took the good guys about thirty seconds to bring this particular chase to its inevitable conclusion as I followed Jamie's instructions to the letter: a left, then a right, then, unhelpfully, a dead end. Leaving the two girls screaming in the back seat, Jamie and I piled out of the motor and ran. For some reason – and I still don't know why I did this – I grabbed the keys from the ignition and threw them as far as I could. There we were, quite hysterically pissed, laughing and running from the law through this industrial estate ringed by security fences and barbed wire. We put on a spurt, sprinting for a good minute or two before the lungs and legs packed in and we paused to get our bearings. Then, faint at first but getting louder, I heard this sort of chink-chink-chink sound. It was handcuffs rattling against the belt of the WPC, by now only about thirty yards away and closing.

We started running again. Over walls, over gates, on and on we ran for what seemed like forever. Then all of a sudden, halfway up an eight-foot-high wall, with the WPC and a growing posse in hot pursuit, Jamie stopped climbing, turned to me and said: 'Hold on a minute. What am I running for? I was a passenger.' With that he dropped down, held up his hands and called out: 'Fair cop.'

I wasn't quick enough to surrender. So by the time they got to me I was hanging by my fingers from the top of this wall, with this WPC bashing me around the ankles with her bloody truncheon. At which, this crowd of plain-clothes policemen who, we later found out, had been hanging about following a spate of warehouse robberies in the area, got to work. They dragged me off the wall, flattened me against the floor and cuffed me. I shouted, 'All right, all right, I'll come quietly,' like they did in the movies, but it didn't seem to do any good.

Once they had established that we were idiots, rather than master criminals, it was out with the breathalyser and under arrest. Then into Poplar nick for a night in the cells with a couple of raving winos. Not quite what I had in mind for the evening. At one stage it looked as though I was also going to be charged with carrying an offensive weapon, but when, despite considerable and under-standable scepticism, they finally accepted that I was a professional cricketer by trade, they conceded the probability that the presence of the cricket bat in the car boot was innocent. They let me out at about 6.30 a.m.

'You're free to go. You can go home,' they said. If only I could. As I left the nick, it slowly dawned on me that I had absolutely no idea where the car keys had ended up. Three hours it took me, scouring the route, before I eventually found them. And then when I finally got home at around eleven, wet, exhausted, humiliated and stinking like a wino's trousers, I had another lovely surprise. Alison's father was a copper. The news had travelled fast.

To be fair, we hadn't exactly been getting on like a

house on fire for a while. I suppose in hindsight the marriage was doomed to failure from the moment the confetti left the box. I just wasn't cut out for it. We stumbled on for a while, for about another year, in fact, but my long absences from home were not always spent alone, and the longer things went on, the worse it became. Alison was in our house south of the river, I just wanted to be with my mates, mucking about, or birding – and so I did. Then I met Mandy.

It was just another ordinary night out with James at the Washington in Hampstead, I think. We met these two lovely girls, got on really well and had a fine time. It was the era of 'ac-i-i-i-d' music and warehouse parties, and it was brilliant fun. I started spending some serious time with her.

Middlesex, having already issued one of the very early 'final warnings' over the drink-driving episode that season, were about to have their patience stretched even further, and so was Alison. Only one of the above relationships remained – barely – intact. In August 1988 I went up to Headingley for the Championship match against Yorkshire, fully expecting to play. When, on the morning of the match, Gatt told me I was twelfth man, it wasn't the greatest news in the world.

For the first half hour of the match, nothing untoward happened, and my absence wasn't noticed. In fact, it was only when fielders started to realize that their calls to the dressing room for assistance were going unheeded that somebody asked, 'Where's the twelfth man? Where's Tufnell?' The answer was that, knackered after rather too much party behaviour, I had decided to find a quiet corner in the pavilion and catch up on some kip. Unfortunately I slept rather too well: through the entire morning session, in fact, much to the consternation of Don Bennett, who had been forced to act as twelfth man himself, fetching and carrying sweaters and drinks and so on for the fielders.

When I finally came round and made my way back to the dressing room, I was informed that my presence was no longer required. Sent home in disgrace, I had another bollocking from the committee to look forward to. Or worse. Happily, the club settled for the former – a very last last warning, they called it – and as a result of my slumbers, the nickname of 'The Cat' was born.

Free to return to home and Alison, I spent the rest of the match at Mandy's. Then I went back to Alison, saying I had been at Headingley the whole time.

I suppose I should have been honest with her and faced up to the situation. Instead, as the affair with Mandy carried on, I was just waiting for Alison to find out, sort of dropping clues here and there, almost hoping she would. Eventually she did. Sorting through some stuff, she came across a load of letters and photographs.

It was very sad. I didn't want to hurt Alison. She had been a good friend and there had been something between us, but it was just irretrievable. She didn't exactly take the break-up well. She got hold of Mandy's telephone number, had a load of cards printed up with 'Mandy's Massage Parlour' written on them and posted them in phone boxes all over London. For the next week or so, until she had her number changed, Mandy kept receiving these calls asking what sort of service she provided.

Soon the divorce was under way and Mandy and I were a solid item. We discussed getting a place and shacking up, and decided that we would move in together once she got back from the upcoming round-the-world trip with her mates that she had been planning for years. I went with Mandy to the airport and saw her off. I kissed her goodbye and told her I couldn't wait for her to come back. The only problem was she never did.

There were a few letters in the first months in which she said she missed me and all that. But as time went by, it became more and more obvious that she had lost interest. I never saw or heard from her again. Alison talked about getting back together, but there had been too much water under the bridge and so I was released into the world of bachelorhood once more, with the inevitable results.

The old man came to the rescue again, helping fix me up in another flat, and Jamie and I just kept on having a laugh. Nothing much was happening on the cricket front in 1989. I was doing enough, but certainly not pulling up any trees, and neither was Jamie. We didn't think our behaviour was particularly untoward, and unless I was imagining it, some of the best laughs we had involved some of the more senior players. But the club had had enough. According to the powers that be, Sykes and Tufnell were becoming too disruptive and had to be separated. One of us had to go.

There are those who believe that Jamie's eventual sacking helped me to come to my senses, to focus on my game more in the knowledge that no one was indispensable. I made a few concessions. After Embers complained that the dressing room ponged like a transport caff, I even promised to smoke outside. But as far as I'm concerned the real wake-up call came when I started to look around the dressing room and became more than a little aware of the emergence and progress of players my own age and even younger. Mark Ramprakash had arrived – a massively promising young batsman with an explosive talent and occasionally fiery temperament to match. Angus Fraser was really starting to come into himself as a line-and-length bowler with 'nip' par excellence. Keith Brown was developing into a fine wicket-keeper-batsman.

Furthermore, particularly after the England side had been decimated by wholesale defections to the South African rebel tour under the captaincy of Gatt, one or two of the guys were being talked about as possible England players. During the 1989 summer series with Australia, Gus was given his chance and showed what he was capable of. Ramps' elevation seemed only a matter of time. Then Gus was picked for the winter tour to the Caribbean.

I was in danger of being overtaken by my peers. It was an uncomfortable feeling and I spent that winter pondering my future. Maybe this really was the time to start smartening myself up. David Gower had been succeeded as captain by Graham Gooch, whose ideas about commitment and preparation were widely known. I have to admit that there may have been room for improvement where I was concerned.

Then again, I thought, sod it. Sod them for booting out Jamie. Sod them all. If they wanted me they could have me. But what gave them the right to try and change me? To misquote Mel Gibson: 'You can take ma life, but you canna take ma Bensons.'

SEVEN

Haircut

All those who are fortunate enough and good enough to be picked for England have fond memories of the performance that opened the door for them. For some it is a century in front of a selector or two; for others, a five-wicket haul. The moment that changed the course of my career and my life forever was when Mike Gatting dragged me down Uxbridge High Street to get a haircut.

By the time we clocked on for duty in the spring of 1990, Gus had returned from the West Indies with stirring tales of exploits on and off the field. Whereas my own experience of the Caribbean during the England Young Cricketers' tour had been, largely, a piss-up, this all sounded suspiciously like what every cricketer is in the game for. Given two chances of upsetting the odds against Viv Richards and company, one of which barked, the team had nearly pulled off a major upset, returning as glorious losers of the 2–1 rather than the usual 5–0 variety. At the same time, they had obviously enjoyed themselves as well, and tales of rum and ginger tickled up what you might call my thirst for action. I decided that I really did want to play for England, after all. But I was determined that it should be on my terms.

In the immediate short term I was helped in my ambitions by the fact that Keith Medlycott hadn't really advanced his claims during the tour. Not that he had had much opportunity, for neither he nor Eddie Hemmings – who had been chosen because Embers had signed up on Gatt's rebel tour – played in any of the Tests. Then when the England selectors started looking around again, the playing conditions in place for the 1990 season could have been made for me. First, the return to low-seamed balls meant that the practice of relying on trundlers to tuck in on helpful wickets was about to disappear. Secondly, the summer was hot and dry, bringing the twirlymen into the game even more.

I began the season in far from auspicious form when, on the first day back at pre-campaign training, the club physio sent me home to get some sleep. But I ended up playing in twenty Championship matches. Embers, who, along with Gatt, was available all summer because of the five-year ban imposed on them for their involvement in the rebel tour to South Africa, played in all twenty-two. We bowled very nearly 2,000 overs between us, took 122 wickets (Embers 57, me 65) and Middlesex won the title. Wallop.

Sending down that many overs and being that involved, it was inevitable that I developed as a bowler more quickly during this season than at any other time during my career. I started to use my brain more, picking up on people's abilities and weaknesses, setting certain field placings, laying little traps and so forth. I was varying my pace more, and my flight, and I was bowling with good control. I also started to realize that, in order to take wickets, you don't have to turn the ball square – just enough. But the thing that really swung it for me, so I am reliably informed, came about halfway through the season with the rearrangement of my coiffure.

The hair was long again now, and a bit unmanageable, to be honest. On occasions the top used to flop across in front of my eyes, so that after I had delivered the ball, I was blinded momentarily in the follow through. By the time we turned up at Lord's for a Championship game against Worcestershire – in which, incidentally, I came up against Ian Botham for the first time, which was a bit oo-er – it was obvious I couldn't go out to field with the barnet flailing about in the breeze. I didn't fancy asking one of my sausage-fingered colleagues to have a crack at trimming it, so the only thing I could think of was to try and tie it up at the back in a pony tail.

I'd be lying if I said I was unaware of the possibility that this might cause a stir. Who could say what effect the sight of my pony tail might have on the MCC members in the Long Room? As I walked through cricket's Holy of Holies on the way out to field, I could almost hear the spirits of the giants of the game, some alive, some long gone, calling to me from their portraits. Douglas Jardine in particular was plainly unimpressed. Mind you, judging by that cap he used to wear he is a fine one to talk.

Perhaps I couldn't hear it for the hair covering my lug-holes, but the game seemed to pass without too much piss-taking. Inevitably, though, the powers-that-be wasted no time in jumping on me again about the usual subjects – my general appearance and approach, etc. – and, as usual, I found it all difficult to get to grips with. Attitude. That was the word I kept hearing. My attitude was wrong.

I never quite saw it like that. In some ways I felt my attitude was too right for some people. Whatever I got up to after clocking off was my business, but the fact was that there was no one with a better attitude than me where it mattered, on the field, trying my hardest to get batsmen out.

There may have been some people at the club who felt that things came a little too easy for me. Perhaps they wanted to see me graft a bit more. The truth is that, had I played the game by their rules, I would have had a much smoother ride. But I just couldn't see that there was more to playing cricket at this level than bowling. The cream and brown snakeskin shoes, the hair, the ear-rings and all the rest ... what did they matter as long as I was doing the job, taking wickets and helping the club win the Championship?

After the degree of success he had enjoyed as England captain in West Indies and a good start to the international season on their return – including his 333 against India at Lord's – Graham Gooch was firmly in the driving seat. Having been left out of the squad for the trip to the Caribbean, David Gower was back in favour now, although seemingly on sufferance, but pony tails and scruffy gits with too much lip did not fit into Gooch's scheme of things.

His greatest friend in cricket, and in life come to think of it, was Embers. Schoolboy cricketers together, mates on early tours, they had the kind of relationship that makes wives suspect their husbands might be on the turn. So whenever Embers perked up on matters pertaining to Gooch and England, everyone in the dressing room listened with more than usual interest.

One day he mentioned my name in that context. 'Look, Cat,' he said. 'I think you have got a good chance of playing for England. You are bowling well, better than any other left-armer in the country, and they are definitely looking.' So far so good. 'But,' he continued, 'you've got to smarten yourself up and buck your ideas up. That means lose the pony tail.'

I knew it was coming and I knew I probably did need a haircut. But I wanted to be the one who decided when to do it, not them. By now I had worked myself up into a bit of serious rebellion. I dug my heels in. 'I like the pony tail. If they don't want to pick me, that's their problem.' I thought no more about it, and when we went to Uxbridge a fortnight later for the next Championship match, against Yorkshire, it was still there. As soon as Embers saw me he took me to one side. 'I'm pretty sure that a couple of the selectors are coming to watch you in this match. That thing has got to go. I'm serious.' And so was I. 'Bollocks,' I told him, or words to that effect. 'I'm sorry, but why does everyone seem to be more bothered about my hair than my bowling?' Too far gone now, I wasn't budging.

Very soon, however, the matter was taken out of my hands in dramatic fashion. During the lunch interval, Gatt tapped me on the shoulder and said, quietly: 'Tuffers, can you come with me for a minute?' Obviously he wanted to have a chat about tactics, the way I was bowling, or a ploy to attack one of their batsmen in a certain way. I duly followed him out of the pavilion and out of earshot of the opposition for the passing on of the secret plans. But he carried on walking. In fact he speeded up to such a lick that by the time I caught up with him I was virtually running.

Then he pounced. He turned, grabbed me, frog-marched me to his car and bundled me in. He drove me down the road into Uxbridge High Street, dragged me out of the car and into the barber's shop and, in the manner of the Master of Ceremonies at Madison Square Garden, announced: 'Short back and sides.' I've never been so humiliated in my life. There was I, slumped sulking in the barber's chair having all my hair cut off while Gatt, like a pissed-off dad teaching his naughty little boy a lesson, sat reading the newspaper to make sure I didn't leg it. We were both still in our cricket gear. Job done, he took me back and made me play without another word.

From then on to the end of the 1990 season, little whispers started being heard. There were a few mentions in the newspapers and the like. I wasn't bowling any differently to how I'd been bowling before the haircut, but there was definitely a change of mood in the dressing room as well. 'Tufnell for England,' one or two of the boys would jokingly chant after a good spell. Except that it seemed to be more than a joke. I kept grooving along the way I had been, paying no real attention to the rumours. Around early September, the squad for the upcoming England tour to Australia and New Zealand was announced. *And I was in it.*

Get your hair cut, play for England. Simple.

Away from cricket, with Alison and Mandy gone, I'd met someone new, a girl from Enfield called Jane McEvoy. We met in a pub, got on well and indulged in a couple of mutual hobbies with some enthusiasm. The other was the raving. Wild times, these, in North London, particularly at home-match weekends. A mob of us used to follow coded instructions and end up in a warehouse in a field outside Waltham Abbey, or somewhere similar. When dawn came we would still be there, whirring round and round in the field, deeply in love with the world, the universe and the cowpats we were dancing in. Then, if selected, a Sunday League run-out in the afternoon.

I must stress that, although we were good mates, there was nothing serious between Jane and me at this stage. I'm not absolutely certain that my approach to the tour down under would have been that different if there had been, to be honest, but, as things turned out, it was like giving Billy Bunter the keys to the tuck shop.

EIGHT

Bad Timing

My first experience of a senior England tour was all a bit too much for me, really, in almost every way I can think of.

The regime was, er, regimental. Fitness appeared to be paramount, and way in advance of the trip we were all given detailed diet and exercise programmes. Micky Stewart, the manager, and Gooch, the captain, led by example and the rest of us were expected to follow blindly and without question. Gower threw up very badly on his first training run at Lilleshall, the ghastly great gothic mansion in the middle of nowhere where we were put through our paces, and whenever I lit one up, I felt as though I was committing a federal offence. This kind of intense physical jerkiness carried on all tour. To some, i.e. Gower and me and a few others, this was clearly impossible. To others, a subtle game of doing just enough was the tried and trusted method. For the majority of the rest, it was jump when you were told to jump. Wayne Larkins I couldn't categorize at all.

'Ned' was a law unto himself. I don't think anyone quite understood the relationship between him and Gooch. A fearsome hitter of the ball, Larkins must have impressed the skipper during their years in county cricket by the sheer brilliance of some of his strokeplay. For, off the field, I never came across anyone less likely to conform to Gooch's ideal of health and fitness. He'd been on the previous tour to the West Indies, but was out of the side for the 1990 home series against New Zealand and India, and most people felt that would be it for him. It wasn't as if the Northamptonshire stalwart was in the first flush of youth, either, being around thirty-seven at the time of departure. He had first toured Australia on the 1979–80 tour, playing only one Test of the three-Test series, making twenty-five and three, and finishing with the modest first-class average of 21.11. All the same, a Northampton brewery saw fit to award him and his county colleague and fellow tourist, Peter Willey, 2,016 pints of beer (seven barrels) as a reward for their efforts.

Between that high point and this latest selection, his career had been chequered to say the least, but Gooch had never stopped rating his talent, so here he was, walking in front of me through the door of a hotel room in Perth, Western Australia, my first room-mate on an England tour on my first day as an international cricketer. For the education I was about to receive, what better teacher could I have had?

No sooner had I set my bags down on the bed than I heard, 'All right, mate, just going to the team room,' and turned to see the door closing behind him. A couple of minutes later, Ned returned. In his arms he was carrying not one, but two cases of Swan lager.

'Fancy a beer?' he asked. Without waiting for an answer, he handed me a can, popped open his own and drained it without appearing to pause for breath. Then he cracked open another and another and another. In fact he repeated the process continuously for about an hour, at the end of which the empties were already starting to pile up, and you could barely see the door for fag smoke. Eventually I thought to myself that surely there must be something else I should be doing and told Ned I was nipping off down to the swimming pool for a splash and a spot of lunch. I asked him if he wanted to come, but he declined. Switching on the telly he said, 'Nah, mate, I'll be right as rain right here.' After lunch a few of us went into town for a reconnaissance mission and so I didn't return to the room until about eight in the evening. As I opened the door, I heard the familiar sound of a can being popped, and looked around to see Ned sitting bolt upright in bed, with the telly still on, his bags still unpacked and a sort of pyramid of empty Swan lager cans growing up the wall. 'Hello, mate,' he grinned. 'Fancy a beer?'

Ned apart, I was pretty overawed to be in this company and, having been given certain advice from Embers and Gatt before leaving, at first I was very careful to do exactly what I was told. Two of the three men in charge of the tour – the tour manager Peter Lush and team manager Micky Stewart – had been there on the last tour in 1986–87, when Gatt had led England to victory. And then there was Gooch, a man who, whatever reservations he would later cause critics to harbour concerning his attempt to impose his beliefs on others, none the less commanded massive respect among the players for his achievements, his ability and his dedication.

They tell me that the main issue to arise from England's 1990–91 Ashes tour was the struggle for supremacy between Goochism and Gowerism, the outcome of which was to define the way England approached, prepared for and played their Test cricket from that moment on. It is a good job they did tell me, for the main issue arising from the trip from my perspective turned out to be having a seriously good time. Off the field, as the tour progressed, the questions to which I sought answers were how much booze I could neck, how many birds I could make the acquaintance of and how much of my tour fee would be left after I had shelled out for all the fines. The answers were: a) lots, b) loads and c) considerably less than there should have been.

I wasn't required for the first few matches, but I soon found a variety of ways of keeping up my spirits. The crumpet was unbelievable. For some reason, whenever I walked into a bar with a few of the boys and the dulcet North London dialect got to work, within minutes there seemed to be a couple of giggling girls eager for an introduction. What was a well-mannered Old Cholmeleian to do? Nothing untoward, you understand, just healthy pursuits, healthily pursued. The trip was proceeding in such an enjoyable fashion that I started to become a little twitchy. Surely something was bound to go wrong sooner or later.

Well, things did start to go wrong soon enough. In spades.

The trouble started when Gooch injured himself in the opening practice game at the Melvista Oval in Perth. We were all up for it, wanting to impress and to get ourselves in shape. But it was only practice, and in my book that means the overriding priority is to make sure you don't do yourself any damage. Yet when Robin Smith smashed a drive straight back towards Gooch off his bowling, instead of waving it on its way, the captain stuck out a mitt to try and catch it. Total commitment is one thing and, even allowing for my innate cowardice in the face of the hard ball, I can tell you that this one was travelling seriously fast.

In any case, the result was gruesome. The gash on Gooch's finger was so deep that you could see right down to the bone. Just after lunch, too. Amazingly, however, the wound turned out to be nowhere near as serious as it first appeared. Lawrie Brown, our terrier-like Scottish physio – whose accent, incidentally, made him sound a dead-ringer for John Laurie in *Dad's Army* – fixed it with butterfly tape. Although even Gooch admitted to some discomfort, he played in the next match against a Western Australian Country XI in Perth, our hosts having agreed that he could do so as a batsman only, and we thought no more about it. The important thing was that there were still three weeks to go before the first Test in Brisbane, so there was more than enough time for Gooch to get himself right.

Of far more pressing and immediate concern to me was the bastard flight we took from Adelaide to Port Pirie to play a one-day match against the South Australian Country XI. In years to come when I have packed up cricket, or when cricket has packed me up, I think I shall write a screenplay for a film entitled 'Guts on the Ceiling: the Story of Flight 111'.

By now most people remotely interested in the career of yours truly will have picked up on the fact that I'm not exactly at my best when airborne. Even on the calmest, millpondiest flight from London to Manchester, for instance, I normally have to be wrestled into my seat and crow-barred out again on arrival. No idea why. Not bad at heights. Maybe it's just the feeling that, for the duration of the flight, my life is in the hands of total strangers. And what if the pilot is on a suicide mission?

But this was something else. The aircraft was a twin engine wah-wah, seating us and not many more. The forecast was bad, with the strong possibility of electrical storms over the mountains, but the fact was worse, far worse. This was the storm at the end of the world. So violent, in fact, that about halfway through, the stewardess employed to maintain calm in such situations first burst into tears and then began heaving grotesquely and absolutely everywhere. At this point, as I sat with my fingernails gripped so tight into the arm-rests that I thought I would have to have them surgically removed, Lawrie cracked open his famous supply of Famous Grouse. Those of us who could actually open our mouths took turns to knock back huge gulps. The bottle lasted about seven minutes. Imagine being strapped into a washing machine spinning out its final rinse. Now imagine the washing machine leaping up and down on the spot as well. You're not even close.

We survived, God only knows how, and when the ordeal was over several of us kissed the tarmac. The match paled into insignificance in comparison, but I did manage to get my first wickets for England, three for 41, as we won comfortably, if somewhat eerily, by the margin of 111. Mercifully the return trip was a walk in the park.

Gooch's injury was about a fortnight old now and in that period he had played eight days of cricket with little or no reaction. The first day of the match against South Australia at the Adelaide Oval passed without fuss, with them making a hatful. Then, while having a net prior to the start of the second day, Gooch complained of acute pain in his finger. At first it was thought it had turned septic. But he was clearly struggling. It didn't look right at all, and neither did he. It was decided that he should go to the hospital for a check-up, and it was a good job he did. The finger had become infected with poison which had spread to the palm of his hand. He underwent surgery that evening and, while no one actually believed his condition was life-threatening, it could have been very nasty. What was not in doubt was that he was out of the first Test, and possibly more than one.

In his absence the captaincy passed over to Allan Lamb, and a slightly more relaxed approach to training, shall we say, was the order of the day. It wasn't exactly on with the red noses, but there was definitely less of an edge to the running around the outfield than there had been when Gooch and Micky had been operating in tandem. It didn't seem to affect performances at first, and in Hobart Lamb scored hundreds in both innings. So we arrived in Brisbane for the Test match in pretty good heart.

The whole experience was a real eye-opener for me. The pitch and weather conditions in Brisbane usually favour seam and swing, so it was no surprise that neither Eddie Hemmings, the senior spinner, nor I made the final eleven. Just being there and involved in an Ashes series, with the ground full and everyone riding on the crest of anticipation, sent the volts buzzing through me. I found it hard to believe I was looking at Dean Jones, Allan Border, Merv Hughes & Co – all massive names – as playing opponents. Before the start of play on the first day, in my youthful enthusiasm and naivety, I ran up to the press box, borrowed someone's phone and rang Embers.

'Do you know what the time is?' he responded.

'Oh, sorry, mate. Wasn't thinking. You'll never believe it. Border, Jones, Healy, all those blokes and they're passing me in the corridor and stopping for a chat. Blimey.

And there are so many people here. I can't believe it. I can't believe it,' I blathered.

'Get back to the dressing room and settle down,' he said.

Naturally I expected everyone to be in the same state as me. I walked into the dressing room ready to knock down walls and shouting, '*Come on, come on*' ... and it was like a launderette on a wet February afternoon. Over there someone was reading a newspaper, another was on the phone. Some of them looked as though they'd done this kind of thing a hundred times before. For the younger ones among us – myself, Angus, Mike Atherton, Alec Stewart and so on – it might have been different, but for some of those who had been around a bit longer, it appeared to be just another day at the office. I don't doubt they were concentrating just as hard and were just as up for it as we were, but to me the overall pre-action atmosphere was, sad to say, a bit of an anticlimax.

We batted first and as the morning wore on it became more and more tense. However anyone else was dealing with the occasion, I was finding it tough. Not as hard as Ned, however. Not only was he out early, but the abscess that had been giving him grief for a week or so had flared up. Outside on the dressing room balcony, he asked me to take a look. It was grim viewing. There was a big angry bubble on the roof of his mouth and I told him he needed to get to a dentist to have it drained. Lawrie had other ideas. 'Eh. Don' you worry about tha',' he said. 'You're cummin' with me.' Lawrie took him inside and it wasn't long before I became aware of a loud commotion coming from within, followed by a series of muffled grunts. It sounded as though someone was being gagged. Curious, I went in to see who or what was making the noise, and was confronted by a scene of some confusion. There on the table amid all the usual debris – jockstraps, old socks and sandwiches – were Ned, with his mouth wide open, and Lawrie, leaning over him with a bottle of Grouse in one hand, what looked like a scalpel in the other and a strange look in his eye.

'Oh my God!' I exclaimed. 'What are you doing?'

'Aw, laddie,' said Lawrie, 'I'm just gonna nick it. I'm just gonna open it up a wee bit so it releases the pus.' And Ned said, 'Yeah. Don't worry, Cat. I've had a couple of Scotches. This won't hurt a bit,' and grinned. Lawrie duly made the incision and Ned hit the roof. For the next three weeks he could barely speak.

Back on the field, the pitch and overhead conditions were making batting extremely hazardous, and in the circumstances our 194 was nothing to be ashamed of. Gower managed to make 61 in a real grafting knock quite out of character with his caricature, and without it we would have been in the cart. With the ball moving sideways off the pitch, no one really knew then how good that score was. Our mood brightened considerably when we bowled them out for 152 to establish a first-innings lead of 42. We were definitely in the driving seat.

But then, after close of play on the second day, came the first of a series of the incidents that eventually led to the big split between Gooch and Gower, with the acting-captain Lamb right in the middle of it.

I'm not making a judgement here. Pots and kettles, etc. But there is no doubt in my mind that the decision of Lamb and Gower to take up the invitation of Kerry Packer to join him and Tony Greig at the blackjack table at Jupiter's Casino that night ultimately had an adverse effect on the team spirit Gooch had been so desperate to instil.

Personally I don't see an awful lot wrong in what they did. But the effect of their trip was to polarize feelings within the camp between the Gooch and Gower factions.

Gower was already out (for 27), and as Lamb used to find it difficult to sleep at the best of times, a night at the tables was probably just what he felt he needed to help him wind down prior to the key innings he would have to play in the morning. Unfortunately, on the resumption the following day the key innings lasted about another ten minutes. We mustered only 114 and then, with the wicket dry and the weather fine, Australia's openers knocked off the required runs by the close of the third day to win by ten wickets with two full days to spare. When the news of Lamb's trip to Jupiter was leaked by an Aussie journalist, the management went lunar. Peter Lush laid down the party line, publicly claiming that Lamb had returned to the team's hotel in good time that evening, at around 11 p.m., a feat which would have required him to leave the casino almost before he arrived.

While Gooch kept his thoughts to himself for the moment, it was clear that this was not the kind of response he had been looking for from his senior pros.

Then I got in on the act.

When we returned to Adelaide for a World Series Cup one-day match against New Zealand a few days later, Gooch was already in an irritable mood. Hacked off that he was still a bystander in the first place, he discovered that any thoughts he might have harboured of extra practice for Gower, or anyone else, the day before the match were scuppered when David informed the management that he had to take a party of punters to a vineyard that afternoon. Interestingly, although there was an open invitation to the rest of the players, there were very few takers. Perhaps some guys didn't want to be seen to be allying themselves too closely to Gower in case it all went pear-shaped later on. Which, of course, it did.

I was in the clear – or so I thought. Not wanted for the limited-overs stuff at that stage, I was about seventeenth man out of seventeen for the game, so I had no worries about another big night. As things turned out, it might easily have been my last on that tour.

It began at one of the many excellent bars the beautiful city of Adelaide has to offer. I had been with a load of the boys, but one by one they had drifted away, leaving me on my own with a couple of lovelies. I had had rather too much to drink, but the chat was in full steam and seemed to be working when they asked me if I would like to pop back to their place. Unable to think of a single good reason why not, I agreed and we bundled into their car. Knowing that, even though I was not required to play, I was still expected to show up at around nine the next morning for the trip to the ground, I wanted to make sure we wouldn't be driving to Ayers Rock, but they insisted that they lived a mere ten minutes away. Threequarters of an hour and a couple of beers in the back of the motor later we arrived, with me now past caring.

A couple more drinks and a bop and the next thing I knew we were all hopping into bed. It was more playfulness than anything Swedish, but there was some wrestling along with the boozing and it was all fairly good exercise. After half an hour or so, the door opened. I ducked under the sheets, thinking 'boyfriend, husband, father, shotgun, horrible death', and was therefore more than pleasantly surprised to find that we had been joined by two more of Adelaide's finest. Helleuuw. These were the flatmates of the two girls I had arrived with, and within seconds they were down to their briefs and in the bed as well. So there we all were, me and these four delicious darlings, all strawberry blonde and all with legs like stairways to heaven, enjoying a little roll around and a few more drinks. Cramped, yes. Cosy, certainly. Glory, glory, hallelujah. The time was flying and I didn't have a care in the world. Cricket? I'm not sure cricket figured too prominently in our discussions.

Once everything had calmed down a bit, I identified the girl whose bed we were actually in and tried to sort out arrangements for the morning. I established that, according to her at any rate, we were about fifteen minutes' drive from the hotel, and told her that on pain of death I had to be there at 8 a.m.

'No worries,' she said. 'I'll set the alarm for 7.30.' Only about a couple of hours kip as it happens, but better than trying to get back there and then.

I don't know what woke me up, but it was definitely not the alarm clock. A little groggily I came to and checked the time. It was half past eight. Oh shit. I went cold. I felt the blood draining out of me. 'Oh my God. Oh my God. Wake up. I am in so much trouble,' I said, uprooting my sleeping companion.

'Zzzzzzzzz,' was her response.

'Oi!' I said. 'What happened to your f***ing alarm clock?'

'Huh,' she said. 'Oh well, you see. I don't know why exactly but sometimes it just doesn't work.'

I grabbed all my gear and threw most of it on as we dived into the car and flew down the highway towards the city. Meanwhile, back at the hotel and unbeknown to me, one or two of the boys, having realized I was not where I should have been, started to think of a covering story.

What they were thinking of when they came up with this one, I will never know. 'Where's Tuffers?' asked Micky Stewart as they were preparing to leave. 'Well,' said Robin Smith, 'sometimes he likes to jog down to the ground early.'

Brilliant.

We finally arrived at about ten past nine, by which time a hundred potential excuses were rushing around my brain. None of them sounded particularly plausible, but I was in a blind brown-trousered panic so I plumped for the least stupid, i.e. I had been in my bedroom all the time but the automatic wake-up call facility hadn't worked. Now time was of the essence. I was for the high jump, come what may, but if I could just get to the ground within about half an hour of the others and in some kind of shape, they might turn half a blind eye. So I came sprinting through the double doors of the hotel, picked up my key and made straight for the lifts, running very fast. The floor covering between the reception desk and lifts being polished marble, and the new shoes being slightly too big, the result of this manoeuvre was like a scene from *Carry On Cricketer*.

First, I slipped and went arse-over-tit, taking out a couple of rubber plants, the information board listing 'Today's Events' and a rather nice vase. Next, coming to a sliding halt right in front of the lift, I heard 'ding' as the doors opened. And then I saw them: three pairs of rather-too-familiar-looking training shoes. Inside them were Peter Lush, Micky Stewart and Graham Gooch. It turned out later that they were on their way to the ground after having attended to some team matter or other. Now Gooch was attending to me.

'Don't say a word,' he started. 'Get your arse upstairs.

Have a shower. Sort yourself out and get yourself down to the ground. I will talk to you later.' I feared the worst. They knew. How could they not have known? I was still in my clubbing gear, stubbled up and looking like something the cat wouldn't dare drag in. I'm dead, I thought to myself. They'll send me home and I'll never play for England again.

By the time I arrived at the ground the story was out among the lads, who were biting their own hands to stop laughing in front of the management. In due course, I was pulled by Gooch and Stewart.

They fined me £500, I think, which I was a bit pissed off about. Looking back, I probably got off lightly, but at the time I couldn't quite get my head round it. If I'd had half a brain, I would probably have realized that with a little cleverness, I could have enjoyed the best of both worlds. But I was twenty-something, footloose and fancy free, and it just seemed that a lot of doors were being opened for me. Granted I was late at the ground and I might not have prepared myself for the match in the ideal fashion. But all I had been doing was enjoying myself. I didn't seem to be doing too much different from some of the more senior guys. The management knew they couldn't lock me up in a box. In fact they did say that there was nothing wrong in going out and having a good time. It was just that I never quite got the timing right. I was simply having too much fun, I suppose. Perhaps my biggest problem was my naivety. That and dodgy alarm clocks.

We lost the sodding match, of course, which made everyone even more cross. Gower, opening in place of Ned who was absent at the dentist, hooked the second ball of the innings for six and was then caught at extra cover from the fourth – a shadow of what was later to happen on the same ground with much more serious consequences. The players were publicly bollocked afterwards by Stewart and Lamb, and the next day we were all called in for what the press called 'naughty-boy nets'.

As December wore on things became more complicated. First up was our action-packed trip to Perth for the next two one-day matches. Gooch could see the way the wind was blowing, and was desperate to get himself fit enough to play and take over the reins again. After a couple of nets with Devon Malcolm he announced he was fit to continue. My net with Devon turned out rather differently.

The incident in question occurred on the eve of the first of two World Series games, against New Zealand, during our final net session. I was a little jumpy at the time because I had just been told that I would be playing the following day. This was going to be it – my first international match for England, the moment that was going to make a bit of sense of my life and I was rather keen not to let anything get in the way. Batting against fast bowling at the best of times has never been my idea of fun. And what I saw in these nets only reinforced my opinion. Not only are they renowned as the quickest, bounciest surfaces in the world but, Devon apart, the young lads recruited from local club cricket to put the batsmen through their paces were busting a gut to make an impression.

In the circumstances, I saw no point in putting myself at risk unnecessarily. The practice nets were coming to a close and I was packing up my gear, getting ready for the showers, when Micky said to me: 'Where are you going? You haven't batted yet.'

'It's all right coach,' I said. 'I'm feeling in good enough nick. I think I'll pass, thanks all the same.'

His response wasn't quite what I was after. 'Get your f***ing pads on and get in that net.'

As I did so, all I could see were images of Robin Smith and David Gower, two of the best batsmen in the world, ducking and diving and doing everything they could merely to avoid decapitation. What chance did I have?

I was thinking to myself, this isn't right. I'm just about to play in the most important match of my life and these idiots want me to go into a terrifying fast net against dangerously hostile bowling. What's the point? Even if I don't get killed, one of these bastards is bound to break my fingers, my hand or an elbow or something and what use will I be to the team then? If my mooching demeanour didn't make plain just what I thought of this, my words must have done. 'I think this is crazy,' I muttered. 'I shouldn't be doing this.'

There was nothing I could do. I had made my protest and no one was listening. So I shuffled into the net, took guard and waited. It was like standing in front of a firing squad. Fortunately Devon understood the situation and the first ball he bowled was a nice sighter. Then, mayhem. One of the young blokes ran in and bowled a genuinely fast ball on about half-volley length. It cut back sharply and hit me straight in the nuts.

So there I was, rolling around on the deck, fighting to get my breath, with the tears welling in my eyes and, behind me, a growing audience of beer-swilling Aussie spectators thought this was the funniest thing they'd ever seen. When I regained the power of speech I let fly: 'I f***ing knew I shouldn't have had this net. I f***ing knew it. What am I doing in here?' At this, the bowler in question leaned towards me and said: 'Get up Tuffers, you f***ing coward. There's another one coming.'

That was it. I was not going to get killed or maimed on the day before my international debut just for the amusement of some Aussie bastards who thought it was fun to use me as a coconut shy. No thanks, I was off.

Gooch, who had seen everything, came up to me and asked me where I was going. I explained my position. Okay, I was a No 11 no-hoper and, of course, you've got to have a net the day before a match to get your eye in. But against blokes trying to knock your head off in the quickest nets in the world? Let's be sensible. Was this going to turn me into Bradman? No. Was I going to get injured? Very possibly. Can someone tell me who was being irresponsible here?

Gooch couldn't have been more sympathetic, or more understanding. 'Get back in the nets,' he said, and walked off.

I lost it then. I threw the bat away and told them they could all go and f*** themselves. This went down brilliantly, and soon I was up before the beaks once more and the cash till operated by the fines committee sprang into life again. Only six weeks into the tour and already I had been done twice. Not the best start to my life as an England cricketer. But this was nothing compared to the events that were soon to define the whole experience, and perhaps the main part of my Test career.

NINE

Fielding Academy

During the fortnight spanning 26 December 1990 and 8 January 1991, the life and times of Philip Tufnell included the following episodes: my Test debut at Melbourne; being sworn at by an Australian umpire; the formation of the Phil Tufnell Fielding Academy; my first Test wicket at Sydney; another alleged row with my captain Graham Gooch; fines for Alec Stewart, Eddie Hemmings and myself for on-field dissent; a catch dropped off my bowling from a hat-trick ball.

It was all happening. And most of it happened to me.

The next piece of bad news for Gooch was not without a smidgen of irony. Although the captain himself was fit again and playing, it was the turn of Allan Lamb to suffer injury. He had batted well enough in Ballarat against Victoria, making 143 against Merv Hughes and Paul Reiffel in the final warm-up match prior to back-to-back Tests in Melbourne and Sydney. And then, as if he had not had enough exercise already, Lamb jogged back to the hotel from the ground, and tore a calf muscle in the process.

Despite the growing number of black marks against my

name, there it was on the team sheet on the first morning of the second Test in Melbourne. And I was ready. No nerves. No time for nerves, I suppose. I would have liked to have got out there sooner than I did. As a result of major rebuilding, there was a big hole where the Southern Stand used to be, but there were still 60,000 in there and an atmosphere unlike anything I had ever experienced before.

Batting first we made 352, with Gower hitting a beautiful hundred and Alec Stewart getting 79. My contribution was a very fine unbeaten nought. Then it was our turn to bowl.

I will never, ever forget my first over in Test cricket. The crowd all seemed to be sitting right above my head, all eyes staring down at me. I wasn't fazed by it. I loved it. I was here. I had arrived.

The first thing I noticed was that the ball, which was not all that old, had all the hardness of an oily rag. The seam had disappeared and there was very little to grip. The next thing I noticed was Dean Jones standing at the other end, sort of eyeing me up.

My plan was to try and bowl tight early on, get into a groove and then see what developed. My plan lasted one ball. I'd just got to the hop in my run-up, immediately prior to the delivery stride, when I looked up and saw Jones *running* down the pitch towards me like an axe murderer. 'Christ alive!' I gasped. 'Now what do I do?' I had to go through with the delivery: I was past the point of no return. But I couldn't bowl it in the place I had planned, because he was coming at me, ready to kill the ball. My immediate thought was to bowl the ball over Jones's head, which, considering this was to be my first delivery in Test cricket, might not have gone down too

e: One of my earliest brushes with the law ... ing a pram while under the influence of ... e-cream.

: My sensible brother Greg with an arm ... d my shoulder in our own personal all-... sports stadium – Wembley in winter, ... 's in summer.

v: In case you didn't believe me, Philip ... Roderick Tufnell, captain of the Highgate ... r School cricket team. With three initials ... Highgate education, how did I fail to ... ne captain of England?

My first Middlesex photocall, at the start of the 1985 season. Among stars like Mike Gatting, Wayne Daniel, John Emburey and Phil Edmonds, I should only have spoken when spoken to. Jamie Sykes and I made sure the club spoke to us rather a lot.

Above: I celebrate my first Test wicket, versus Australia in the third Test of the 1991 Ashes tour at the Sydney Cricket Ground, by rucking with the Aussie umpire Tony Crafter.

Right: Graham Gooch and I had our disagreements, but I respected his dedication.

Left: Gooch had no complaints when I bowled out West Indies at The Oval in the sixth Test of 1991 to help us earn a 2–2 draw.

Above: Practising my penalty-kicks at Lancaster Park, Christchurch on the 1991/92 tour to New Zealand.

Left: My parents, Alan and Sylvia, on their wedding day.

Getting the winning habit, as the Kiwis crumble in Christchurch, 1992.

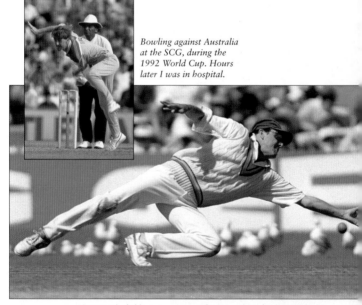

Bowling against Australia at the SCG, during the 1992 World Cup. Hours later I was in hospital.

Very nearly fielding on my second trip to Australia, 1994/95.

...dras palmist assures me that my fortunes ...e 1993 tour to India will improve – once ...home that is.

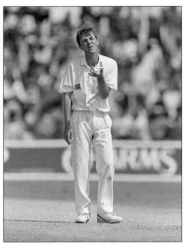

Failing to get a handle on Indian batsmen.

The headline treatment: I learnt that my ex-wife Alison had taken up a new career from a reporter on the News of The World...

EST STAR'S
WIFE IS
ON THE
AME

WORLD EXCLUSIVE

ONCE SO HAPPY: Phil and Alison on their wed

ENGLAND cricket hero Phil Tufnell's ex-wife is **working as a prostitute.**

Pretty blonde Alison Tufnell charges punters £150 a night for sex.

Close to tears she said: "I'd give my right arm to stop what I'm doing. I've become addicted to it—and to the money.

"I do it seven days a week."

The News of the World discovered 26-year-old Alison's secret while probing the murky world of escort agencies following the brutal murder of

By JAMES WEATHERUP and

Phil booked in the Test hotel No Limbo at Lord's yesterday England's ex-wicket hero West Indies earlier this...

He split with Alison when she became a prostitute and before they were officially...

...Later the Daily Telegraph *reports on me getting my just desserts.*

Tufnell is fined for hitting ex-girlfriend

PHIL TUFNELL, the England and Middlesex cricketer, was fined £800 yesterday after admitting two charges of assaulting his former girlfriend.

Tufnell, 27, was also ordered to pay £250 compensation to Miss Jane McEvoy, the mother of his 21-month-old daughter Ellie.

Enfield magistrates heard that when the spin bowler returned from England's tour of the West Indies in April, he was disappointed that Miss McEvoy had not met him at the airport.

He went to their home in Osborne Road, Palmers Green, north London, and she told him she was leaving him. They parted that night.

Three days later, Tufnell arrived home and found Miss McEvoy and her brother

Phil Tufnell Jane McEvoy

his daughter again. In the row that followed, the couple ended up fighting on the floor.

The second assault came two days later, after Tufnell was told he could not see his daughter at a nursery because staff were "afraid he might kidnap her", said Mr Francis. Miss McEvoy arrived and Tufnell slapped

Above: A rare success in India on the 1993 tour. Navjot Sidhu is sent packing.

Right: Trying to bowl the ball-on-a-string.

Ian Salisbury's elevation from net bowler to squad member in India had a totally negative effect on my already fragile confidence.

Atherton succeeded Graham Gooch in
with a clear mandate for change. He was
nly more tolerant of my on-field
ssion.

The man who made playing for England fun
for the first time. Ian Botham's return to the
Test scene against West Indies in 1991 made
me see things in a different light.

atel, the Kent left-arm spinner, who
got an unexpected call to travel to
alia in 1994 on the night I spent in the
iatric unit in Perth.

Yorkshire's Richard Stemp. At least Min got
a Test eventually. Stemp was included in a
couple of squads, but never played.

At the start of the 1994 tour to West Indies I might have taken the instruction to let my hair down a shade too far.

Pleading for justice against a Victorian batsman on the 1994/95 tour to Australia. Generally speaking Australian umpires and I did not always see eye to eye.

well. Finally I forced myself to get the thing down to the other end of the wicket. Then Jones, without seeming to break stride, hit it past my ear like a shell.

'Hard luck, Cat,' came the voice of Gooch from somewhere to my left. 'Keep going.' Keep going? I had only bowled one sodding ball.

'Pull yourself together,' I told myself. 'Just bowl it.' Just bowl it where, exactly? I had a sudden vision of a Test career analysis reading: 1–0–millions–0. Don't call us.

For the next ball Jones adopted the same method, but seemed to start running even earlier. I just managed to fire it in so that he had no room to swing his arms. Flushed with the success of not being smacked to the rope, I got a bit giddy. I decided I would just hold the next one back a fraction and give the ball a little more air, so that when he gave me the charge this time he wouldn't quite get to the pitch. I would be ready and waiting, Mr Jones, for the catch.

Nice idea. Shame about the result. I held it back well enough, but all that seemed to do was give him more time to spot it, mark it and leather it. Trouble was, he leathered it straight back again, this time even harder than the first so that I had no time to move a muscle, let alone get a hand to it. It hit me full on the right ankle, at which I let out an agonized scream.

From my position on the deck, it took me a few moments to realize that there wasn't a great deal of sympathy forthcoming from my colleagues. In fact, after I had stopped rolling around on the floor and managed to struggle manfully to my feet, I noticed that not one among them had moved an inch to offer assistance. They were all just standing around staring at me. 'This,' I thought to myself, 'is a *very* hard game.'

During our second innings it very quickly became much, much harder. We had dismissed them for 306 in the first dig, thanks to some brilliant stuff from Angus, who bowled his bloody great heart out as usual. That gave us a lead of 46 and, without getting carried away, very handy we thought that would be too. At 103 for one in our second innings, with Ned and Gooch both on fifty-odd, all the talk in the dressing room was of what sort of target we should set them in our declaration. The pitch was slow and it would be difficult to bowl them out a second time, so it was vital that we should give ourselves enough time. To make that happen we needed to press on now. Down in the dungeon of a dressing room, Gus and I were idling the time away when Gooch, trying to force the pace, played at a wide one from Bruce Reid and was caught. No cause for alarm, we thought. There were plenty more runs to come. Even when we lost a couple more in quick succession at tea on that fourth day we were 147 for four, 193 ahead with power to add.

Then the roof caved in. As the wickets fell, the noise grew louder and louder and the panic became more and more hysterical. In a flurry of bats, pads, boots and gloves in the dressing room, followed by a flurry of the same out in the middle, we lost our last six wickets for three runs (Tufnell completing a pair of undefeated noughts, incidentally) and we were well and truly in the shite. I have never been so frightened at a cricket match before or since, nor more disappointed. The feeling that this was all slipping out of our control, and the reaction of the crowd, increasing by a notch on the dial with every dismissal, combined to unleash an almost tangible sense of fear. The whole thing seemed to happen in a matter of seconds.

We tried to persuade ourselves that we had a slim

chance of victory, but we fully understood that in order to pull it off we needed every little slice of luck to go our way. Nothing did. Gus, after his heroic efforts in the first innings, was starting to struggle with the hip injury that was to place a huge question mark against his future. Devon was lively, but the pitch, now dead, gave him nothing. Although I was accurate enough, there was not a lot going on out there for me, either, against Geoff Marsh and David Boon, who was in one of his most obdurate moods.

We were bowling as much for pride and experience as anything else. If they were going to win, we wanted to make sure they would have to do it tough. And what better personal incentive could I have had than to be out there chasing my first Test wicket? Enter, stage right, Peter McConnell, the Australian umpire with whom I was about to share a brief but intense relationship based on mutual contempt.

As so often happens in these cases, the trouble came out of nothing. It happened in about the fifteenth over of my spell and it happened like this: I was concentrating like mad, intent on keeping things as tight as possible, and on the way back to my bowling mark I happened to ask the umpire how many balls were left in the over. I believe it was the first thing I had said to McConnell in the entire match. His response was charm itself. Without even so much as a half-turn of the head he muttered: 'Count 'em yourself you pommie c***.'

'Sorry?' I replied. 'You what?'

There was no response.

'Look mate,' I carried on, 'all I did was ask you how many balls there were to go in the over. I'm not having that.'

By this time, everyone watching but not hearing was thinking, 'There goes Tufnell again, showing dissent to the umpire.' And when Gooch marched over towards us, the boys in the press box were not the only ones thinking the bad boy was in hot water again and maybe, bearing in mind my previous misdemeanours, about to be boiled alive.

'Excuse me, umpire,' said Gooch.

'Here it comes,' I thought. 'Bye-bye Melbourne. Bye-bye Australia. Bye-bye Test career.'

'I heard what you said,' Gooch continued, 'and you cannot talk to my players like that.' You could have tied my tits together with candyfloss. Bugger me if the old sod wasn't sticking up for me. Very big respect to Graham Gooch, here. None whatsoever to Peter McConnell. He was clearly unsettled by Gooch's rebuke and obviously embarrassed. I was mightily relieved.

It wasn't long, however, before the umpire struck back.

I was probing and searching and, the longer I went without it, almost praying for my first Test wicket. The moment finally arrived a few overs later. David Boon stepped back to cut a short ball, miles away from his body, and gave it everything. The result was the biggest nick I have ever seen in my career before or since, straight through to Jack Russell. I ran down the wicket towards Jack shouting and screaming and carrying on like a lunatic. Whatever else happened in my life, I would not be going to my grave without a Test wicket.

Now, I fully understood that the general practice in Ashes contests was that nobody walked without being given out. I did think in this case Boon might have made an exception. After all, he had clearly smashed the cover off the bloody thing. Anyway it was obvious he wasn't going to go of his own accord, so I turned to McConnell for the formality of the appeal. He looked me straight in the eye and said: 'Not out.'

'You f***ing bastard,' I said.

'Now *you* can't talk to *me* like that, Phil,' he said.

We never did manage to get rid of Boon. He and Marsh duly completed the job and the result was that after two Test matches we were 2–0 down, having lost by the not inconsiderable margins of ten wickets and eight wickets.

Although the mood was generally gloomy within the camp, I have to confess that I didn't share it. I was having a great time: fun and frolic off the field, and now actually playing for England at Test and one-day international level on it. I felt the world was my lobster. And some strange occurrences at the Sydney Cricket Ground were about to enhance my reputation no end among the Australian sporting public. In fact, by the time we moved on from that even more beautiful city, I had become a sort of cult figure.

The next thing that happened to me was the formation of the Phil Tufnell Fielding Academy. The day/night World Series match at the SCG on New Year's Day drew a large crowd and Australia were struggling a bit at 82 for four when Steve Waugh came in to join his brother Mark. Crucial time, crucial partnership, pulses racing. Then came the moment. I bowled a ball to Mark that he knocked short. Steve reacted quickly and hared off for the single, but Eddie Hemmings got to the ball faster than anyone thought possible. Mark realized there was no chance of a run, turned and stayed in his crease. Steve kept on coming and joined him at the striker's end with the ball already in Eddie's hands. Steve, having sussed the situation, started to walk off, and I do believe he actually began taking off his gloves at this point. All we had to do to finish off the run-out was for Eddie to lob the ball back to me and for me to break the wicket at the bowler's end.

Eddie lobbed it all right, nice and gentle and loopy straight towards me, and I was there, standing behind the stumps in textbook position, ready and waiting. What could possibly go wrong? To this day I cannot believe what happened next. Out of nowhere, the ball hit my hands like they were saucepans, Teflon non-stick saucepans. Then it gathered pace, sprouted wings and flew ten to fifteen feet away.

Steve had given himself up so completely that I still had plenty of time to go fetch, run back and nick off a bail. So what did I do? Panicked. With both batsmen still stuck at the striker's end, I sprinted after the ball, picked it up, and hurled it at the stumps as hard as I could. I missed by miles. And with no fielder backing up, Steve just shrugged his shoulders and jogged back to the crease to make his ground. Meanwhile nearly 37,000 people were looking at me, bellowing and hooting and shaking with laughter.

Not for the first time I looked around for a spot of support from my colleagues. It was a familiar picture. Alec Stewart, keeping wicket, was looking down at his boots. Gus was walking away with his back to me, trying desperately to control his mirth. Gooch, surely Gooch would have something to say. He did. He said: 'You c***.'

Then the sadists operating the giant screen proceeded to show the entire episode from every conceivable angle, over and over again in slow motion. Each time I looked up hoping that a miracle might occur, that the whole thing might turn out to be a hallucination or a trick of the floodlights. It never did.

We lost heavily. Gooch said afterwards that the

performance of the batsmen was the worst he could recall during his captaincy. Good job he didn't mention the fielding. The academy was born.

The roller-coaster ride continued a few days later in the Test match at Sydney. They won the toss, batted first and scored 518. But proceedings were far from uneventful. My run-in with McConnell at Melbourne had left an after-taste that became even more sour here. We felt we were not getting the rub of the green with close umpiring decisions. When a couple more fifty-fifties didn't go our way in the first innings, a certain degree of grouchiness crept in which resulted in one or two of the boys indulging in conduct unbecoming. Eddie and Alec Stewart were fined for dissent and there was some tut-tutting from the boys in the press box. But that was nothing compared to what was about to come my way. While the occasion should have been one of the highlights of my career, it turned out to be anything but, and the result was another black mark on a report card that was rapidly becoming as black as a report card covered in black marks could be.

My first Test wicket was proving increasingly elusive. I felt I was bowling reasonably, keeping things nice and tight, but as time went on I started to get a bit panicky. A few shouts for leg before had been turned down by McConnell and Tony Crafter; a half chance or two didn't carry; and all the while I kept imagining the smirk on McConnell's face growing wider and wider.

And then it happened.

Greg Matthews, the off-spinning all-rounder, had been batting well to score a century that appeared to be making the game and the series safe for Australia. He came down the wicket to a flat full toss and got it too low on the bat. The result was that he spooned the ball high towards

Hemmings at deep mid on. I think my heart actually did miss a beat. I shouted, 'Catch it, Eddie. Pleeeease,' then turned away. I couldn't look. I'd had one perfectly good wicket taken away from me by McConnell at Melbourne and there'd been a few close ones here. I simply couldn't bring myself to watch. All I could think of was: 'Please let me get off the mark before I fade away or get run over by a truck. Please.' I looked at Alec, who was staring intently towards the position where Eddie was going to try to take the catch. When I saw a little grin on his face, I knew it was okay. I couldn't resist a little dig at Crafter. I told him: 'I suppose that's not f***ing out either.' And then I turned and ran towards Eddie without a second glance. I just kept on running. I saw nothing else, I didn't see the 40,000 people in the ground or any of my team-mates.

What may have contributed to the subsequent controversy was that on that second day, when the Aussie tail-enders hacked out some runs to which they were not entitled, our fielding became pretty shabby. Gooch later called this passage of play 'the most shaming day of my cricketing life', and when we got back to the dressing room he told us what he thought of our performance. However, the first I learned of the fact that I had 'snubbed' the England captain was when I read about it in one of the Australian newspapers the following day. What were they talking about? Snubbed Gooch? When? Where? How?

The answers were as follows. In the immediate aftermath of Eddie taking the catch, Gooch had apparently come up to me and tried to shake my hand. I, according to the report, had ignored the captain's gesture and run straight past him. The truth is that Elle Macpherson could have been standing in front of me as naked as the day she was born and I wouldn't have noticed. A rather more attractive proposition than our stocky off-spinner, I grant you, but I only had eyes for Eddie.

Whether Gooch was upset by this perceived slight or not, I have no idea. He has never mentioned the incident to me, and I imagine that if he had been seriously pissed off about it, he would have said something. He had already had plenty to say to me about my behaviour before that. I suppose the bad-boy business was really starting to kick in at this point. I was an easy target. The team was being bashed about and those critics, inside and outside the team, who were looking for scapegoats found that I fitted the bill nicely.

In the short term, we responded positively to Gooch's bollocking. Athers dug himself in for a big one – 105 in a day and a bit – and Gower spanked a lovely 123. Gooch then threw down the gauntlet by declaring 49 behind on the fourth afternoon. When we got a couple out that evening they were a little less chirpy than they had been, and the final day was set up nicely. They didn't know whether to have a shit or a shave, to be honest; whether to press on for runs and have a dart at us, or consolidate and kill the game. It was then that I had my little moment in the sun.

I'd already got Boon out, caught by the skipper off Jack Russell's glove, which got us a little interested. They still had the big guns of Border, Jones, Steve Waugh, Matthews and night watchman Ian Healy to deal with, but if we could get among them, the picture could change radically. Then it did. Gooch caught Border round the corner, sweeping, off my bowling to make it 129 for four. Game still alive. Next ball, Dean Jones followed his usual pattern and came at me, running. Again, as I had done at

Melbourne, I held the ball back, and again, as he had done at Melbourne, he smashed it straight back towards me. Unlike at Melbourne, however, this time I caught it. Two wickets in two balls, Australia 129 for five. Now then ...

Steve Waugh came in to face the hat-trick ball and we shut out the daylight. Everyone was around the bat. All of a sudden the Aussies in the crowd who had been laughing their socks off at us stopped laughing. Waugh pushed forward with his bat behind his pad, the ball flipped past the pad and went straight off the full face of the bat towards Gower at silly point. For a moment David was obscured from my view by another fielder and instinctively I leapt in the air, believing as much as hoping that he had held on. He just failed to do so. What a hat-trick that would have been: Border, Jones and Steve Waugh! I think I might have been forgiven a few late nights for that little lot.

We still had a great chance and pressed really hard. Eddie and I bowled over after over, but as time went on, most of us became convinced that nothing short of knocking out all three poles would have been sufficient. Failure to keep such observations to myself cost me another fine for dissent. Rules are rules and all that. But I counted five bat-pads – and my arithmetic is terrible.

If only Gooch had brought Devon Malcolm back earlier to have a go at the tail, things might have turned out differently. My first five-wicket bag in a Test match was no real consolation for the fact that we just let them off the hook. Although Gooch and Gower smashed it everywhere, a target of 255 in 28 overs would have required miracles. The Ashes were out of reach.

For the rest of the tour Gower and I, and one or two others it appears, proceeded to find more and different ways to piss Gooch off. First there was the Tiger Moth incident at Carrara, when, having borrowed a few dollars from Peter Lush for the purpose, Gower and John Morris buzzed the ground where we were busy playing Queensland. Gower and Morris were relieved of a grand each, and 'Animal', despite making a hundred in that same match, never played again for England. After that came Gower's last-over-before-lunch dismissal in the Adelaide Test, watched by a stony-faced Gooch, and then we completely fell to pieces in the final Test at Perth.

It was here that I produced a performance which, in terms of my current relationship with the captain, was probably the last straw. My fielding was at about its worst point by this stage. I had simply lost all confidence and it is fair to say that most of my time in the field was spent praying that the ball wouldn't come anywhere near me. The academy had been fun when it started, and among the thousands of words of abuse I'd received, my personal favourite was: 'Tufnell, lend me your brain. I'm building an idiot.' By now, though, much of the humour had long since gone out of it.

On the field I had started to imagine that Jones was deliberately picking on me. He would push the ball towards me, knowing that in normal circumstances there would be no chance of a single, and then he'd take one anyway, banking on the fact that I would cock it up. When I came a little closer to try and cut off the single, he would push the ball past me for two.

The batting display that earned Gooch's undying contempt came when I literally gave my wicket away against Merv Hughes in that game at Perth. The pitch was quick and bouncy and these boys were a shade too hot for my liking. When earlier I had bowled Craig McDermott with a peach of an arm ball, my joyful farewell to the big fast bowler was met with a stare and the following reply: 'You've got to bat on this in a minute. Hospital food suit you?'

By the time I went out to do so against him and Merv in the second innings, with us crumbling to inevitable defeat, those words were dancing around my head. I managed to carve a couple over the slips, which didn't strike them as funny at all, and then I received a monster of a ball that reared up from a length and which, had I not deflected it with the tip of my thumb, might have taken my head clean off. Despite a big appeal, the umpire did not seem inclined to give me out. I decided the time had come to take the law of self-preservation into my own hands.

'Ow, my thumb,' I wailed. 'I think you've broken my thumb,' I said and walked off. The umpire's finger brought my batting in the series to an end none too soon. When I got back to the dressing room, several players had towels in their mouths. 'Sorry, mate,' I said to Gooch as I sat down. He looked at me as though I had nicked his wallet.

'It's been like farting against thunder,' he told the press afterwards. 'A nightmare. I've been unable to get the best out of my players and motivate them sufficiently. Our attitude in touch-and-go situations is nothing like that of the Australians, who have always been competitive. At the end of the day it's the careers of these players that will suffer. They won't make it and they'll only have themselves to blame. Our fielding has been the worst I've ever seen in any team.'

Did he mean me? He surely did. Clearly, in his comments about attitude and so forth, he was also referring to Gower. Once we moved on to New Zealand for some more one-day stuff, Gooch invited his long-time colleague out for dinner and a chat to clear the air. That worked. Gower didn't play for England for another eighteen months. Although I didn't know it then, I was about to join him on the outside looking in.

TEN

The Cut of my Jib

I hadn't exactly been the kind of textbook tourist that Gooch, Micky and their work ethic had been all about. All the same, I returned home from my first senior tour under the impression that I had done okay. Socially, my horizons had been widened somewhat. A year before, I had been one of the lads down the White Hart pub in Southgate. For the past couple of months I had been rubbing shoulders with legends like Gower and Lamb, drinking wine and champagne. Yes, please. And apart from having had a quite brilliant time off the field in almost every other way imaginable, on it I had played my first Test, taken my first Test wicket, racked up a five-for and very nearly snared a hat-trick of huge names at one of the great arenas of world cricket. Furthermore, I had forced my way past Eddie Hemmings to become the first-choice spinner. All in front of big enthusiastic crowds. Not bad for starters, eh?

It wasn't long before I discovered that I seemed to be in a minority of one in this belief.

After every overseas trip, the manager and captain used to submit their tour reports to the officials at the Test and County Cricket Board. These would then be passed on to the counties for their perusal, and before long, rumours began to circulate around Middlesex that the sections concerning me were X-rated. By all accounts it was the kind of report that schoolkids try to snatch from the hand of the postman and feed to the dog.

I was summoned before the county committee and given what I suppose amounted to a grilling. It was a little confusing, because every sentence started with, 'Your tour report said that you bowled very well, Philip.' It was the subsequent buts that were not quite so flattering.

By the start of the 1991 season, word had spread, it seems, not only in the Middlesex dressing room but elsewhere on the circuit as well. I got the feeling that other players were a bit sheepish when they came into contact with me. Mates were giving me funny, sympathetic looks. It was as if someone in my family had died and nobody was sure whether I'd been informed yet.

I wasn't deaf to Gooch's remarks at the end of the Perth Test, but I bowled well for the club in the early games and no one had said anything to me on an official basis. I knew that there were probably going to be changes to the Test team, but I didn't for a moment believe I was going to be one of them. Then suddenly I was. The squad for the first Test against West Indies at Headingley was announced and two names were conspicuous by their absence: D.I. Gower and P.C.R. Tufnell.

In my place was Richard Illingworth, the Worcestershire left-arm spinner. I didn't look any further. All I could think of were the nods, winks and whispers that had been following me round like a growing swarm of midges ever since I got back from the tour. I had been dropped, pure and simple, and as far as I was concerned my Test career was over. Down in the pub that afternoon

I told my mate Horace: 'That's it. They won't pick me again. I've upset a few people and that's the end.' The next day I took what was left of my tour fee out of my bank account, walked into a second-hand car showroom and bought a Porsche. Retail therapy, I think they call it.

Illingworth hadn't been in the final eleven at Headingley, as England relied on seam and swing on a pitch that traditionally helped those elements far more than spin. Thanks to a brilliant century from Gooch, England won, however, and it was highly unlikely that they would be making too many changes for the second Test at Lord's. When the squad for that Test was announced, no matter how many times I turned on Ceefax to see if there had been a mistake, my name was still nowhere to be seen. Illingworth's was. All my fears were now confirmed. If this was the way they wanted it to be, good luck, I thought. What was this all about, anyway? Go and stand in the corner until we send for you?

Now, picking me or otherwise on cricketing grounds was one thing, but all the information that was reaching me suggested that I was being excluded for every other reason except my cricket. Attitude, character, call it what you will, the message was that they didn't like the cut of my jib. Excuse me, but exactly who were these people making judgements about my life and my behaviour? What were their credentials? What gave them the right? Anyone making the link between now and my mind-set of early adolescence, award yourself five points. My attitude was this: you lot are having a go at me again. Up yours.

In the immediate short term, I carried the feeling with me to Sheffield for Middlesex's game against Yorkshire, to be played at the same time as the Lord's Test. As it happened, that match became one of the first big turning points of my career.

I was at my brilliant best from start to finish. What was I doing there when I should have been at Lord's? What's up with you? What are you looking at? Spoiling for a fight, when Embers asked me what field I wanted for a certain batsmen, I said to him, 'Don't ask me. You're Gooch's mate. You're the man who knows it all. You set the field.' I sulked and shuffled and scratched my arse through the entire match. I was a disgrace, if I say so myself. On the third day I surpassed even my previous very high standards. A mis-hit drive off my bowling sailed over the fielder at mid-off but bounced way inside the boundary before going for four. I lost it. I had a right go at Gatt for not having positioned the man on the line and I gave it the full monty – swearing, kicking the turf, refusing to carry on until I got my way and had the man back on the boundary rope for the catch. I can think of no better word to describe the episode than tantrum, with all the suggestion of childishness that it implies. Gatt came right back at me and we had a shouting match, at the end of which he decided that the only solution was to send me off!

Nobody said a word to me for the rest of the match, which, perversely enough, finished with me and Simon Hughes as the last pair batting out six overs or so to cling on for the draw. Perhaps I knew what was coming and had decided I had better pull my finger out, although if I'd been run out off that risky single I took in the last over I'm not certain that would have gone down too well either. Sure enough, at the end of the match Gatt told me he wasn't having it and suspended me for the next match. That might not have been too harsh a punishment, except for the fact that the next match was the NatWest first-round match against Ireland in Dublin, a two-day trip that invariably turned out to be a magnificent piss-up. Gutted!

It was then that Embers took me to one side and gave me a bollocking. 'You selfish little prat,' he started. 'Who the hell do you think you are? Buck your ideas up. You can't keep relying on other people to set your fields for you, you can't keep blaming other people if your fielders aren't in the right positions. You have got to start taking on a bit of responsibility for yourself, your bowling, your field placing, your behaviour. You can't just keep running to me or Gatt and expecting us to do your work for you. We've got enough on our plates looking after our own game without having to wet-nurse you all day long. Grow up.'

This was a wake-up call. Embers was the one senior player at the club who had always been on my side. He had stuck up for me in countless situations where Gatt had lost patience, and I had come to regard him as my minder and my mentor. The others could say what they liked, but for him to take me to task in this way was serious.

I took a look at myself. The first thing I realized was that my reaction to not being picked for England was pretty pathetic. I was sulking, pure and simple, thinking only of number one. Yet there was more to it. The more I looked, the more I started to believe that the real problem was not too much confidence, but too little. A pattern was beginning to emerge in as much as my behaviour seemed to rely almost totally on my success as a bowler. When I wasn't bowling as well as I should have been, I became irritable, self-conscious, even a little paranoid. I felt that people were looking at me and saying, 'He's not very good after all.' My self-esteem would dip, I would react and then, more often than not, I would go and get lashed to top up with Dutch courage. I had become too self-absorbed. I was either on top of the world or down in the dumps. There didn't seem to be any middle ground.

Embers' words hit hard. Prior to that, my reaction to all the bollockings from the club had been to shrug my shoulders and ignore them. This time, what was said and who was saying it meant something. Whether or not it did any good in the long term I don't know. I can't say I became a changed man or anything like that. And I found it difficult to comprehend everything that seemed to be required of me. On the one hand, my little eccentricities and a few tales of after-dark deeds seemed to keep my colleagues amused enough. 'You're a character,' they told me. 'Don't change the way you are.' But when things went wrong, it was, 'Pull yourself together. You can't carry on the way you are going. You've got to change.' Perhaps that was a contradiction I was never going to resolve, or never going to want to, to be honest.

Another thing I found was that sometimes people would take too literally some of the things I said. Try this as an example.

Team-mate to Tufnell, looking slightly shabby, first morning of match: 'What's up, mate?'

Tufnell to team-mate: 'Oh, you know, bit of a headache. Must have been the ten pints I had last night.' Chuckle.

Team-mate to Tufnell: 'Ten pints? Blimey.'

Tufnell exits dressing room.

Tufnell returns to dressing room.

Committee man to Tufnell: 'Philip, can I have a word? Don't you think ten pints is rather excessive the night before a match?'

Tufnell: 'I beg your pardon?'

The immediate impact of Embers' comments was far less complicated, however. It was the realization that far too many people were getting far too pissed off with me far too often.

The fact is that had Richard Illingworth – a bloke for whom, incidentally, I have always had a lot of time – taken the opportunity to establish himself in the England side, that might have well been time, Tufnell, please. As it was, however, defeat at Trent Bridge and then in Birmingham meant England were 2–1 down going to The Oval. Gooch was desperate to win the final Test and square the series, particularly after having come so close to a similar result in the Caribbean during their previous encounter. Desperate men sometimes employ desperate measures.

Strange things began to happen. Just prior to the selection meeting, I heard and read suggestions that I might have been growing more mature in my approach. Was I? According to whom? Or was this information being put about by the selectors to explain their impending U-turn in policy over yours truly? The fact that I had been bowling well and with a fair degree of success in county cricket might also have had something to do with my return to the colours. Not wishing to be ungracious about this, or ungrateful for the second chance, chaps, but in years to come it often struck me that some people's perception of a player's 'attitude' and 'character' seemed to depend on how many runs or wickets that player was taking at the time. Or was this merely a case of Gooch becoming a little less rigid in his thinking?

It's fair to say that my private life was somewhat less hectic than it had been in Australia. Jane and I were now an item and we were having a lot of laughs. She had a bit of fire and spirit in her and the raving exploits of the previous summer were again pursued with some vigour. Acid House parties were still in vogue, we liked going to them, and the lifestyle clearly wasn't affecting the cricket. No harm done.

So when I turned up at The Oval, I had mixed feelings. I did want to succeed – desperately. But I went there determined to be myself, to prove to Gooch and the others that I could be an England bowler on my terms. At this time of my life my attitude was that off the field my life was nobody's business but mine. All I ever wanted and expected anyone to do, and all anyone was actually entitled to do as far as I was concerned, was to judge me on what I did with a cricket ball in my hand.

And then into the dressing room, for the first time in two years, exploded Ian Botham. *This* was what I had signed up for.

It is hard to describe the wave of relief that washed over me when I heard the noise with which Botham announced his entrance. The sound itself is hard enough to describe, emanating as it appeared to do from a deep underground cavern, then booming from his mouth like the horn of an ocean-going liner announcing its imminent departure. Incorrectly aimed, the vibrations from one of Botham's belches might be capable of laying waste to a small market town. To me, though, it sounded like the music of the gods. As I sat in the corner of the changing room at The Oval, not quite knowing how to react to having been given a second chance, watching this living cricketing icon completely grip the attention of every single person just by being there, I offered up a silent prayer.

'Thank God,' I thought. 'Thank God there is someone

here who will stop everyone looking at *me*. Thank God there is someone here who is not blindly going to obey the regime if he doesn't think it is right. Thank God Beefy has come to save me.'

'Come on lads,' said one of the hierarchy. 'Let's do a couple of laps.'

'Yeah, right. In a minute,' said Beef.

And I thanked God again.

With all that was going on between Gooch, Gower, myself and others, the atmosphere inside the England dressing room during those last two Ashes Tests had been extremely tense. No one quite knew if it was okay to talk to X or be seen with Y. It was office politics gone mad. And now this. This bloke came in and single-handedly threw all that nonsense out of the window, lifted the mood and took all the worry and the tension out of proceedings. His message was simple: do your thing, take no shit, enjoy yourself. For me it was as if someone had ripped down the curtains that had been blocking out the sunlight. And it was the same on the field. Whereas in Australia the blokes in the slips were so petrified of missing a chance that they looked as though they had pineapples stuck up their arses, Beefy was actually standing there in the slips with his hands on his knees making stupid faces.

At last I was playing in a Test match where people were not going around frightened of their own shadows, caught up in the nerve-racking fear of doing something wrong and letting the side down. At last it was all right to have a laugh on the cricket field when playing for England.

Beefy's sense of fun was infectious. Although we were determined to win, the experience just wasn't so deadly headbanging serious as it had been before. Instead of me thinking, 'Don't let the ball come to me in case I bog it up,' I was thinking how bloody marvellous it was and how lucky I was to be out there.

On and off the field his presence had an effect. Robin Smith, who had worshipped Beefy from the first time he came in contact with him, made a sparkling hundred. Botham himself made 31 before failing to 'get his leg over', as Jonathan Agnew and Brian Johnston fell apart trying to tell the nation, and we made a highly useful 419 – including a well-crafted two by me, prior to having the living crap scared out of me by Patrick Patterson.

They had moved quite happily to 158 for three when I came on for my first bowl on the Saturday. Desmond Haynes, my Middlesex buddy, was cruising. Clayton Lambert, the left-hander renowned as a fierce walloper of the ball and who felt all spinners were put on the earth for his own personal gratification, was equally well set. And as I prepared to deliver my first ball, I noticed with some trepidation Clayton actually laughing out loud as he swung his arms and rehearsed a huge mow towards deep mid wicket. Deep as in halfway down the Harleyford Road. Here was a good test of my new-found *joie de vivre*. Sod it, I thought, if he wants to have a go, let him. I popped one up just outside off stump, nice pace, little bit of turn. He launched himself at it and sent it about 150 yards almost perpendicularly straight up in the air. Ramps was never going to drop it: 158 for four.

Viv Richards was suffering with piles, so Jeff Dujon came in next, to be cleaned up by David 'Syd' Lawrence at 160 for five. But after I had Malcolm Marshall caught by Botham in the slips for nought at 161 for six, the moment could be delayed no longer.

I have to say that there are very few batsmen whose

mere presence actually struck fear into my heart. Plenty of bowlers, yes, but very few batsmen. And Richards was the scariest of them all. The way he strode to the wicket, with that incredible swagger of his, carrying his bat like a club – he made time stop. Spectators and players alike went deathly quiet in his presence, out of sheer respect. And there he was at the other end from me. My boyhood hero, the bloke I had watched on my television smashing very good bowlers to all parts, getting ready to bat against little me. He looked absolutely gigantic. Inside me a tiny voice was crying 'he-e-elp'.

Searching for a crumb of comfort or even encouragement, I sought out Beefy. Surely to God, if anyone knew what I should do next it would be him. The two men were soul mates, blood brothers. From their years playing together with Somerset and against each other in Test cricket, they each knew instinctively what was going through the other guy's mind. Somewhat unhelpfully, Beefy was pissing himself.

There was nothing for it. I simply had to bowl the ball. I did. I gave him my best looping, spinning, ball-on-a-string. It was cleverly flighted and dropping on a perfect length ... and Viv played it with his dark eyes closed. Then he looked at me from under that peaked West Indies cap, a strange, piercing look of contempt. 'Is that the best you have, Philip?' said the look. 'Is that it? Is that what I walked all the way out here to bat against?' And I thought to myself: 'Jesus Christ almighty. This bloke is going to whack me f***ing everywhere.'

I tried to walk back to my mark but my legs were like jelly. For a split second I actually thought I was going to faint. Then, somehow, I pulled myself together. What's the worst thing that's going to happen here? I asked, but left the question unanswered. Come on, *come on*, I urged myself. If he's going to come gunning for me, there's nothing I or anyone else can do about it. So I bowled the next ball, held it back a fraction and saw him coming at me full pelt.

Now when Viv came at you, he used to do it with a leap. He used to cross his legs in mid air so high that you could almost see the sole of his leading boot coming straight for you. And in that moment I was convinced that he was going to hit this ball harder than anyone had ever hit a ball in the whole history of cricket. So I did what I had to do. I made myself as small a target as possible. Down on my haunches and turning sideways, I assumed the cricketing equivalent of the crash position. When he started the huge heaving motion from the top of his backswing, the gust it created nearly blew the hair out of my head.

I knew. There wasn't any doubt in my mind whatsoever. It was a certainty that if Richards hit the ball the way he looked as though he was going to hit it, I was a dead man. But he didn't hit it the way he looked as though he was going to hit it. Out of the corner of my half-turned-away head, I saw it pitch, turn and bounce – and then I saw and heard him just get a little nick on it as it passed through to Alec.

My first reaction was shock. I was numb. 'What do I do now?' I thought to myself. 'Appeal, you idiot, appeal.'

Now there was utter confusion. In the same action as taking the catch, Alec had whipped the bails off to stump him as well. And now the umpire at my end, Merv Kitchen, was looking across to the square-leg umpire John Holder. Holder looked nonplussed, certainly not as if he was about to give Richards out stumped. 'Don't look over there, Merv,' I said. 'He nicked it; he nicked it.'

'That's out,' said Merv.

What? What do you mean, 'That's out'?

Wake up. Think. Think quickly. How to celebrate? Big running, whooping stuff, perhaps? No. No. Don't be a ponce. This is Viv Richards, here. The King. The masterblaster. Something more befitting the occasion. I had it. I strolled down to the other end and quietly shook hands with Alec as though this was the kind of thing I did every day of my life. Mind you, when I spotted my brother and his mates celebrating his stag day in one of the boxes, leaping and jumping and punching the air, I very nearly did forget my sense of decorum.

After that the fun continued: Curtly Ambrose, caught Botham again for nought, 172 for eight; Courtney Walsh, caught Gooch for nought, 172 for nine; and finally Patterson, caught Botham once more for two, 176 all out. All bowled by Tufnell, who finished with six for 25, including a spell of six wickets for four runs in 33 deliveries.

There you go. I was back.

To be quite honest, although I had bowled pretty well and kept my nerve in certain situations, I have to say that the batsmen contributed a large amount to my success. It was as though they had wound themselves up to bash me out of the game and once they started they just couldn't stop themselves. No matter. I'm not complaining. As a bowler you take days like these in compensation for all those when you bowl like a god and finish up with sod-all. My abiding memory was that it was all so much fun. In between overs, when I walked back to my fielding position on the boundary, there were cheers and roars and applause from the crowd. Quietly, under my cap, I was giggling to myself like a schoolkid. When I ran up the steps at The Oval at the end of their innings, I was met halfway by Greg, who grabbed me and hugged me. Neither of us said it, but I'm sure we both thought the same: if only Mum could have been there. I took some calming down in the dressing room, as you can imagine, but there was no time to dwell on what I had done, because we enforced the follow on and went straight out to field again.

Having taken six in the first innings I naturally assumed another shedload would be coming my way in the second. It didn't quite work out like that. Forty-six overs, six maidens, one wicket for 150. Talk about back to earth with a bump. Richie Richardson got at me a bit and made a dashing hundred, and this time Viv made a commanding sixty in his final Test innings. The ovation he received when he left the field for the last time with a bat in his hand brought a little lump. And they managed to set us a nasty little 140-odd to win.

It was at this point that I really started to appreciate for the first time what Graham Gooch was all about. Here we were, on the threshold of what might be one of the great Test match wins, needing a tricky last-innings total, and I looked at Goochie, strapping his pads on and muttering to himself, pumping himself up and gritting his teeth, and realized there was no one else in the world I would have wanted to go out there and try and knock them off for us. From then on, although I may not have fully agreed with his methods, I saw where he was coming from.

It was a jittery time out there. Gooch made 29 to steady our early nerves, and by the time he was out at 80 for three, we seemed to be almost there. Robin Smith got out at 80 for four and it was left to Alec and Mark Ramprakash to take us to the very edge of victory. Although I wouldn't for anything have wished on Ramps his dismissal one run short of the line, it was somehow hugely fitting that Beefy should go in and knock his first ball for the boundary that clinched a drawn series against West Indies for the first time since 1973–74.

Champagne? Fill her up, please. Then fill her up some more. There were some amazing scenes: big crowd going bananas; massive celebrations; showers of champers and beer; and Botham at the heart of most of it. I don't recall leaving the ground and have no idea how I got home. The next thing I have any kind of clear recollection of was being woken up the following morning by Jane hitting me over the head with a rolled up copy of the *Sun*.

'What the f*** is this?' she enquired, shoving the paper under my nose. Through the mist, an image started forming. It was of me, standing none too steadily between two girls with their boobs hanging out and dressed only in G-strings, holding a bottle of Moët in each hand and with the maddest expression you have ever seen. Then it all came flooding back. Someone at the ground had suggested we should carry on drinking, and I ended up at a nightclub owned by someone's mate, where a group of dancing girls were doing a show. I was a bit pissed, they came over and had a few drinks and a few laughs and the owner asked if he could have a private picture to frame and put on the wall of the club. So we all stood up and adopted this party pose, the flash went off and that was that.

Now here was that same private photograph adorning page three of the newspaper with the largest circulation in the known universe. And now here was Jane attempting to cure my hangover by smacking me over the head with it. Why can't anything in my life be straightforward?

Things were about to become even more complicated.

I retained my place for the final Test of the season, against Sri Lanka at Lord's. This was going to be a brilliant occasion for me – a Test at my home ground, the fulfilment of a dream dreamed by my old man ever since he had forced me back into the game seven years earlier.

When the phone rang in my hotel room at around 11 p.m. on the eve of the match, I was just getting ready for bed. My first thought was that Botham was bored, couldn't sleep and was rounding up a few of the troops for a little libation.

'Phil Tufnell?' enquired the voice on the other end. 'I am a reporter from the *News of the World*.'

'Of course you are, Beefy,' I replied. 'And I'm Joe 90.'

'No, no, Mr Tufnell. I'm serious,' said the voice. 'I am from the *News of the World* and we will be running a story this weekend saying that your ex-wife Alison Squires is now working as a prostitute. Were you aware of this?'

I didn't know what to say. This really was news to me. The reporter wanted me to react; that was obvious. He wanted me to say something daft to spice up the story even more. Yet if I said nothing, then maybe that would sound worse, as if I had something to hide. I plumped for the 'so what?' approach. 'What has that got to do with me?' I said.

'Well, you were married to her and she is going to say some things which might cause you embarrassment. I'm just telling you we are going to run the story and offering you the right of reply.'

'I have nothing to say,' I told him. 'As you have said, I am her ex-husband. We are no longer together. That part of my life is over. Her life is her own concern now,' and I put down the phone.

My feelings were a jumble. If this was true, and of

course anything was possible, my immediate thought was concern for Alison. We hadn't spoken since the split became final, and the break had been as clean as these things can be. I just hoped that, whatever she was doing, she knew *what* she was doing. And then I thought about the publicity that was inevitably coming. I didn't sleep much that night, but decided to tell the management and the other players what was about to happen first thing the next morning. There was a bit of stick flying around. Perhaps the lads thought the best approach was some mild piss-taking. But although I tried to put it out of my mind and just concentrate on the cricket, I found it tough going. On the Sunday I was up with the lark and made straight for the newsagents, half hoping that the whole thing had either been a hoax or that the *News of the World* had decided against publishing the story. They hadn't, but I had not anticipated what I saw next. At the very worst I was expecting a ten- or twelve-paragraph story tucked away on one of the inside pages. Instead, when I looked at the pile of papers stacked up to my waist, there, on the front page, was the headline written in massive letters: CRICKET STAR'S WIFE ON THE GAME.

I spent the rest of the day reeling, and by the time I reached the ground on Monday, it seemed that everyone in the place was either reading or had read a copy of the paper. I was in a daze. A fortnight earlier I had helped bowl out West Indies to win the Oval Test and my name was splashed over the back pages of the national papers for all the right reasons. Now this. For the first time in my career I was front-page news.

Beefy tried to help. He had been there before, too many times to keep count. 'Ignore it,' he said. 'Tomorrow's fish and chip paper.' I tried to, but I didn't really succeed. The name-calling from beyond the boundary wasn't great, either.

In the short term, fortunately, there was bowling to be done. Hundreds from Alec and Gooch against Sri Lanka's gentle medium-pacers had enabled us to set them 423 to win from 132 overs. We snuck a couple out on the Monday evening, then bowled them down the next day. I finished with five for 94, my third five-for in four Tests and against three different sides, after Australia at Sydney and West Indies at The Oval. And by the end of the match I thought I had succeeded in pushing the story out of my mind.

With a winter tour to New Zealand and the 1992 World Cup in New Zealand and Australia on the horizon, I should have been on top of the world. I knew it was odds-on that I would be picked but, try as I might in the days ahead, I remained uneasy. The *News of the World* had barged open the door, and now everyone else was piling through. Very strange how it happens. One day you are just a run-of-the-mill bloke doing your job; the next day you are public property. Everyone wants to know you, to get close to you, to analyse you.

I had achieved a certain amount of notoriety down under the previous winter, but nothing on this scale. Could they really have been talking about me?

Step right up, ladies and gentlemen. Come and see the next wonder of the media circus; Tufnell's his name, or Scrufnell, or the Artful Dodger. Is he the saviour of English cricket? Is he the bad boy of English cricket? You decide. Drives a Porsche, you know. Flash git. Bit of a rebel, you know, expelled from public school. Burnt down the gym, didn't he? Ooh yes. Always in trouble, with the law, with Middlesex, with England. Wore a pony-tail. Is he a poofter? Now his ex-wife's on the game. Did he leave £30 on the bedside table? Drives a Porsche, you know. Flash git. Wait folks, here's the sad bit: mum died when he was very young. Misunderstood, misrepresented, misquoted, misfit. Likes a drink, likes a fag, what else I wonder? I've heard he likes the wacky-baccy. Sshhh. Likes the ladies, though. See that photo in the *Sun*? Maybe he swings both ways. Feet at ten-to-two. Can't trust him, but what a laugh! Middlesex nearly kicked him out. Middlesex should have kicked him out. Refused Gooch's handshake when he took his first wicket, didn't he? Can you believe it? You name it, he's done it. Fines? He's had 'em all. Just ask the England management, eh Philip? Oversleeps, overpaid, over-rated – drives a Porsche, you know. Flash git.

Hold on. Hold on.

Now, everyone involved in sport accepts that they are in the entertainment industry. There would be no sport if no one watched it either live or on television, and the modern camera techniques mean that the viewer is as near to being on the field in the heart of the action as it is possible to be without actually being there. And with that false closeness comes a false intimacy. When it is decreed by the newspapers that you are to be the flavour of the month, there is nothing whatsoever you can do about it. The newspaper editors justify their actions by citing the people's right to know. The people's right to know what? Then they send their reporters to find out. I'm not only talking about the tabloid papers here, either. Where their guys will dress up information gathered as news stories with appropriately catchy headlines, the writers in the broadsheets will sometimes use exactly the same material to build what they would describe as an analytical appraisal, but which can be just as intrusive and just as hurtful. Nobody just writes about cricketers as cricketers any more. Character, attitude, approach and behaviour have become as much a part of the big picture as technique, ability or skill. So what makes Phil Tufnell tick, then? If the answer is not newsworthy, interesting or sensational enough, find one that is.

All papers have writers who fancy themselves as amateur psychologists. Some are better at it than others and everyone is entitled to their opinion. But sometimes their conclusions are so unfair, so far off the mark that they would be funny, if it weren't for the fact that people read them and take them seriously. As for the advice you are always given – namely to take no notice – get real. How are you supposed to take no notice when your name is plastered all over the front page of the screws?

Some of the motivation for this microscopic attention must be jealousy. What's he done to deserve all that? Why should he be bowling out West Indies? Why not the rest of us?

The mood spreads to the man in the street. I remember one occasion soon afterwards when some bloke came up to me in a pub, slightly pissed, and asked if he could buy me a pint. I thanked him and accepted the offer, spent five or ten minutes with him and chatted about my bowling at The Oval. Very nice. Later I heard from someone else that this bloke had been in another pub the next night shooting off his mouth. 'I was with Tufnell the other night,' he told his mates. 'What a lad! Ten pints we had. I carried him out. Then we met some birds. Then we went down the Chinese and he ended up puking everywhere. And he never once put his hand in his pocket. Flash git.'

My natural paranoia started to kick in in a big way. And this extended to the game. It might not have been the case, but I felt that my reputation was now preceding me.

Before my success, a lot of people in the game – players and umpires and others – just thought I was a bit of a nutter, I think. Had my success now made me a target?

The squads for the winter tours were yet to be announced at the time my frustration boiled over in an incident at Trent Bridge in a game for Middlesex against Nottinghamshire. Ramps and Keith Brown had made hundreds in our first innings and Notts were struggling to avoid the follow on. Eddie Hemmings swung a ball off me high towards Norman Cowans. It was a sitter, but Norman missed it. I had a tantrum, kicked the ground, the usual tricks, and the umps had a quiet word. The next day the papers were full of it. According to them I had been severely reprimanded by the officials. There had been a major bust-up between Norman and me. High drama. Bad boy of English cricket living up to his reputation.

It was just ridiculous and it was just because it was me. The bandwagon was rolling. How many times in his career had Gus kicked the ground in frustration? When he did it, it showed the right spirit, it showed he cared, it showed he was worthy of respect. When I did it, it showed I was a yob.

I was so concerned about the stories that I actually rang up Gooch. I knew that the selectors were meeting while this series of Championship matches was going on, I knew they would have heard about the incident, and I was worried as to how they might react. Luckily we managed to have a reasonable chat. 'I think it's all getting a bit out of hand,' I said. 'We had a bit of a row, but it was nothing like as serious as it was reported.'

'Don't worry,' he told me. 'Just keep your head down.'

Two days later the squads were announced and I breathed out.

ELEVEN

Kiwi Fruit

As the tour was still three months off, there was time to take stock. During the early stages of my relationship with Jane, her parents had been highly sceptical about their daughter's new boyfriend. The main reason, I found out later, was that Alison had rung them up and told them I had given her a dose. That probably explains why, at my first meeting with Michael McEvoy, he warned me that he would break my legs if I did anything to hurt or upset Jane. How those words would later come back to haunt me.

After Alison, I was still very dubious about long-term relationships, and although I enjoyed being close to Jane, at twenty-five any thoughts of marriage were not mine. There were so many girls ... so little time. So I arrived in New Zealand once again considering myself a confirmed bachelor. And once again, I did what confirmed bachelors do.

In the break between the end of the season and leaving for the tour, we had trained and prepared well. It had been hard work, but somehow not as rigid as I had feared, and once we arrived the cricket was almost non-stop success as well. There was a nasty early scare, when one of the

New Zealand cricket writers implied in an article that I was a chucker, providing a topic that various Kiwi cricketers and commentators managed to keep alive through suitably ambiguous references.

The feeling within the camp was that this was a not very convincing attempt to unsettle me before the Test series started. In fact, it did affect me for a brief spell, during which I would look around and see cameras being pointed at me from all kinds of peculiar angles. But the talk soon faded before any real damage was done. Graham Gooch and Micky Stewart fully supported me, pointing out that in five years of first-class cricket and a full Ashes tour I had never once had my action questioned, let alone been 'called' for throwing. After that I just got on with bowling – and everything seemed to fall into place.

The Kiwi crowds, who had had such fun at my expense a year earlier, soon found their voice again – 'Tufnell's a wanker' being their particular favourite – and their aim. During the first one-day international in Auckland, which we won at a canter, certain members of the audience decided I should be used for target practice and one or two were pretty good shots. I enjoyed giving them as good as I got and, while it was raining fruit only, the situation was well under control. It was quite warm out there, so a nice piece of mango, banana, or even a peach or two was very refreshing. It was when some bloke started throwing pot noodles at me that I drew the line.

When I complained to Derek Pringle afterwards, proudly listing the items I had bravely withstood, he was far from impressed. 'What do you know about being pelted by the crowd?' he inquired scornfully. 'The last time I fielded down there someone threw a bat at me.' Derek always did, and still does have a way of eclipsing a story with a tale of his own, or with his extraordinary knowledge on a wide range of utterly obscure subjects.

Born in Nairobi and brought up in the bushland before being educated at an English public school and Cambridge University, he possesses the certainty of conviction common to many of the descendents of colonial adventurers. Invariably he began his ripostes with the words, 'What do you know about,' then whatever it was the previous speaker had identified, as in being pelted by people in the crowd/real ale/any unknown rock band you care to mention/traffic jams/the legendary doctors of jazz, Washboard Sam and Harold 'Stoneballs' Aloysious/room service in the James Cook Hotel in Christchurch/wine/the mating rituals of the African water buffalo/cricket/anything (delete as applicable). Top bloke, Derek, and the most gentle of giants, but winding him up brightened many a dull afternoon on tour.

Following the rigours of ducking and weaving against the West Indies' fast men, our batsmen enjoyed themselves immensely in New Zealand. No disrespect, but Danny Morrison, Chris Cairns, Chris Pringle, Willie Watson and the fantastically named Murphy Su'a (the 'a' of which, in the time-honoured fashion of saluting opposing goalkeepers, was pronounced as in 'you're shit aaahhhh') did not pose quite the same threat as Curtly, Courtney, Malcolm Marshall and Patto had done.

In the first Test in Christchurch we made 580 for nine, even without a contribution from Gooch, who made two. Alec Stewart hit 148, Robin Smith 96, Allan Lamb 93 and Chris Lewis 70. That meant we were controlling the game, and once again I was in the great position of having a huge total to bowl against. I took four of the first five wickets to fall in the first innings and, with them struggling at 91 for five, things were going swimmingly. Then one of the ghosts of my past came back to haunt me. Dipak Patel, who along with Graeme Hick and Phil Neale had helped make my Middlesex debut such a misery, came out and, just as he had done in 1986, hammered me everywhere. His counter-attack took them within range of avoiding the follow on, until quite out of the blue Derek unleashed a magnificent throw from the boundary to have the poor sod run out for 99.

They did have to bat again, before tea on the fourth day. But by then, on a pitch that was slow and getting slower, they should have been capable of saving the match. With only the final session remaining, they had reached the safety of 201 for three and everyone in the ground – which, to be fair, was not that many – was convinced that they had done so. Several interested parties had already made their excuses and left. One Sunday newspaper journalist, whose name escapes me, had left the ground for a relaxing punt on the river Avon. Visiting dignitaries from the Test and County Cricket Board – A.C. Smith, the chief executives and other bigwigs, whom we collectively called A.C. and the Sunshine Band – had seen enough, as had the representative of our sponsors, Tetley Bitter, while a game of cards had started up in the press box.

Why not? New Zealand were only three wickets down, the vastly experienced left-handed opener John Wright had reached 90-odd and taken root, and to win we needed to take more wickets than had fallen on any of the previous days. To make the task even more unrealistic, Dermot Reeve had left the field with food poisoning and Daffy was limping.

How we did it remains one of the great mysteries of recent Test cricket. Before we went out for the last two hours of play, Gooch urged, 'The game is not over until the last ball has been bowled,' but the response was largely lip service.

I had taken one of the three second-innings wickets that had fallen, but by this time I had bowled an awful lot of overs. Almost as many as the 39 I'd sent down in the first innings. I was trying hard enough but nothing much seemed to be happening and I could see a few of the boys in danger of dozing off. Then, quite unexpectedly, we noticed that Wright was getting a bit fidgety. His problems seemed to begin when he reached 99 a few minutes before tea. I don't think he was quite sure whether he should try to score the run he needed for the century there and then, so that he could clear his mind of it then set himself again after the break, or settle for shutting up shop and getting the run afterwards. He dithered and scratched, then finally plumped for the latter. This was fun. No matter what I bowled, he was going to force himself not to take any risks.

After the interval he carried on batting like a stuck record for another ten or fifteen minutes. I was aiming the ball into a spot of rough outside his off stump and he was determined not to play across the line. When he did try an attacking push, the field was set so that there was no way through, and he was obviously becoming more and more frustrated. Then, suddenly, he went at all levels. Despite the fact that he still had the best part of two hours in which to score his hundred, he charged down the wicket towards me hopelessly early, I fired it in and as the ball went past him, his cry of 'Oh, nooooo' said it all.

By rights we should still have been nowhere near, as Martin Crowe, one of the very best batsmen I ever bowled to, was more than comfortable. But a few minutes later, with the pressure growing, I managed to nick out Mark Greatbatch and Shane Thomson. Dipak didn't know whether to block or attack and ended up getting caught slogging. They were seven wickets down with an hour and five minutes of play remaining, and when I snared Cairns for a duck they were 241 for eight.

Time, runs and wickets were all as vital as each other. The equation was this: New Zealand needed to survive either until the close of play or until ten minutes before the scheduled close, provided they overtook our score. Then, even if we bowled them out and needed only one run to win, the ten-minute break between innings would mean we were counted out. At tea, their vice-captain Ian Smith had packed his bags and announced that he was looking forward to a cold beer. When he was bounced out by Lewis at 250, the last pair came together with half an hour remaining and 18 runs still needed for them to draw level. It was the tensest passage of play I had ever been involved in.

Crowe was the key and he was batting like a master. Every run was priceless. With about fifteen minutes to go, Ramps, on his first tour and fielding as substitute for Daffy, pulled off an amazing save to turn what looked like a certain boundary into a single. By the time I began my 47th over of the innings and my 86th of the match, Crowe and Chris Pringle had chiselled out 14 crucial runs. Four more, or one more over, and we would all have shaken hands.

With all the fielders in tight to save the singles, Crowe gambled on hitting me over the top to score the boundary that would save the game. It was his one false move. He skied the ball high above wide mid-off, prompting an instant of pandemonium when it seemed everyone on the field was calling for the catch. Finally Derek Pringle shouted loudest, circled underneath it and, even though it started to curve away from him in the air, held on to it for dear life.

From 211 for three, they had plunged to 264 all out and I had taken six wickets in 70 deliveries. Several hundred beers later, someone pointed out that my seven for 47 in the second innings out of eleven for 147 in the match represented my third consecutive five-wicket innings in three Tests. One thing was certain: we didn't hear any more talk about chucking. Instead Crowe said afterwards, 'Tufnell is clearly one of the best slow bowlers in the world.' Blimey! A slight change from what Gooch had been saying a year before.

I never used to analyse my performances too deeply, for I always felt that I might disappear up my own analysis. Embers used to say that the quality about my bowling which impressed him more than anything else was my ability to hold a ball back with no visible change in my action. The delivery that did for Viv Richards at The Oval was one of the best examples of this. I call it my 'ball-on-a-string'. Not quite as catchy as Muhammad Ali's 'rope-a-dope', but I hope it describes the (virtual) action of being able to pull the ball back from where the batsman thinks it is going to land. When Crowe fell in similar fashion here, my confidence went through the roof. At this point in my embryonic Test career, I felt as though I could bowl out any batsman alive.

We won again in Auckland, on a pitch that started damp and on which Gooch scored one of the best wet-wicket hundreds I've ever seen (playing and missing about fifty times) and Lamb battered sixty in quick time to set them a target they were never going to reach. After completing his panto season, Beefy arrived soon afterwards in time to prepare for the World Cup – Oh yes he did – and injuries dictated that he be pressed into action for his 100th Test at Wellington a few days later.

Our only low spot of the trip came when, on the final day of that Test and with the match going nowhere, 'Syd' Lawrence, our huge and huge-hearted paceman, suffered an horrific injury. Syd ran up to bowl like an elephant whose tail was on fire and delivered the ball like a heavyweight boxer launching a right cross from his boot straps. He couldn't try any less than 100 per cent if you paid him. Off the field he was just a big, awkward, smiley kid. At Wellington, in the middle of his full, rampaging delivery stride, he got his studs caught in the hard ground and cracked his kneecap clean in two. You could hear the noise, like a gunshot, all round the Basin Reserve.

No one felt like continuing the match, which ended soon afterwards in an irrelevant draw. Syd never played for England again. He went home almost straight away and spent years fighting the gloomiest prognosis. He even made several courageous comeback attempts for Gloucestershire, before finally admitting defeat. Although we tried to hide the feeling from him, those of us who were there that day feared the worst from the moment he fell.

As for my off-field exploits, it was on this tour that I learned the truth about what you can and what you cannot get away with and why. The fact is that as long as you are winning, you can get away with anything. When you are winning, all the larks and pranks are considered funny. When you're not you start to find that some of those fun and games are no longer tolerated. I couldn't work that out. To me, what's funny is funny whether you're winning or losing. My behaviour was no different to what it had been in Australia the year before, involving the same number of liaisons, the same number of units of alcohol and the same number of scrapes. Yet, because we were playing well and wiping the floor with the Kiwis, it was *carte blanche*. Maybe Gooch had eased up a little from the strict discipline he had tried to impose twelve months before. Maybe, with Beefy around for half the tour, he knew he wouldn't get very far trying to lay down the law with his senior professional. Whatever, I was intrigued when I later read Gooch's description of my approach as 'first-class'. The only difference I could discern between now and then was that whereas Australia had kicked our arses, we had taken New Zealand to the cleaners.

The World Cup was different. This was where we really came into our own. I started going out with an Australian Penthouse pet who snored like a helicopter. And we reached the final.

I had not been expecting to make the cut. The selectors had chosen Richard Illingworth to join the squad for the World Cup, and I assumed that once the Tests were over I would be sent packing. But my bowling persuaded them to keep me on.

Botham was to open the batting, as a very early version of the pinch-hitter. He had done so as an experiment in the final one-day match at the end of the New Zealand tour, making his highest score in this form of the game, and he continued to open throughout the World Cup campaign. Typically, though he failed with the bat in the first match against India in Perth, he then won the man of the match award and the game with his bowling and fielding.

A strong side in all departments, we maintained our

momentum with a win against West Indies, and would have thrashed Pakistan – most probably putting them out of the competition – had the rain not intervened in Adelaide, where we bowled them out for 74 and were 24 for one in reply. So we were on a roll when we arrived in Sydney for a showdown with Australia.

The occasion was magnificent and the setting perfect: a match against the old enemy. What better combination to inspire Botham's last show-stopping solo performance at international level? First he took four wickets for no runs in seven balls, including a peach of a delivery to bowl the Aussie skipper and his great rival Allan Border, going on to complete his best bowling figures in one-day cricket of four for 31. Then he went in and cracked a half-century to make the rest of our task a formality.

Sadly I missed almost all of that part of the performance. I hadn't been feeling great in the few days prior to the match, but, on the day, felt just about good enough to play. Almost as soon as we started fielding, though, I began experiencing these terrible stabbing pains in my gut. I managed to get through my bowling spell, just, but came off the pitch at the end of their innings feeling absolutely awful. Before he and Beefy went out to bat, Gooch gave a team talk that my colleagues later informed me was all but drowned out by the sounds emanating from trap one of the water-closet area. It was me donating the entire contents of my stomach to the Sydney Metropolitan drainage system. I came out of the bog looking like death and feeling like someone had taken all the blood out of my body. I was carted off to hospital, where I spent the night shot full of painkillers. They did loads of tests but couldn't find anything wrong, so I stayed on and took part in one more match, the defeat against

Zimbabwe in Albury that was the upset of the tournament. My only other memories were beating South Africa on the rain-rule to get into the final; some bloke dressed up as the Queen taking the piss in the pre-final dinner, at which Beefy and Gooch walked out and Peter Lush ordered the rest of us to 'stay in your seats, boys, don't move'; and the final itself against Pakistan in Melbourne.

To this day Pringle is convinced he had Javed Miandad plumb leg before from his first ball, at a time when his wicket would have given us a stranglehold on the game. To this day, every time Derek bumps into the umpire in question, the Jamaican Steve Bucknor, he asks if Javed is still not out. To this day, Steve has always responded in the affirmative. When we batted, Beefy got a bad decision and smashed his bat to bits in the dressing room in frustration, Wasim Akram started swinging the old ball round corners, and we were not quite good enough on the night. Running round the ground at the end and waving goodbye to the England fans among the crowd of nearly 90,000 who had supported us was a bit of a tear-jerker. We felt we were the best team there and we felt we should have won the Cup. Did we just run out of puff at the end? The number of little niggling injuries we picked up as the tournament reached its climax suggested that might have been the case.

We drowned our sorrows – many feared dead – and departed, deflated and exhausted, the second-best one-day team in the world.

When I got home Jane told me she was pregnant.

TWELVE

Out of Control

If I had my time again I wouldn't change a thing. Isn't that what we are all supposed to say?

Well if I had *my* time again, there are an awful lot of things I would definitely not do. Most of them occurred in the two-year period that began on my return from the 1992 World Cup and ended in the early summer of 1994 in violence, recrimination and court proceedings. All of them involved Jane and our beautiful daughter Ellie, who was born on 18 September 1992.

When I look back now at some of the things I did then, I go cold. I find it difficult and distressing to review a period of my life in which from time to time my thoughts, emotions and actions were out of control, causing pain to those closest to me.

For a lot of what happened I cannot excuse myself, nor do I seek to do so. Some of my behaviour was simply appalling. I can only offer explanations and attempt to describe the forces working within me. Almost certainly, none of that will ever be accepted by Jane and her family – and they will probably not be in the minority. All the same, I cannot gloss over the facts of my life during these dark days. They happened. I wish to God sometimes they hadn't, but they did.

The news that Jane was expecting came as a complete shock. We had been living together as boyfriend and girlfriend prior to my departure for New Zealand but, as I have said previously, there were no thoughts at all of a permanent relationship, certainly not marriage or children. That is not to say that I don't like kids: far from it. Whatever else happens in my life, I will always love Ellie, and the appearance of her half-sister Poppy – thanks to my second wife, Lisa – has brought me nothing but joy.

But prior to Jane's announcement, I had no desire to take on such huge responsibilities and even less idea of what they might actually entail. Since I first put on long trousers, my priorities had been extremely well defined: have a laugh, have a few beers and *cherchez la femme*. While the benefits of having someone cook, wash and run around for me had somehow persuaded me that married life with Alison was the right thing at the time, the thought of settling down to family life again just hadn't entered my head. In any case, in the immediate short term I was not actually fully committed to the relationship with Jane.

So when she told me I was going to be a father, I think it is fair to say that my initial reaction was bewilderment. As time passed and the idea took hold, my mood changed. I came round to thinking that if that was the way it was, I would face up to it, stand by Jane and try to make the best of things. The mood did not last very long.

There was no one close to me who could help me think through what the whole business of being a parent actually meant. My brother Greg had not yet become a dad. My own dad was by now living in retirement in Spain, getting his bald head brown, and Mum had died before I had the chance to discuss such matters with her. None of my mad mates had come near to fatherhood, at least not deliberately, and the reaction of the people I worked with – mostly single cricketers who, like me, had spent a good deal of their professional lives drinking, having a good time and trying to get laid – ranged from disbelief to out-and-out ridicule.

Time and again the conversation got round to changing nappies, being woken up at 3.30 a.m. and again at 5 a.m. and abandoning all ideas of fun and frolic. No one said a positive word to me. No one said, 'Phil, this is what happens – the first few months will be a struggle, but after that, you become involved in a great adventure.' No one suggested that the experience would be anything other than exhausting, debilitating and restricting. And the nearer the birth came, the worse I felt. I became incredibly anxious about what was going to happen to me once the baby was born. I just wasn't ready to live the life I was about to be committed to. My thoughts were filled not with what I would be gaining but what I would be forced to give up – namely the freedom to do exactly what I wanted, when I wanted, and with whom. I became utterly depressed.

My state of mental health was not improved when my body blew up in early May. Although the trouble I had experienced in Sydney had never been satisfactorily diagnosed, there had been no recurrence by the beginning of the 1992 season. One morning at Lord's, however, not long before the start of a Middlesex match, the pains came again even stronger than before. I pulled out of the game, the doctors did some tests and told me they wanted to open me up to find out precisely what the problem was. I refused and went home. The Test series against Pakistan was not far away and I wanted to play. Good thinking.

Two weeks later, I awoke in the middle of the night feeling as though someone was trying to rip open my guts from the inside. Sweating and shivering, I couldn't stop throwing up. I must have blacked out, because the next thing I knew I was waking up in the hospital again to be told that my appendix had burst and they had operated to remove it.

They wanted me to stay in for at least a week, but after a couple of days I was bored stupid. I got up, realized I could walk around a bit, phoned up my mates and said: 'I've had enough of this. I can't smoke, I can't drink. Come and get me out of here.' I still missed the following two months of the season, including the Lord's Test, where, in my absence, the leg-spinner Ian Salisbury was given his Test debut, and I didn't play for England until August in the last Test.

Recovered from the operation but frustrated by events, I once again turned my gaze towards my navel. I was spending less and less time at home. Once I was fit enough to play for Middlesex again, the normal cricketer's life on the road saw to that. And the more I was away, the more convinced I became that I was not cut out for what was about to happen. It just wasn't right. I should have been feeling excited and happy at the prospect of the birth of my first child, but I wasn't. I really didn't know what I should be feeling; all I knew was that I wasn't feeling it. Instead I was nervous and scared. I saw a deep chasm opening up in front of me. This was not what I was supposed to be doing. It was not that I didn't want the baby, it was just that the more I considered it, the more I became frightened of the responsibility. I felt trapped. And I tried to escape the only way I knew how.

This was not a case of the normal few beers after a game. This was a few beers after the game, then a few more, then downward to oblivion as quickly as possible with something stronger. Sometimes something a lot stronger. It reached the stage when, if I was not actually playing, I was almost certainly drinking. The booze made me brave again. I *was* somebody; I was Phil Tufnell, England cricketer. I had a few wickets. I had a few quid. I had a Porsche. I was a bloody legend. Who was I to be sitting around at home watching the telly?

One thing I wasn't was an alcoholic. Oh, no. Alcoholics can't control their habit. I could. I could stop whenever I wanted. I knew what I was doing. Oh, yes.

I couldn't see it at the time – as far gone as I was, I couldn't see anything much – but the reality was that I was pouring myself down the drain. By now the reason for my drinking had become largely irrelevant. The drinking itself had taken over. They say that when you start drinking you drink to forget, then after a while you drink to remember what it was you were drinking to forget in the first place. I know the feeling, but I was also drinking for the escape, for the feeling of being out of it itself. I was pulling myself to pieces. God only knows what I was doing to Jane.

It was then that the rows started in earnest. Huge, flaming rows. They would start out of nothing in particular, progress through the 'you never wanted this baby in the first place, did you?' stage and on to the 'I'm carrying your child and all you're doing is pleasing yourself' level. Then came the stuff being thrown, the screaming, the blind rage, the utter frustration and despair. All the rows ended the same way, with me walking out and slamming the door.

At the same time I began to pretend none of it was happening. In the same way as I blanked out the circumstances of my mum's death for years after the event, I behaved as if the pregnancy and the impending birth were simply not taking place.

The event itself was symptomatic of everything that was going on and everything that was going wrong. When Jane went into labour I was out on the town. I had been to a benefit function for one of my team-mates, didn't fancy going back home too early for the usual row, so I went on with a few of the boys and finally arrived home at around 3 a.m. When I rolled in, trying to be quiet so as not to wake Jane, I spotted a note on the hall table. Jane had gone to the hospital and, much to the disgust of her parents, when I arrived I was clearly the worse for wear.

When I watched Ellie come into the world, my emotions were churning. I was overcome at seeing her and Jane and knowing they were okay. I felt a strong love for mother and daughter, but at the same time I was just so anxious about everything. Jane stayed in for the night. I fled. The next morning I went to the pub at opening time and stayed all day and when, a couple of days later, Jane brought the baby home, she found me sitting there, still drunk. Jane said later that this was the moment she felt she had become a single parent. I can't blame her for thinking that. Ellie was a beautiful gift, and part of me wanted to look after her and give her all the love and attention I could. But at the same time that part was being drowned out by the noise in my head that was shouting, 'Get me out of here.' I didn't deliberately set out to hurt anybody. It was just that I was nowhere near mature enough to handle my own life, let alone somebody else's – and especially not that of a little helpless bundle like Ellie.

The memory of which gives me no pleasure or satisfaction whatsoever. Only shame. Over the next year or so, there was plenty more where that came from.

Cricket did not prove much of a distraction or comfort during these turbulent times. My one match of the season for England at The Oval ended in a victory for Pakistan that clinched the series for them 2–1. We had desperately wanted to win to gain revenge for the World Cup, and the desire among Gooch and the other players to do so was increased by the feeling among them that the Pakistan fast bowlers had been tampering with the ball. Their mutterings exploded into outright accusation after the one-day international at Lord's.

My full and complete personal experience of the controversy was the one delivery I faced in our second innings at The Oval. Having just taken guard from the umpire Dickie Bird, I looked down, looked up again and heard the stumps being trashed behind me. Don't ask me if the Pakistani bowlers fiddled with the ball. I never saw it *after* Wasim let it go, never mind what he might have been doing with it beforehand.

The selection of the squad for the winter tour to India and Sri Lanka provoked more controversy. I was glad to see Embers, and Gatt as well, back in the fold after their rebel bans had been lifted. (South Africa had been readmitted to international cricket, following the dismantling of apartheid, and all sporting sanctions were lifted.) The prospect of playing Test cricket with the man who taught me so much about spin bowling was one I relished. But Gower was omitted, as were Salisbury and Jack Russell, and this raised a real stink among a group of dissident MCC members.

After his spell at Gooch's pleasure, Gower had been

brought back for the Old Trafford Test against Pakistan, and had become England's leading run-scorer of all time. He helped to win the Headingley Test, so his subsequent omission was bizarre, and never credibly explained. The MCC dissidents, led by a man named Dennis Oliver, loved Jack because he was so clearly and genuinely mad, and they saw Salisbury, the only leg-spinner to play for England in living memory, as the last survivor of an endangered species to be preserved at all costs. Eventually Oliver's army forced MCC into a vote of no confidence in the selectors that was defeated only on the second ballot. Even later, maybe as a concession to them, Sals was invited to join the squad.

Most of which passed me by, to be honest. I was in, and frankly, apart from the Embers factor, at this stage that was pretty much all I cared about. By the time we departed for Delhi just after Christmas, the situation at home was slightly more stable. Or maybe we were kidding ourselves. It was a wrench saying goodbye to Jane and Ellie, with whom I had formed a strong bond almost despite myself, but somehow I think I felt that once I was away from them, for the duration of the tour at least, the reality of our situation would be postponed. And who knew how I would feel when I got back?

THIRTEEN

Done India

A land of colour, excitement, passion, drama, beauty and charm. And I am sure that for many visitors the reality of the Indian experience lives up to the ideal, wholly or at least in part. Personally speaking, it did my head in.

Everyone we met on the 1992–93 winter tour to India and Sri Lanka was as helpful as it is humanly possible to be. It was just everything else that I found over-whelming. They say India is an assault on the senses. It was. It gave me a headache.

I suppose if I had listened in school, I might have been a little better prepared for the culture shock. I might have been better prepared for the poverty, the sheer number of people, the smell, the mosquitoes, the sickness, the heat, the cold, the fog, the smog, the noise, the rats, the beggars who cut limbs from their children to increase their street value, the people with no legs shuttling themselves around on boards … But I hadn't and I wasn't.

It didn't take long for the possibility to occur to me that there might be a few minor differences between life here and in Tufnell Park. My first clue came about fifty seconds after I had taken my bags off the airport carousel. The porter who had strenuously and genuinely beaten off a crowd of his colleagues for the privilege of fetching and carrying my luggage – a walking skeleton with bow legs and a set of teeth like a bashed-up piano – then placed the whole lot on the top of his head as though he was building a house of cards. Then he *ran* towards the waiting team bus.

Impressed, but fearing I might be about to become the stupidest tourist victim of all time, I ran after him. His balance was incredible. Nothing moved from its original position. Then all of a sudden, and right in front of me, he screeched to an abrupt stop, removed the bags one by one, squatted in the gutter and performed a spectacular bodily function. Without further ado, he hitched up his rags, picked up the cases, sprinted to the bus and placed them precisely and carefully on the overhead rack.

Welcome to India.

As anyone who witnessed my performance in the bar at the Taj Palace hotel in Delhi on New Year's Eve could testify, I was in a fragile enough psychological condition as it was. Fuelled by a couple of gallons of margharitas, I was busy reviewing a year in which my personal life had gone haywire when, from nowhere, a massive, angry sadness swept over me. Just before midnight I tried to ring Jane from a telephone in the bar but the line kept going dead. Fed up, I walked over to the pianist whose dirgey playing had been getting on my nerves and asked him if he couldn't find anything more cheerful to play.

I was out of it and getting worse, and now I started picking arguments. I wanted to fight someone, to lash out, and I definitely wanted another drink. When the barman suggested I might have had enough, I disagreed, violently. The barman, fearing how things might develop, went off to fetch the manager of the hotel. Fortunately, one of the press guys arrived in the bar just before him, took one look at me, sized up the situation immediately and stepped in. First he smoothed things over with the manager, who was hell-bent on making an official complaint. It took some doing, but in the end the journo managed to persuade him that I was upset because of having to leave my baby daughter and that I had reacted badly to a combination of the booze and the malaria tablets. And then he dragged me off to his room.

He told me later that he felt the only way of making sure I didn't get into deeper trouble that night was for him to pour so much Bushmills down my throat that I would eventually pass out. And so he did, before hauling me back to my room at around 5 a.m.

Over the next three months I was to come across sights, sounds and, most particularly smells, that I had never experienced before or since. The whole tour was like an acid trip through the looking-glass to a cross between wonderland and hell with everything in between. And it left me completely beaten-up-exhausted.

The beggars were the first thing you noticed. Wherever we went, and particularly in Calcutta, Madras and what used to be called Bombay, the streets were lined with all shapes, sizes, varieties and ages. Some ancient, some barely old enough to walk, some with all their fingers, toes and faculties, some with very few, and all of them pleading for scraps of food or money. These were not the kind who populate the cardboard cities near Charing Cross railway bridge. Horrendous as this existence may be, such a life would be beyond the wildest dreams of these wretches. These people literally had nothing but the rags they stood up in. And no one seemed to be taking a blind bit of notice.

The Indian people might have considered such sights as part and parcel of their everyday life, but they weren't part and parcel of mine. I was to learn that most middle-class Indians actually seem to despise these poor souls; policemen beating them away from taxis and cars, or the drivers themselves chasing the beggars away from the tourists became a regular sight. And I never got used to it.

Indian society is complex, I kept being told. The problems of the poor are insurmountable, was the message, so do not concern yourself with them. According to Hindu religion and culture, the explanation of a caste system and the existence of these living dead can be found in a solemn belief in reincarnation. In short, as I understand it and as a former England football manager lost his job trying unsuccessfully to explain, Hindus believe that those born into such poverty and degradation were paying for sins committed in former lives. For obvious reasons, I find such a concept unutterably terrifying, and confess to being totally unqualified to comment on the religious beliefs of anyone. All I know is that the poverty I witnessed was dreadful and harrowing.

On this particular trip I don't really think any of us got used to India full stop and there were good reasons why the tour was more challenging than most.

First among these was the fact that it coincided with an outbreak of communal violence that cost hundreds of civilian lives all over the country. None of us knew where Ayodhya was, nor what the temple there represented. All we knew, thanks to the regular television bulletins and newspaper headlines, was that as a result of its destruction, extremists on both sides of the religious divide were killing a great many people. The idea was unsettling.

On England's previous visit to India, in 1984–85, the assassination of Mrs Gandhi had forced the England team to take refuge in Sri Lanka and, when they returned, the British Deputy High Commissioner, Mr Percy Norris, was shot and killed *en route* to his office in Bombay the morning after he'd entertained the touring party at his home. This time round, although we kept being assured by officials that we were perfectly safe, one or two of us felt anything but, and as the tour progressed and the bloodshed increased, so did that feeling.

As if that little lot weren't enough to put a man off his stroke, there was also the question of travel. Just for good measure, on top of everything else that was going on, the Air India pilots chose this moment to take industrial action. The government acted swiftly to recruit replacement fliers from the neighbouring Soviet republic of Uzbekistan, and jolly good they were too. Unfortunately the arrangement contained one vital flaw: none of the air traffic controllers spoke any Uzbekistani and none of the Uzbekistani pilots spoke English. The resulting incidents caused flying, at the best of times reputed to be more hazardous here than anywhere else on the planet, to become even more of a lottery than usual.

We played the game for a while, prepared, if not entirely happy, to leave matters of security and transport in the hands of our tour manager, Bob Bennett, along with his contacts at the High Commission and the relevant Indian authorities. We did the flag-waving bit, met the locals, had photographs taken wearing silly turbans and riding elephants with doped-up snakes wrapped around our necks. And then, shortly after we arrived in Lucknow to play a three-day match against an Indian Board President's XI, one or two of us decided enough was enough.

When we checked in at the hotel, we were informed that there would be armed guards on every floor. If we wanted to leave the hotel, we should not do so alone but in groups, and those groups would be ferried about in the back of an army jeep surrounded by armed specialists riding shotgun. Under no circumstances were we to walk to the ground, even though the journey would have taken about as long as it took for you to read this last sentence. When we got there, we were confronted by the sight of five thousand armed guards among the crowds of ten thousand who turned up to watch us practise and play. Yet all the while we were being assured that there was no cause for alarm.

If there was no cause for alarm what were all these chaps with rifles doing, exactly?

Frankly, the security in the hotel was a joke. Hardly any of the rooms had doors you could actually lock. At one point three blokes with guns, who were clearly not regular army, wandered off the street into a room occupied by myself, Robin Smith and Neil Fairbrother. All they wanted was autographs, but had they been so inclined they could easily have taken us out.

The final straws for Robin and me came soon enough. First it was announced that the one-day international match scheduled for Ahmedabad had been cancelled because, owing to an escalation in violence and killings in the area, the officials there could no longer guarantee our safety. Then another 'incident' involving an Air India jet landing on its nut forced the resignation of the government minister responsible for the air transportation system – a man who had earlier personally guaranteed our safe passage around the country.

'We've been assured that the tour will not be affected by

what is going on. The Indian Board hopes there will be no further disruption,' was the message. Robin and I and many more among us did not want to leave it to hope. We wanted some answers. In a meeting at which all the players and management were present, a few pertinent questions were asked. Why were we playing a game of cricket in a stadium in which half of those present were carrying rifles for our protection? Why, when there had been so many bombs and killings in Ahmedabad, had we had to wait until the Indian authorities decided they could not guarantee our safety before the match was called off? Why were we blindly flying around the country when the internal air system was a dangerous shambles? And why wasn't anybody telling us the real story of what was going on? We were not diplomats, or soldiers, or aid workers. We were cricketers.

The response? For God's sake, Tuffers, aren't you proud to be over here playing for England? Pardon me, but has anyone ever heard of pride deflecting a bullet or disarming a bomb?

I felt sorry for Graham Gooch, for I don't think he was ever really there at all. The moment we touched down in India he announced that his marriage was over, and he seemed preoccupied throughout. Later, when we arrived in Calcutta for the first Test, he was too ill to play but forced himself out there anyway, and the whole thing gradually fell apart for him. He reflected afterwards that he probably should have given up the captaincy at the end of the previous summer, but in the event stayed on one tour too long. Many believe he did so out of loyalty to Keith Fletcher, his mentor and former team-mate at Essex, as he took on his new role as England team manager in succession to Micky Stewart. At this stage, Gooch seemed to be caught in two minds. On the one hand I think he had a certain amount of sympathy for the way we were feeling. On the other, as captain, it was up to him to lead by example and carry on regardless.

In any case, having got precisely nowhere this way, we enlisted a spot of help from outside sources. The press boys had been monitoring events closely and one or two of them knew exactly how some of us were feeling. When one of us had a quiet word with one of the Sunday paper boys after play one day, the journalist agreed to write something that would bring to light our concerns and which might put pressure on the TCCB in England to take steps.

Robin, speaking on behalf of a group of us, told the reporter that the players were genuinely concerned about what was happening in terms of security and transport. He said we wanted action to be taken that would guarantee our safety. He suggested that, if it were thought sensible and practical, the England squad should abandon the tour temporarily and seek safe haven somewhere, at least until the worst of the violence subsided. Considering the England team did just that on the previous trip, when Sri Lanka offered a helping hand in very turbulent times, a trip there might have been the ideal solution. Then, if the level of violence remained dangerously high, consideration should be given to calling off the tour.

The reporter sent back the story, which was embellished back home by some quotes from wives and girlfriends – and the shit hit the fan. When news got back to Lucknow of what had appeared, the management went ballistic. There was an inquiry. Who said what to whom? At the ground, one of the daily papermen asked me for a comment and I gave him one, half for quoting, half not.

'Done the elephants, done the poverty,' I said. 'Can we go home now?' Later Robin was reprimanded for talking to the reporter. But he and I insisted that instead of flying back from Lucknow to Delhi, we would take the train.

Back in England, the next day's papers were full of follow-up stories claiming that the players involved were wimps and traitors. All very well, viewed from several thousand miles away, but we were the ones walking around with armed guards following our every step. We were the ones who might just get in the way of an extremist's bullet. We were the ones answering increasingly desperate phone calls from home. We were the ones who felt isolated and unprotected. And for what purpose? So that we could have a few games of cricket? The fact is that we were genuinely worried about our safety and genuinely pissed off that no one seemed to be taking the situation seriously.

From a personal point of view the tour was about to go from bad to worse.

When the squad was originally announced, I was looking forward to starting at Test level the partnership with John Emburey that had been so successful for Middlesex. I'm sure he was too. The benefits of us operating in tandem were obvious: we knew each other's game inside out by now and instinctively knew how to work together in the business of laying and baiting traps for particular batsmen. We were convinced that what worked for Middlesex could work for England. And then, shortly before the first Test was due to start in Calcutta, the rumours started.

Ian Salisbury had been invited out to India to help the batsmen prepare for the leg-spin of India's Anil Kumble. Whether it was the pressure being placed on the selectors by the MCC dissidents that caused the change of heart, I suspect no one will ever know. While they were certainly not going to back down over Gower or Russell, maybe they felt that by including Salisbury after all, they might silence some of their critics.

Whatever the reason for it, the addition of Salisbury had a wholly negative effect on me and Embers. Maybe this is another of my many character flaws, but I have never been one of those blokes who conform to the cliché of 'responding well to competition'. My response was to start wondering if the selectors and captain had lost confidence in my ability. I felt uneasy, as though all of a sudden people were doubting me. Just as I had after returning from the Australian tour of 1990–91, I felt that the selectors were casting around for alternatives – and this time I couldn't for the life of me see why.

Off-the-field problems notwithstanding, I had started my Test career with five-wicket bags against Australia, West Indies, Sri Lanka and New Zealand. Yet, for some people, that didn't appear to be enough. Considering my state of mind when the tour began and my concern at the situation we found ourselves in, this was bad news for my sense of well-being.

I kept reading and hearing that Salisbury was such a competent all-round cricketer. He could bat well, field well and he was a good team man. Although it was never spelled out, the comparison that kept coming out loud and clear between the lines was: 'As for Tufnell, he doesn't know which end of a bat to hold, he fields as though he has two left hands and he's a selfish ne'er-do-well you couldn't trust as far as you could throw.' If the management were trying to provoke a reaction from me they got one. I went into my shell.

I must emphasize that I have nothing whatsoever against Ian Salisbury. I've known him for years and we have always got on well. I also respect his ability as a bowler, and I'm sure he would have enjoyed more success in the game had he not been the only one of his type available to England. It was just that Embers and I had been the first-choice spinners. By bringing in an alternative, the management put us firmly on the back foot straight away. How the Indian batsmen like Mohammad Azharuddin and Sachin Tendulkar would have loved the idea that England were so unsure of their front-line spinners that they had sent for the back-up bowler before the series had even started! More specifically, Salisbury's presence represented a direct threat to me. We both spin the ball away from the bat and it seemed highly unlikely that both of us would be picked in the final eleven. But if they weren't going to pick him, what was he here for?

We did not have long to wait for the answer. Against all predictions, and in the face of the example of the Indians who had picked three spinners – Kumble, off-spinner Rajesh Chauhan and left-armer Venkatapathy Raju – we went in with four quicks – Devon Malcolm, Paul Taylor, Paul Jarvis and Chris Lewis – and Salisbury. The explanation given by the management was that he had been bowling better than Embers and me in the nets.

Back home, chairman of selectors Ted Dexter reacted to our eight- wicket defeat by commissioning a study into the effects of pollution on English cricketers. As one of the most ingenious excuses for a thrashing in the history of world sport, this should have a regular spot on *They Think It's All Over*. (By the way, whatever happened to the findings?) The truth is that in the prevailing slow-turning conditions we were hopelessly outclassed and under-equipped. An ill Gooch apart, the batsmen – having prepared at Lilleshall on quickish, bouncy 'spin-mats' that had as much in common with the pitch in Calcutta as beermats – had little idea how to use their feet to the Indian spinners, who took seventeen of our twenty wickets. Salisbury took one. Our most successful bowler was Graeme Hick, who took five with his part-time off-breaks. On a wicket devoid of pace, our four pacemen took six between them. Azharuddin, the Indian captain who had faced calls for his head prior to the match, slapped the bowling to all parts in his 182.

Embers and I said nothing. He was being diplomatic; I was quietly fuming. And it was in this mood that we arrived in the clearer seaside air of Vishakhapatnam to play against the Rest of India in a match that turned out to be the backdrop for one of the 'finest' moments in my career.

I think the management realized that their selection for Calcutta had been a big mistake. Intelligence was forming that the wickets for the remaining back-to-back Tests in Madras and Bombay would be pretty similar. So all three spinners were picked to play in this final warm-up. Gooch, trying to get himself better, missed the game and Alec Stewart was appointed captain. But before scoring on the first morning, he burst a blood vessel in his finger and took no further part until the last afternoon. In his absence the captaincy passed to Embers, which placed him in the position of wanting to try and bowl himself into the side, but at the same time having to give his rivals, myself and Salisbury, a proper bowl as well. Still resentful at having to prove myself in the first place, I struggled for rhythm and tempo. I'm not saying I didn't have the will or desire to fight for my place. It's just that what had happened was such a huge knockback.

What made matters worse was that one of the umpires, Jayaprakash, decided I was overstepping the popping crease in my delivery stride and kept no-balling me. Eleven times. Now I may be a lot of things, but I am not, was not and never have been prone to regular overstepping. I was puzzled, so I asked the fielder at mid-on to check what I was doing wrong. At least then I could adjust my run-up accordingly. But no one who fielded in that position could see a problem. Although I was cutting the crease with my front foot, the deliveries were perfectly legal. Pissed off enough as I was, it now seemed that everything that could go wrong was going wrong.

I felt under so much pressure. I just thought everyone was looking at me and saying to themselves, he's gone. There I was bowling for England as though I was a Middlesex Under-15 triallist. Three bowlers into the probable two Test places wouldn't go; nothing was happening for me; and now I was being no-balled by some bloke who, in my opinion, didn't know the rules. The whole thing was a right schemozzle.

Then, at last, a change of luck. Tendulkar came down the track to drive me and I did him in the flight. I knew I had him the moment the ball beat his outside edge, and I began celebrating accordingly. Tendulkar was already established as one of the best batsmen in the world. To get his wicket would not only have given me the greatest satisfaction, and helped my cause for reinstatement no end, it might also have had a profound psychological effect on him and his senior team-mates. So when Richard Blakey missed the stumping chance it was more than my fragile state of mind could cope with. Suddenly everything

I had been feeling boiled up inside me. I blew, noisily, obviously and maniacally. The result was an outbreak of childishness that still causes me to blush every time I think about it.

It was later reported that the object of my anger was Richard Blakey; that I swore at him and called him all the names under the sun for missing the stumping. That is just not so. I swore all right, colourfully and repeatedly. I swore all over the place until I was blue in the face, but I was not swearing at anyone or anything. I was swearing at everyone and everything. It was a blind rage, the kind you see from kids being dragged round supermarkets, the kind which bring down the house and have everyone cringing with embarrassment. And I was not finished there. At the end of the over I called Jayaprakash a cheat, snatched my cap from him and booted it all the way back to my fielding position at fine leg. If there is one cricketing incident in my career that I would seek to eradicate, this would be it. I really, really shouldn't have reacted the way I did.

I understood straight away that there was going to be trouble – and there was. Jayaprakash complained to the management, and I knew that when I got back to the hotel it would be trousers down and six of the best again. So I devised a plan. The management were bound to come looking for me, so instead of going to my room to await the inevitable phone call, I went to Robin Smith's and hid in his bog. Maybe I felt that if I could stay out of their clutches long enough they might forget the whole thing. Daft, really. All that happened was that the longer they spent trying to find me, the angrier they became.

I was in a right state. Robin tried to calm me down over a few beers, but all the frustrations had built up and now they were spilling over. I didn't want to be there any more.

I hated this feeling of being on trial. I felt humiliated. My life back home was falling apart and too many things kept going wrong. Then finally Bob Bennett found me. He told me there was to be a disciplinary hearing in front of him, Fletcher, Alec as the acting-captain and Embers as the replacement acting-captain. No, I did not have time for a quick beer. They had been searching for me for two hours.

I played it brilliantly. Instead of going in there, apologizing, and taking what was coming, I started off by flinging open the door and enquiring: 'Right! What's the f***ing matter with you lot?'

Silence.

'Come on, come on. What the f*** is the matter?'

Silence.

'All right, all right. I'm sorry. I was wrong. I didn't mean it, okay? I don't wanna be here. I don't wanna be here sitting in front of you lot giving me a load more shit, right? My guts have gone, I feel terrible, I don't want to be hearing what you are saying. I didn't want to do wrong but I did. Let's just forget about this episode. I've been stupid, I've been a bad boy. Now do what you've got to do and just let me get back to my room.'

The fight-fire-with-fire approach went down extraordinarily badly. After I had finished shouting and screaming I noticed that the chins on the faces of my judges had hit the floor. Then they threw the book at me. You can't behave like this: fined £500.

After the others left, Bennett stayed and put his arm round me. 'We're still behind you, Tuffers,' he said. 'We all want you to do well. Just get yourself together.' I took his kind words at face value and was grateful for them. As I left the team room, I kicked a whole load of empty beer bottles down the corridor, smashing several.

The next person I bumped into was the Reverend Andrew Wingfield Digby. Appointed by Dexter on an official basis as a sort of pastoral counsellor, Andrew was by now a semi-permanent fixture. Later, when Dexter was replaced by Ray Illingworth, Wingfield Digby was banished on the basis that if players needed such guidance and assistance they were no good to him – very northern, I'm sure. But in this instance Wingfield Digby was extremely helpful. He was the only bloke among the hierarchy who listened rather than talked. He made no judgements about what I had done, but merely let me have my say. That in itself was therapeutic. Then I went back to my room, grabbed a couple of bottles of something and made for the rooftop balcony. Sitting there, looking out over the sea and the stars, I felt the rage subside at last.

The next morning, when I looked up at the site of my ruminations, I noticed that the particular piece of balcony I had been sitting on appeared to be held up by a few strands of string. As the realization struck me that I could have plunged to my death at any moment, I burst out laughing and soon afterwards felt an awful lot better. Perhaps, after all, bringing things to a head in this way had helped me get rid of all the poison. Whatever, I went out to bowl and took four wickets in five overs. The excitement of the previous day was gone and forgotten.

At the ground the press boys wanted to know what action had been taken against me. The content of the discussions during the disciplinary hearing was kept relatively quiet, but the fine was duly announced. Fletcher told them simply: 'Phil has to learn to keep his emotions in check.' Later, another reporter managed to extract the following off-the-record remark from one of my judges:

'The thing you have to understand about Phil is that he is a great bowler and a complete dickhead.'

Although I returned to the side for the second Test in Madras, there was no fairytale transformation for me or the team. In the immediate short term, things only got worse. On the day before the match I was persuaded to go and see a palmist, who read my future and told me that things were looking up. She was very specific. She said my fortunes would improve substantially after 21 March. When I returned to the hotel and told Mike Atherton what she said, he informed me that 21 March was the last day of the tour.

She didn't foresee the prawns, though, as in the prawns that Gooch and Gatt ate in the hotel's Chinese restaurant the night before the match and that subsequently rendered the captain unable to walk, let alone play. Gooch wasn't the only one suffering. Soon after the start of play, both Robin and Gatt left the field with their insides turning inside out, and that was about as good as the match got for us.

India scored millions, or 560 for six to be more precise. I bowled 41 overs, Hick and Salisbury 29 each, and Navjot Sidhu and Tendulkar just collected at will. They bowled us out twice to win the match by an innings and 22 runs – and with it the three-match series. I did gain some consolation in the second innings by making a magnificent 22 not out. At the time of going to press this remained my highest Test score, but I do feel that there is a hundred in there somewhere. Well, a 23 at least.

This was pure joy for my bat sponsors, BDM. During our week in Delhi at the start of the tour, one of their representatives had come into the dressing room and asked if any of us did not have a bat sponsorship. Funnily enough I happened to be the only one. I did a deal, took a couple of his bats and the next day he turned up at the hotel with a suitcase full of rupees – thirty thousand of them, worth around £750. To this day, I still have no idea what the initials BDM stand for, nor what the company makes, but endorsing whatever it is was a source of great pride to me – and I'm still open to offers, by the way.

Another big defeat in Bombay meant a three-nil whitewash, as a result of which we became the only England team to suffer a hundred per cent failure in a Test series against India. My final moment of glory came in a last-wicket partnership in the first innings, during which I guided Graeme Hick to his highest Test score. Even though I had made my own career-best in Madras, I unselfishly gave young Graeme as much of the strike as possible and we shared 68 for the tenth wicket in 83 minutes. My contribution was an exquisite, undefeated two. Truth be told, I had my eye on the longest nought in Test history, declined several clear opportunities to get off the mark, then missed the record by seven minutes when an inside edge slewed past the keeper and Hicky nearly threw me down the other end.

Despite this triumph they battered us again, and those looking for reasons went through the book, taking their pick. Scruffiness and facial hair were identified as two of the biggest problems. A photograph of the presentation ceremony at which several of us were not looking at our best was latched upon, as was a shot of Bennett wearing ill-fitting shorts at a press briefing afterwards. Cheap shots, as far as we were concerned. Some of those who had a go should try running around the outfield under a hot Bombay sun for two and a half days, diving around dusty outfields and losing pints of bodily fluid in almost every way you can imagine, and then see how immaculate they look. Poor old Bob had been suffering from a slipped disc for half the tour and had forced himself out of his sick bed for the aforementioned press conference, on the understanding that no pictures would be used. Then they did him like a kipper. However unfair, the photo appeared on the front page of the *Daily Telegraph* and *The Times* back home, fitting neatly into some people's clever ideas of how to take the piss. As for the suggestion that our cricket would have improved had we all shaved more regularly – of course, why didn't we think of that?

At least my batting had given me an excuse to celebrate: I finished the Test series fifth in the averages, higher than Alec Stewart, Robin Smith and Graham Gooch. Not that I pointed this out to them any more than two or three hundred times.

The rest of the tour was filled with the mix to which we had by now become accustomed. Beautiful palaces full of glittering opulence – like the silver train that carried the port bottle round a silver track on some Maharajah's dining table – and elsewhere, horrible poverty. The usual scares in the air, including the occasion when the hydraulics failed as the plane was landing in Bangalore and the boys got out to see a hole the size of a coffin in the fuselage, and a game of hunt the rat on one train ride from God-knows-where to God-knows-where-else. Then later some random violence towards us in the final one-day internationals. At Jamshedpur a six-inch metal spike thrown from the crowd only narrowly missed Devon Malcolm's head. Fletcher complained afterwards that 'someone could have been killed' and we were assured of tighter security in Gwalior, where Alec Stewart was duly crusted by a lump of concrete.

I have to say that bowling against Sachin & Co in these conditions was an education. Never before or since have I come across batsmen who possessed such wonderful technique against the turning ball. All batsmen in India are brought up on a mixed diet of leg-spin, googly, off-break and slow left-arm in turning conditions – and that is just one of the reasons why they have become so difficult to beat in their own country. During Australia's current period of world supremacy, for example, winning a series in India has been the one prize that has eluded them. The injured shoulder that later required surgery was not the only reason Shane Warne was made to look ordinary here in 1998. By all accounts Sachin used his feet and smashed him everywhere.

What struck me about how these guys played against me here was that they had a completely different attitude to playing spin bowling from anything I had ever come across before, either in Test or county cricket. Their footwork and their wristwork were exemplary; their ability to read the ball on length was uncanny; they were so nimble on their feet and so flexible. I lost count of the number of times I felt I had lured one of them so that they were not quite at the pitch of the ball to play a stroke, only to find that they would come again, take another step and get to the ball easily. On the odd occasion when they were still not quite where they could be comfortably in control of their shot, a break or turn of the wrist would get them out of trouble. I felt that I bowled well. But at the same time I couldn't escape the feeling that the batsmen were in control and that, to them, I was just another spinner to be milked at will for two or three runs per over. Their approach was almost clinical.

I would have liked to have bowled at them on the

fourth or fifth day of one of the Tests when the pitches started to break up and turn, but the way the matches panned out that didn't happen. And, looking back, perhaps I should have been more aggressive. After the incident at Vishakhapatnam, I took a conscious decision to make sure my behaviour was beyond reproach and it may be that, as a result, I missed the spark, lacked the edge. Maybe I should have set different, less conventional fields to them. But overall I gave as good as I had. I went into my craft, mixed up my deliveries, my pace and my flight and put as many balls as I could in the danger area – and they played me with sticks of rhubarb.

I felt I let myself down. I went out there on the back of taking loads of Test wickets and with a bit of a reputation, but I never really got into them at all. I would dearly love to go back to India one day and prove to the players and the crowds, who are among the most knowledgeable and enthusiastic in the world, that I'm a better bowler than they saw on that tour. Certainly I would have a better chance now with the experience gained first time round. The bottom line is huge respect to their batsmen. If you are going to be made to look ordinary, it's better to be made to look ordinary by masters.

Sri Lanka? Bloody hot. Bloody lost. Done the poverty, done the elephants, done the mosquitoes, done the tantrum, done in. *Now* can I go home?

Thank you.

FOURTEEN

Jesus Wept!

I returned from India in just as much of a spin as when I left, and with no clear idea how I was going to handle home life again. Although I had learned a lot from bowling on those wickets against the Indian batsmen, I had nothing to show for my efforts – and the little game of football I had had with my England cap in Vishakhapatnam, added to my earlier response to the bombs, bullets and near-misses at thirty thousand feet, ensured that I didn't score too highly when the management cast their votes for man of the tour.

In fact, for a short time at least, things were slightly more settled at home. My feelings of having been cast in the wrong part remained as strong as ever, but I was getting my head round the idea of Jane and Ellie and myself as a unit a bit more. Once the season began, though, and I slipped back into the familiar circle of absence from home, nights out with the boys, and the rest, it soon became clear to me that I was still not cut out for settling down. I didn't have the willpower. To be honest, I didn't have the will. And to forget all my troubles, forget all my cares, I'd go downtown – and down and down and down.

My professional life was about to become just as jumbled up.

Gooch was persuaded to carry on as captain for the 1993 Ashes series – once again, I think, against his better judgement. The selectors didn't want a new captain taking over before such an important series, but I think Gooch realized that, although he was still near the peak of his powers as a batsman, he had little left to give as a leader. The glory of the 1992 World Cup campaign had worn off. The size and the manner of our defeat in India and Sri Lanka, as well as the residual resentment of the pro-Gower lobby, meant that his credit was running out. From the point of view of personnel, there was a clamour for an infusion of younger blood, and it became obvious that, unless Gooch and his side were successful against Australia, big changes would be made. Then Shane Warne bowled what might become the most famous ball in history.

When the Australian squad was announced, the name of Warne meant little to most of us. About the sum total of our knowledge was that he was young, blond, bowled leg-spin, had been carted to death in his first Test, but could turn the ball and was rated by those who knew. The learning curve was about to go vertical.

Embers having been one of the early casualties of the Indian experience, Peter Such, the Essex off-spinner, was selected for the first time, and we both made the final eleven for the first Test at Old Trafford. Damp weather meant the groundstaff had been unable to get the pitch properly dry, so when we bowled on the first day, the ball was gripping into the surface, particularly at one end. Such came on before lunch on the first day, took six wickets to my two, and we bowled them out for 289

Without the opening batsmen Mark Taylor and Michael Slater, who scored 124 and 58, they would have been in all kinds of strife.

At 80 for one in reply, Gooch and Gatt were battling but winning when Warne came on to bowl his first ball in an Ashes Test.

Now, when a new boy arrives in Test cricket preceded by a bit of a reputation, the natural response of those who are already there is that any respect he acquires will have to be bloody well earned. At twenty-seven, I didn't exactly regard myself as a gnarled old pro, but the question, 'Who does this bloke think he is?' may have wandered across my mind once or twice. The view from the players' balcony at Old Trafford is side-on to the wicket, and when we assembled around the dressing room television that day to find out, it has to be said that most of us were fully prepared – and also strongly hoping – to be unimpressed. Gooch and Gatt were the best players of spin in our game; they would sort Warne out, no problem.

Jesus wept.

The ball started on the line of middle and leg stumps, but swerved further down the leg side in the last yard of flight so it pitched outside leg stump. Then it turned like you would expect a cartoon cricket ball to turn, appeared to gather pace off the pitch and flew past Gatt's outside edge to hit the off stump threequarters of the way up. The last time I saw that look on Gatt's face someone had nicked his lunch.

The legend was born. Warne took four wickets in the first innings and, even though the pitch had dried out by then, four more in the second. Only Gooch, in a hundred that ended when he punched the ball to stop it looping off his body on to the stumps and was given out handled the ball, came close to looking comfortable against him. First blood to Warne and Australia.

Then, at Lord's, they absolutely murdered us and the stock of Gooch and Dexter fell even further. In view of the increasing demands for new players, Gooch's selection of his Essex colleague Neil Foster, at thirty-one – four years and a South African rebel tour after his last appearance for England – appeared to some to be an act of pure contrariness. It turned out to be one of the less inspired selections of all time. On a pitch as flat as a fart, Australia racked up 632 for four. The opening attack of Foster and Andy Caddick produced the combined analysis of nought for 214 in 68 overs. I took two for 129, and also unwittingly did some bloke out of a king's ransom. This punter had had a bet on their first four batsmen scoring hundreds. When Taylor (No 1) made 111, Slater (No 2) smashed 152 in his first innings at Lord's, David Boon (No 3) passed his century and Mark Waugh (No 4) reached 99 the bookie in question must have been packing a suitcase. One more run and he would have had to pay out the small matter of £200,000. It never came. I bowled Waugh without addition.

Athers might have saved the match had he not been run out going for the third run that would have given him a hundred, but our seventh Test defeat out of seven meant that the lynch mob were out in force. At the press conference afterwards they demanded to know *on behalf of all England* why this was happening, what was going to be done, *and when were we going to get some young players?* When Dexter tried to lighten the mood by mumbling something about Venus, their response was stony silence. One of them told me later that Dexter got the mood all wrong. He tried to make light of events an they were sitting there thinking: 'Excuse us, but your side has just lost seven Tests on the trot. What are you talking about?'

Heads rolled. Mine was one of them and I didn't play another Test that summer.

Ironically, the cricketing highlight of my season – and one of the major achievements of my career – coincided with the next Test. I didn't set out at the start of Middlesex's Championship match against Glamorgan in Cardiff with anything more than the normal desire to prove the selectors wrong for dropping me. And my figures of one for 114 in 45 overs, as Adrian Dale and Viv Richards both made double-centuries in their first-innings 562 for three declared, wouldn't exactly have had them eating their words. But the fact that we overtook them with hundreds by Gatt and Embers demonstrated the nature of the pitch, and by the time Glamorgan began their second innings at 12.10 on the final day, the draw seemed the only possible result.

I don't exactly know what happened this day or why. Granted the pitch had begun to wear slightly, but from the moment I came on to bowl my first over, the eighth of the innings and the last before lunch, the Glamorgan batsmen seemed intent on committing a kind of ritual suicide. The big moment came when Richards strode to the crease in best *High Noon* fashion at 62 for three. Halfway through my run-up he stepped back from his stance and stopped me. We exchanged a few pleasantries and then I had him caught off the glove first ball. He wasn't happy, and it may have been just as well that this was the last time I ever bowled at the masterblaster. I dread to think what carnage he might have inflicted in revenge. Then they folded, collapsing from 25 for no wicket to 109 all out. I finished with my career-best figures of eight for 29 in 23 overs and we knocked off the runs to beat our main title rivals with ease.

Embers bowled really well, but only had one wicket to show for his efforts, and as we left the field I turned to him and said, 'Don't worry, mate. You'll get an eight-for in the next match.' I was wrong. He only took a six-for in the next match, against Warwickshire. He got his eight-for in the match after that, against Hampshire.

In my absence from Test action, there were all kinds of fun and games. Dexter initially succeeded in his increasingly frantic attempts to persuade Gooch not to walk. Changes were made at Trent Bridge, including the introduction of Graham Thorpe, who made a century in the second innings, and the papers' choice of Mark Lathwell, a young opener from Somerset whose presence at the top of the order was accommodated by Gooch dropping down to the middle. A draw was achieved and the church bells rang out. They were quickly silenced by events in the fourth Test at Headingley, where Australia marmalized us again by an innings and 148 runs and, with the Ashes gone, Gooch finally quit. Mike Atherton took over with a mandate for starting from scratch with a young team, whereupon he dropped Lathwell, reinstated Gooch at the top of the order, and picked Embers (aged forty) as one of two off-spinners at Edgbaston (Such was the other). On the final morning, an announcement of which the new captain had no prior knowledge was made over the public address system, stating that Dexter had resigned. Then at The Oval, to general astonishment, Gus Fraser returned after two and a half years out of the side because of his hip injury to take eight wickets, win the man of the match award and the match.

Athers and I had more or less grown up together as

England players. We went on our first senior tour together, to Australia in 1990, and had always got on well. A bit of a dark horse, he was nowhere near as dour off the field as he liked to make people believe and he and I shared one or two interesting moments in various bars on various tours. But what now? Burdened with the responsibility of captaincy and having to take the whole thing a tad more seriously, would he know me not, as Prince Hal discarded Sir John, or what?

As I had not been picked for the last four Tests of the summer, there was no guarantee that I would make the plane for the winter tour to the Caribbean. Embers and I had done well for Middlesex and, with Gus available for all but the final Test, we all did our bit to help as we won the County Championship with some ease. We officially became champions as early as 30 August – the earliest winners since 1979, apparently – and lost just one match, the last of the season, to Worcestershire.

I soon enough found my answer to the Falstaff conundrum. Athers knew me. He had got his way over picking younger players: there was no Gatting nor Emburey, and Gooch had made himself unavailable for the tour anyway. No sign of Neil Foster, either. Rather this was the new generation from which Athers hoped and intended to build the next Test team, however long it took.

I was pleased that Athers had kept faith in me, but once the squads were announced, the wait until the tour started was all a bit of a mess. Jane and I were surviving, rather than living, together. I wasn't around much and, naturally, when I was there the atmosphere was frosty. We were arguing and it wasn't much fun. I was drinking too much, all the while resenting the fact that I was and that this was not what it was supposed to be like. We were both sticking at it for Ellie's sake more than anything else. So when the time came to go, apart from the obvious sadness at leaving Ellie, the only emotion I felt was relief.

From the moment I arrived in the Caribbean in January 1994, I let the feeling go to my head. Back in West Indies, the scene of my past triumphs as an MCC Young Cricketer, I felt like I had been let out of jail. There I was in Antigua, at a lovely hotel on the beach, with the hot sun on my back, blue seas, blue skies, money in my pocket, plenty of stunning-looking birds and a load of mates to have a laugh with. Oh, and some cricket somewhere along the way as well.

Rightly, in my opinion, the management – comprising Athers, the team manager Keith Fletcher and the rather detached M.J.K. Smith as tour manager – decided that the best way to acclimatize for the arduous tour ahead was a couple of weeks of no more than gentle practice. The campaign was going to be long and hard, so the boys may as well let their hair down while they could. Chris Lewis shaved his off and proceeded to suffer sunstroke, but that was nothing to my response.

I think I might have taken the idea a shade too far.

Having already been told that I would not be playing in the first warm-up match, against an Antiguan XI, I went for it, totally. From the moment we arrived at Miller's bar on the beach, a twenty-yard walk away from our hotel, it was all on. I sat there sipping rum and ginger, with the music playing and the waves lapping, watching the suntanned lovelies running around in their bikinis, thinking to myself that this was the best bar in the world and listening to the devil on my shoulder playing our tune. As far as I can recall he carried on playing it for the first six weeks of the trip, and I never tired of hearing it.

We trained pretty hard during the days to be honest, but the sun sets at around 5.45 in those parts and once it is down, the nights draw you in. Everywhere you looked Antigua seemed to be full of bars and full of crumpet. It was extraordinary. You'd be sitting at a beach bar in a pair of shorts and a polo top, you'd kick off your shoes, and someone would wander in off the beach, catch your eye, and a few rum punches later you'd just stroll off together. 'Hello' became the magic word, and who was I to argue? It was *Le Sans Frontières – It's A Knockup* – and I played my joker over and over again. People were ducking and diving and slipping and sliding all over Antigua. And then one night, on the eve of a well-earned day off I hasten to add, we were invited to a barbecue laid on by the British Airways crew at their hotel, a ten-minute walk up the hill.

Otherwise engaged for most of the evening in one of the bars at Nelson's Dockyard on the far side of the island, I wasn't too bothered either way. There was a little something waiting for me at our hotel, I knew, and she had promised to wear the rather fetching leopardskin underwear she had told me about. But the rest of the boys in the taxi wanted to drop in to see how the party was progressing and I was outvoted. I was rather the worse for wear and announced my arrival by staggering about all over the place crying: 'I'm here, girls.' Yet somehow I must have made an impression, because the next thing I knew I was looking into the piercing blue eyes of a beautiful creature with long blonde hair. Her name was Lisa Barr, she was a stewardess, and within minutes we were both chatting and laughing as though we had known each other for years. She had no idea who I was and no interest whatsoever in what I did for a living. We laughed at the same time and at the same jokes and seemed immediately to be on the same wavelength. We chatted for hours until realizing we were the only ones left in the place, and parted company with the promise of meeting on the beach the next day. The assignation with the safari lingerie completely slipped my mind. I never saw its owner again.

Lisa and I met as arranged and got on just as well sober as we had done the night before. We really enjoyed each other's company, nothing physical happened, and when I left for the match in St Kitts a day later, we said goodbye fully expecting that it was the last we would see of each other.

Suitably refreshed I managed to get my focus back on the cricket. After what had happened in India, I had made a promise to myself that I would no longer bowl for a quiet life. Out there, following the fracas in Vishakhapatnam, I had tried to keep my nose clean and ended up having it bopped with aggravating regularity by their batsmen. If people told me to calm down, maybe this time I wouldn't calm down, maybe this time I would use the anger and aggression as weapons. With my reputation firmly established by now, the likelihood was that I was going to get shitbagged whether I behaved myself or not, but this time when I returned home I wanted to be able to look at myself in the mirror and say that I had bowled and played according to my instincts and not someone else's idea of how I should behave.

At St Kitts, in the game against St Kitts & Nevis, the inevitable happened. Some bloke got a clear nick on a bat-pad catch to Nasser Hussain and started to walk off, but in the absence of any appeal the umpire called 'not out'. He only had one eye, as I recall, and that must have been shut. Sure enough, I booted the ground in time-honoured fashion and for the next couple of overs bowled as though

I wanted to deck anyone who got in my way. The difference was that this time Athers took me to one side and said: 'Don't worry if you get some stick for this in the papers. As far as I'm concerned that was fine. I want you to be aggressive. We are trying to win a bloody series.'

I was impressed. Athers saw the way I was and he put himself out for me. Sad to say, my response was not what it should have been. The next time he had words with me, at the end of the first Test in Jamaica three weeks later, it was to warn me that my participation in the remainder of the series was in grave doubt.

As the first Test approached, it was becoming pretty clear that neither myself nor the other spinner Ian Salisbury would be picked. The pitch at Sabina Park was quick and bouncy and spinners rarely turned the ball off the straight there. So, knowing I would be about sixteenth man out of sixteen, I lapsed back fairly dramatically into party mode. In Kingston I bumped into some fellow with a shock of black hair streaked with a white flash who, for obvious reasons, called himself Don King, and he told me that in this place, he was the man. Anything I wanted, I was to go through him. He took me to some right dodgy clubs in the heart of one of the most dangerous cities in the world that just oozed menace, degradation and depravity. Right up my street, really.

The night before the Test was due to start, he took me to this 'night-club' called Pisces, or Atlantis – something to do with fish at any rate – and it was the business, even by Don's lofty standards. I remember walking through a doorway down a dimly lit passage that opened onto a courtyard round the back. As I followed Don into the yard, I peered through the fug that is unique to the Jamaican brand of Woodbines and noticed quite a few of the clientele sporting deep facial scars. At this point I thought to myself, 'Perhaps, on second thoughts, it is rather late,' and, hoping that no one had noticed my coming in, started tugging at Don's sleeve. Don saw the look on my face, sat me down and said: 'Don't worry, man. You're with me.'

The music was deafening, the bass thudding out like someone was hitting me on the head with a rubber hammer (on second thoughts maybe someone *was* hitting me on the head with a rubber hammer). The girls on stage demonstrating various artistic dance poses appeared so discomfited by the heat that they were forced to remove most of their clothing – in some cases, all of it.

As you might have guessed, this was not my debut appearance in an establishment of this kind but what happened next made the experience a first. At the end of a seemingly interminable rap event and near to the time when I decided I'd had quite enough of this night, five blokes seated in the row in front of me suddenly sprang to life, pulled out their handguns and started shooting into the night air. Whether this was their way of showing their appreciation at the efforts of the artistes, I never found out. I was too busy running for my life, with Don a close second.

The upshot was that when I arrived at Sabina Park the next morning, I was in need of a little shut-eye. We won the toss, lovely, lovely. Athers and Alec Stewart went out all pumped up and bristling for the challenge of taking on Curtly, Courtney and the two Benjamins, Winston and Kenny. I wished them *bon voyage*, retired to the physio's room and prepared a bed for myself.

The cricket played on that first morning was sensational stuff. The West Indies quicks ran in fast and, aided and abetted by the fire in the pitch, subjected our guys to the most rigorous examination of technique, temperament and sheer guts. The boys passed with distinction, ducking and weaving when necessary, taking the blows and standing up and striking out when the opportunity arose, and had progressed to a highly creditable 70-odd without loss at lunch. I know this because I read it in the next day's newspaper. The fact is that I slept through the whole lot, and when Athers returned to the dressing room at the interval and found out, he quite understandably went bananas.

'That is pisshole,' he told me. 'Alec and me are out there busting a gut for this side, a side that you are part of, and your idea of supporting us is to bugger off for a kip. I put myself on the line to get you on this trip, you've been on the piss for a month and now you can't even be bothered to stay awake to watch the first morning of the series. That is out of order and I am very, very disappointed.'

I tried to make a joke of it. 'Well, er, you know, Athers, mate, you know I'm a terrible watcher. It was so hot in the dressing room and, er, you know, that's why you all call me The Cat.' This was not a good idea. Athers didn't say another word, but if you could bottle the look he gave me and market it for sale to the parents of unruly children, you could buy the yacht now.

He was right. I held up my hands. It was poor. Very poor. Incredibly, there was worse to come.

Athers and Alec had gone on to share an opening stand of 121, but then we fell away, collapsing to 234 against some good swing bowling by Kenny Benjamin who took six for 66. We had them 23 for three but Brian Lara, Keith Arthurton and local man Jimmy Adams pulled things round. They made 407 and then bowled us out a second time for 267. Once again Athers took a fearful battering and showed his immense courage, while Graeme Hick later profited with 96. Towards the end of our innings they targeted Devon Malcolm for the treatment and it all got a little hairy. At stumps on the penultimate day, West Indies had reached 87 for two, requiring a further eight runs for victory.

This night the drinking began as an attempt to drown sorrows, but by the time I had returned to my room accompanied by one or two attractive assistants, the wake was in full swing. We were jumping and bumping and ranting and raving, and I distinctly remember seeing the sun rise just before I passed out.

When the alarm call came an hour or so later, it was like someone was trying to make a hole in my head with a blunt drill. Boozed up and knackered, I felt terrible, as terrible as it is possible to feel while still being alive. Some bastard had emptied the contents of several ash-trays into my mouth and everything in the room stank of booze. I simply could not move. I was in no fit state to carry on living, let alone attend the last rites of the match. So I rang Dave Roberts, the physio, and told him I was suffering from a stomach upset, which I suppose was technically correct. 'Is there any point in me going down to the ground?' I asked him. 'After all they only need a couple and I won't be required for twelfth man duties or anything.'

'Well, you sound dreadful,' he said. 'Don't worry. Just stay in bed and get yourself better. I'll let Athers know you're not well.' I settled back into the arms of Morpheus, content in the certain knowledge that I had got away with it.

When Athers realized I hadn't made it to the ground he

asked if anyone knew where I was. Roberts assured him that there was no cause for alarm. 'He rang me in the hotel and told me he had a bad stomach,' he explained. 'I told him to stay in bed.'

'You have to be f***ing joking,' Athers replied. 'Three hours ago he was in the room next to mine swinging from the f***ing chandelier.'

Oops.

At the end of the match, Athers came straight to my room. 'Stomach upset, my arse,' he began. 'Look, Cat, you have got to buck your f***ing ideas up. You've been giving it too much of a crack here. And now the cricket has started and you are still jumping around until all hours while a Test match is being played. You may not want any sleep, but what about me, what about the rest of us? Get your priorities sorted out. I'm warning you; if you don't buck up your f***ing ideas, your arse is on the next plane home. I won't warn you again.'

I apologized, again, just as I had done on the first morning of the match. But by now I could see that my words were just sort of bouncing off him. What can I say? Here I was again, in trouble for the third tour out of four. No excuses, no mitigating circumstances. I was getting a bit carried away with the freedom and the fun. When, if ever, was I going to learn? Streetwise? Don't make me laugh.

I respected Athers totally and what he had to say. It wasn't a case of him getting on my case because he could, but because it had to happen. And he made his point even more forcefully when Salisbury was picked ahead of me for the next two Tests in Georgetown, Guyana, and Port-of-Spain, Trinidad. By the time I finally managed to get a game in the fourth Test in Barbados we were 3–0 down, the series was over and, thanks to Curtly Ambrose, we were in some disarray.

If I hadn't been in the dressing room to see the effect that Hurricane Curtly had on our boys during those two sessions in Trinidad, I wouldn't have believed it. It was a bit like standing on the beach at the start of *Saving Private Ryan*, in the middle of the appalling devastation, knowing that no one was firing at you. There is a scene in that film where one of the soldiers has his arm blown off and he is wandering around in a daze carrying the dismembered limb in his other hand. I saw a few of them at the Queen's Park Oval. The really crazy thing about us being bowled out for 46 was that when we started the second innings with a target of 194 to win, we genuinely felt we were favourites. We had a whole day and fifteen overs to make them and no prospect of bad weather to thwart us. But by the end of those fifteen overs we were 40 for eight. The wickets fell so quickly that no one could get themselves properly prepared. Inside the cramped changing area it was chaos as people grabbed bats, pads, boxes and helmets – and nobody seemed actually to be breathing.

Beaten up and trampled upon as we were, it was fully expected that we would sink without trace in Bridgetown. After all, this was the impenetrable fortress of West Indies cricket. Not only had they won their previous twelve Tests at the Kensington Oval, but they hadn't lost here for fifty-nine years. Remarkably, in the face of all expectation, we managed to achieve what many believed to be as likely as me giving up smoking.

It was a match full of incident, drama and brilliant cricket. There were Stewart's hundreds in both innings as he became the first England player to achieve such a feat against the West Indies, Angus took his Test-best eight for

75, and the gradual build-up of tension and excitement as Andy Caddick and I helped bowl them out a second time to win the match had everyone on the edge, on and off the field. The Barmy Army was in full swing and the hordes of English supporters who arrived to watch the final two Tests on the holiday islands of Barbados and Antigua lapped it all up.

Some of those present that fateful last day do say that the quite astonishing catch taken at full pelt over the shoulder to dismiss Lara was not only the highlight of the match but also its pivotal moment. Modesty forbids, etc. – oh bollocks, Catch of the Century.

In amongst that lot there had also been a spot of bother during their first innings, when I chased a ball to the far boundary, tried to get my boot in front of it before it hit the wall, wasn't sure whether I had or not, picked it up and threw it in. The batsmen, thinking the ball had gone for four, stopped running and as the ball arrived at the bowler's end someone nicked off the bails and appealed for a run out. According to the Laws of the Game, as the umpires had not signalled a boundary one of the batsmen should have been given out. The umpires called to me and asked if the ball had hit the wall, I signalled that I didn't know, and the episode was brought to a farcical conclusion when they ruled not out but gave three runs and not four. If they had only completed three runs, how could the decision be not out? We all got a bit aerated at the time, I recall. Some tosser on the radio called my action 'disgraceful', while Everton Weekes – one of the great West Indies trio of Frank Worrell, Clyde Walcott and Weekes better known as the three Ws – chose this moment to describe me as 'an oik of the worst sort'. Pleased to meet you, as well, Mr W, I'm sure.

At any rate, nobody cared too much about that when we clinched the victory.

It should have been one of the most satisfying experiences of my career. Sadly, most of it passed me by. I was thrilled with the victory of course, but other matters were pressing on my mind.

While I had been living the life of Riley, inevitably things had been building up at home. Before I left, it appeared that a parting of the ways was only a matter of time, and I think Jane came out to Barbados with the rest of the wives and girlfriends more or less in a last-ditch effort to try and save the relationship. I was pleased to see her, and for a couple of days spent together without any distractions we got on pretty well. Then one afternoon following training, I came back to the room to find Jane sitting on the bed staring into space.

Jane obviously knew that I had been seeing other girls at home and here, and our constant rows about that and my drinking had worn us both down. Thus far, however, I think she had made a decision to ignore such behaviour, for Ellie's sake as much as anything else. But now she had discovered what she thought was concrete evidence of my infidelity. After Lisa and I had parted company in Antigua I had written her a note. I told her what a nice time I had had and suggested that we might meet up again in the future. But I never got round to posting it. Jane was sitting there holding the letter in her hand.

'What's this, Phil?' she asked, quietly but obviously upset.

Even then I couldn't confront the situation head on. I explained that I had met Lisa and we had had a few drinks and that I was writing to her to say thanks, but that nothing had happened to get excited about. Jane obviously didn't believe a word of what I was saying, and I can't say I blame her, and the rest of the week was very strained. There were no tears, no tantrums. I think Jane just realized that this was the last straw, there was nothing to be gained by fighting, and that bringing the relationship to its sad conclusion may as well wait until we got home. She was upset, but determined. I was just all over the place.

When we left Barbados straight after the Test match, me for the final Test in Antigua and Jane for London, the parting was tearful. Jane said she needed time to think.

The flight to Antigua was one of the lowest points of my life. I realized that by not putting up more a fight, by not trying harder to persuade Jane that the episode with Lisa was innocent, by not making any real effort to convince her that we still had something worth trying to preserve, what I was demonstrating was that I didn't actually want us to be together any more. I rang home from Antigua a couple of times, but we didn't seem to be getting anywhere on the phone. Then the night before the match I asked if she would be coming to the airport to meet me at the end of the tour. Her answer said everything that needed to be said.

'No, Phil,' she told me. 'I won't be there.'

I spent the night at the bottom of a glass.

Once I began to think straight again, fortunately there was one final game of cricket to be played. The unpleasant reality that my personal life was once again falling apart around my ears could be postponed for a week or so at least.

When they were 12 for two on the first morning, the prospects were encouraging. Even at 191 for three anything was possible. At 593 for five declared, however, the picture had changed somewhat. The little matter of Brian Lara's world-record 375 had been placed before us and we were all found wanting.

Funnily enough, we thought we had him in big trouble early in the innings. After Chris Lewis got him jumping about with a couple of short ones, Lara sent for some eye drops. 'Oh, yeah, right,' we thought. 'Something in your eye there, Brian, like a little bit of fear, perhaps?' Next thing we knew he was making the ball scream for mercy, and several hours later, so were we. After he played and missed for the first time in the innings, Angus, the bowler in question, decided to try and rattle Lara with a bit of sledging. First he stood there staring at the great man from only a few yards away, then, as we waited to hear what he could possibly come up with that would make the slightest impression, Gus suddenly burst out laughing.

'What's the matter, big man?' someone asked.

'Well,' replied Fraser, 'I was going to call him a lucky bastard, but I've just seen the scoreboard. He's 317 not out and that's the first time the ball hasn't hit the middle of the bat.'

When Brian scored the run to overtake the record held by Sir Garfield Sobers, the match came to a complete stop. In the stand next to the pavilion the speakers in Chickie's Disco started blaring out the theme tune of the tour, 'Feeling Hot, Hot, Hot', Lara kissed the turf, Sobers strode out to shake his hand surrounded by a swarm of cameramen and photographers. Near me on the boundary some old couple hitched their cauldron of boiling hot corn soup over the fence and set up shop on the outfield, while Gravy, the transvestite car mechanic with an outrageous outfit for every occasion, was leaping and jumping like a grasshopper on acid. For about twenty minutes nobody seemed to care that there was a Test match going on, or rather not going on.

Athers and Robin Smith both made big hundreds and we saved the game comfortably. Then all my thoughts turned to the uncertainty of what I would find back home.

At the end of most tours, players are desperate to get back to their homes and their loved ones. This time I didn't really want to leave.

FIFTEEN

Gone to Hell

For me, the flight back from the West Indies in the spring of 1994 was an even more uncomfortable experience than usual. As I've mentioned before, in normal circumstances I consider air travel to be about as pleasurable as having your testicles barbecued, but on this particular journey I was even more apprehensive than usual.

The taxi ride from the airport to Palmers Green was awful. As we got closer, my imagination raced over all kinds of possibilities. What had Jane decided? Did she want us to try again? And if she did, did I? The only thing that was crystal clear in my mind was that I was desperate to see our little girl. Everything else I would just have to play by ear.

When I walked through the front door and called hello, there was no response. I put down my bags, looked round the house and realized there was no one at home. I took my cases upstairs and noticed that Jane's stuff and everything that had been in Ellie's little room was gone – all of it. So I went downstairs, sat there in my empty kitchen in my empty house, only hours after returning home from a three-month tour of the West Indies, thinking to myself, 'Why? Why have I made this happen the way it has?'

I sought the answers in the all the usual places and in the manner to which I had become accustomed. I called up a few mates and went down the pub.

Soon after I returned to the house, Jane arrived, on her own. She didn't say much, but she put the kettle on and we sat down and had a cup of tea. Then she came straight to the point. 'I've thought it all through,' she began, 'and I think we should split up.'

I don't know why those words had such an effect on me. Maybe I just wasn't expecting her to come right out and say them. Maybe I was expecting her to be less cut and dried about the situation. Deep down I believe we both knew that this was the right thing to do, but when Jane sat there and spelled it out so starkly the words left me cold.

There was no rage or anger – I don't think either of us had the heart. The usual things were said, but we were just talking ourselves round in circles. Finally, when I said I wanted to see Ellie, Jane told me that our little girl was at her mum's house but she soon went and fetched her. I was so happy to see Ellie, but within five minutes Jane took her off to bed. The next morning, with everything still up in the air, I went to the club to report back for duty.

When I got home, the first thing I noticed was a large van parked outside my front gate. The next was the sight of Jane's two brothers removing items of furniture from my house and placing them within it.

'Oi! Hold on,' I shouted. 'Just where do you think you're going with my sofa?'

'Er, you'd better have a chat with Jane,' one of them replied.

She was there in the house, but said nothing when I asked her what was going on, and the brothers carried on as if I wasn't even there. The atmosphere was completely different from the way it had been before. This time it was far more of a confrontation. When I started having a go at the brothers, who backed off, Jane told them to leave so that we could try and have a conversation. All the time my priority was wanting to see Ellie, but as we talked Jane just kept putting the subject off. Then it started to get a bit grubby: I'm having this; you can't have that; this is the way it's going to be. Next it became aggressive, and very soon the aggression escalated into a full-scale row.

'Take what you like,' I said, 'but you've got to let me see Ellie.'

'I'll tell you when you can see Ellie,' she replied. 'I'll decide.'

The last thing I remember with any clarity was: 'I'm putting this in the hands of the solicitor. I'm taking half the house … and you are not going to see Ellie.'

I flipped. We started screaming at each other and fighting, rolling around, kicking, lashing out. I was grabbing her and shouting that she had to let me see my child. As the grabbing developed into slapping, she dug her nails into my cheek and scraped them down the side of my face. Then I shut her in the cupboard.

Realizing that I had gone too far, I let her out within a couple of minutes and eventually we both calmed down. Jane left. My face hurt, everything hurt. Everything was wrong. Physical violence has never been my style and to act in this way towards anyone, let alone the mother of my child, is something I bitterly regret and will continue to regret until my dying day. All I can say is that I was out of control and beyond all reason, fired up by red rage at the prospect of being prevented from seeing Ellie. Someone, it didn't matter who, was telling me that I couldn't see my daughter. I temporarily lost my mind.

The next day I rang Jane at work and asked her again to let me see Ellie. She told me I couldn't; we argued; I pleaded. She said I could see her on Saturday or Sunday, knowing full well that I was playing for Middlesex at the weekend. I told her I wanted to see Ellie now. She said that Saturday or Sunday were the only days she would allow me to see her. I said that was not fair.

I asked her if Ellie was at the crèche at the David Lloyd Sports Centre, where Jane normally dropped her off when she was working. When she said she didn't know, I realized that she must be, told Jane I was going there now and was going to see her, rang off, jumped in the car and drove.

As I walked through the reception doors and approached the crèche I noticed three or four nursery nurses, all in a line, barring my way. 'It's all right,' I told them. 'I have just come to see my daughter.' They refused to budge. One of them told me, 'I'm sorry. That will not be possible.'

'Look,' I said, 'excuse me and all that, but I've just come to see Ellie.'

'Sorry, but I can't allow you to,' said the nurse. 'I've been telephoned by Miss McEvoy and told not to let you anywhere near her.'

'This is ridiculous,' I said. 'What are you talking about? You have no right to stop me from seeing my daughter.' I tried to force my way past them. Suddenly a couple of security staff appeared and a stupid struggle ensued. I insisted that I was perfectly entitled to see Ellie and they started getting heavy, shoving and pushing me around. The scrimmaging was in full flow when Jane walked through the door.

'What are you doing?' she asked.

'Listen Jane, I have come to see our little girl. That is all I want to do. I don't want any trouble. I just want you to let me see my daughter and then I'll go.'

She turned to me and said: 'You are never going to see her.'

The rage returned. The words burned into me. I felt frustrated and angry. I slapped Jane round the face and walked out. I knew everyone was looking, I knew it was stupid, I knew I shouldn't have done it. But I couldn't stop myself. I went home, got the Scotch out and cried my eyes out.

Later that evening – I'm not sure when as I had lost all track of time – there was a knock on my front door. I opened it to see four policemen on my doorstep.

'Are you Philip Tufnell?' asked one.

I nodded.

'We are arresting you on the charge of assaulting Jane McEvoy.'

I was in a daze. The only thing that struck me was that there were so many of them. I couldn't work out why there were so many coppers just for me. I went quietly. I locked up the house and was taken to Enfield Police Station. They were quite chatty in the car, as it happens. As soon as we arrived they booked me in, charged me, took my fingerprints and my photograph with the serial number in front of me, and packed me off to a holding cell. Then they came and took me for interview.

This was all going a bit fast. I hadn't called for a lawyer. To be honest, it hadn't really occurred to me, and when we were sitting in the interview room the tone of questioning seemed reasonably sympathetic. I think they could tell from the gouges on my face that whatever assaulting had been committed the fighting was not all one way.

They told me what I was being accused of. As I told them my side of the story, they pretty soon seemed to have realized that they were dealing with what they would have called a routine domestic incident. I was taken back to the cells. The duty solicitor explained that I would be appearing at Tottenham court the following morning and that we were going to apply for bail. Could I go now? No, I had to spend the night in the cell.

That was pleasant – an open bog and a ledge with a blue plastic mattress on top, and bloody cold to boot. I didn't sleep a wink and by the time morning came I was in mint condition. They came for me at about ten o'clock, slapped on the handcuffs and walked me to the van. It was a cage on wheels that I shared with about ten other blokes. The conversation revolved around what they were all up for and it was charming stuff. Grievous Bodily Harm was about the least serious misdemeanour.

In due course I was taken to another holding cell – all porcelain tiles, hard stone floors, windows too high off the ground to look out of, and blokes shouting to each other, 'Six months? I'll do it on me 'ead.' And I was sitting there thinking, 'What the f*** am I doing here?'

I was taken up to the courtroom, looking like shit. I hadn't shaved, I hadn't slept, I was wearing a pair of jogging trousers and a T-shirt, the scars on my face were throbbing. Vaguely I could hear someone in the distance talking about extenuating circumstances ... previous good character ... no threat to society ... Mr Tufnell deeply regrets ... The someone turned out to be the duty solicitor and I suddenly realized that he was talking about me.

He told them a bit about who I was and that, apart from the five minutes at our house on the day I got back from the West Indies, I hadn't seen Ellie for three months. They set the date for the trial on the charge of assaulting Jane and granted bail, on condition that I didn't, as they put it, 'interfere' with Jane or Ellie. The solicitor told me not even to try to make contact. Go home, lock your doors, be a good boy and get yourself a lawyer. I took some of it in, but not all of it.

A free man again, I telephoned a mate to come and collect me, but when we approached the house it was surrounded by reporters. I ducked down in the car and my mate kept driving. We parked round the corner and sat there for a while then came to the conclusion that there was nothing for it but to run the gauntlet. I rushed past them and locked and bolted the door with the flashes going off. They started pushing notes through the letterbox, the usual stuff: 'Phil, we're on your side. Tell us the story and we'll pay you this and give you that ...'

Then the tone changed. One of the reporters shouted out: 'Phil, who's this mystery girl, then?'

It hadn't taken long. The reporters knew about me hitting Jane and they knew I had been arrested and charged. Fair enough. But now the element of the 'mystery girl' had been introduced. I had never mentioned anything about another girl. The subject had not been raised in the courtroom. So where exactly had the information come from? And what had been said? Next the phone started ringing. 'We'll pay you for the whole story, but we want to know about the other woman ...' Just for good measure, Jane rang and started having a go.

I slammed down the phone, then rang Greg and my dad in Spain and told them what was happening. Dad said he was coming straight over, a lawyer was set up and the wheels of my defence were put in motion. Greg spelled it all out rather neatly. 'You've been a very stupid boy,' he told me. Dad said much the same. So we were all agreed.

Then I did something without thinking. I rang Jane back and told her I wanted to see Ellie. Within about ten minutes of me making that call, the police returned and arrested me again, this time for contravening the conditions of my bail. 'Hello, Phil,' said one of them when they turned up. 'I'm afraid you are in big shit now.' The press boys couldn't believe their luck. More flashes, more pictures. They were having a field day. Back to the cells, back to the open toilet, back in the jug.

I don't know how my lawyer managed to sort things out. Pleaded insanity, I presume. However he did it, he succeeded in persuading those that had to be persuaded that I had been in such distress at the time of the hearing that I hadn't fully understood the conditions of bail. There was considerable truth in this. But when the lawyer got me out again he made it clear he was very, very pissed off with me. In fact, he went absolutely berserk. 'Do not, under any circumstances, ring her again,' he screeched. '*Do I make myself perfectly clear?*' He had.

The reporters were still there when I got home – and they stayed for another day or two. I rang the club and spoke to the chairman of the cricket committee, Bob Gale, who was very understanding, told me to take some time off and see how things developed. The next day some photographs appeared in the papers of me with scars all over my face.

It was around mid-morning that the threatening

phone calls began. At first I would pick up the phone and there would be no one on the other end. After a few of these, a man's voice said: 'I'm going to come round and kill you.'

I felt a shiver run down my spine. In the moment I heard those words I felt sure the caller meant what he said. I got in touch with the police straight away. I wanted them to know of the calls but they told me there was nothing they could do. The calls continued.

It was around this time that I decided to get in touch with Lisa. With questions being asked about the so-called 'mystery girl', I didn't think it would be long before people put two and two together and tracked her down, and I felt I had to warn her that the pack was in pursuit. She was concerned about my well-being and asked if there was anything she could do to help. I desperately wanted to get away from the house and the area for a couple of days, just to clear my head, so when she suggested I should go and stay with her, and Dad agreed to look after the house, I was off like a rocket.

At last, away from the madness; some peace. We spent a lovely couple of days down at Lisa's place in Sussex. Away from the hassle and aggravation, you could almost believe that the whole thing had been a ghastly nightmare. Then, on the second evening, the threatening calls began again. God only knows how they got the number.

The time came for us to go back to London for a meeting with the solicitors. We hoped that back home the coast would be clear by now, but even though it was late when we got there, the photographers were still camped outside the house and they duly got the picture of 'the girl'. It was bound to happen sometime or other. Neither of us wanted to spend our lives in hiding, and we hoped that they would now leave us alone. Amazingly, they did. They had what they came for and now they went.

I was still in distress over not being allowed to see Ellie, but at least I was in the company of friends and people I trusted. Dad, Lisa and I were just beginning to feel that the worst might be over.

We were wrong. The next day I discovered that my car had been stolen. That evening, as we sat in front of the television, tucking into fish and chips, I heard a rattling at the front door, as though someone was trying to force a key. Thinking it was the press boys back for more, I ran out into the corridor, where there were two glass doors – a porch door and the front door.

As I went through the porch door, closing it behind me, the front door was kicked open. There in front of me was Jane's father, holding a half brick in his hand and coming at me. The next thing I knew I felt a crack on my head. As we grappled, I went flying back and through the porch door, with the glass smashing around me. Within seconds all I could see was red as the blood streamed into my eyes. Dad and Lisa rushed out to see what the commotion was and, not knowing if McEvoy was on his own or with a mob, Dad shouted to Lisa to go out the back door and run for it. McEvoy was raving, shouting and screaming that he was going to break my hands, and we were fighting and shoving and pushing. Then Dad leapt at us and drove us both back out of the front door, down the steps and into the driveway.

Now McEvoy came at me again, grabbing my wrist, twisting it and shouting: 'You'll never f***ing play cricket again, you bastard!' and when I finally pulled away, it took both Dad and me to hold him down, Dad grabbing him round the neck and me hanging on to his legs. As one of the neighbours came running out, Dad shouted to him to call the police.

We struggled to restrain McEvoy but the police arrived incredibly quickly, took him away and charged him, and sent for an ambulance for me. Once McEvoy had gone, we realized that we had no idea where Lisa was, but found her back in the house. She told us she had jumped over the fence and hidden in the next-door neighbour's garden shed.

Dad went down to the police station and gave a statement. I went off to hospital, with blood all over me and my shirt completely red, to have eight stitches put in the top of my head.

Looking back on this part of the story, I have to say that I hold no malice towards Michael McEvoy. In his shoes I would probably have done the same. I have two daughters now, Ellie and Poppy, and if anyone behaves towards them in the way that I behaved towards Jane, I would doubtless react in much the same way. I was wrong. I hit Jane, and that was totally out of order. At the time I was pissed off with McEvoy, but I understand his motives totally. A lot of what I got I deserved.

In the immediate short term, though, all the roles seemed to be reversed. As far as the police were concerned now he was the villain. He was the one being charged with assault. I was the witness with the arm being put around my shoulder; I was the one having my injuries photographed as evidence; I was the one giving the statement about what had been done to *me*. Funny old game, as they say. The next day McEvoy was taken to Edmonton court, where he was charged with assault and making a nuisance phone call.

Once the club were informed they did all they could to

help. They offered to put me and Lisa up in a hotel, although we didn't stay long. On the first night, when we went out for a meal in a nearby restaurant, we had barely sat down when about seven photographers burst in and started snapping. We decided we'd had enough of running. We went home, tried to sort a few things out and waited for the trials.

I felt I owed Middlesex for their understanding attitude. With that in mind, nothing much else to do, and in an attempt to return to some kind of normality, I asked if they wanted me to make myself available to play. There was more than a month to go before the trial, and as so often in the past, cricket seemed to offer a bit of sanctuary. After all, it was my job. Understandably, they didn't want to rush me, but it was decided that the best thing was for me to play in a second-team match to get back in the swing, and then we could all take a view on the proper course of action after that.

The exercise did not go exactly according to plan. The match was against Yorkshire at Uxbridge in mid-May and, in the absence of any announcement that I would be playing, the occasion was mercifully free of newspaper attention. The first team didn't have a game, so Gatt came down to see me for a chat and to watch me bowl.

I approached the match determined that for a few days I was going to push the trial, the trouble and the turmoil out of my mind. It started off all right. We fielded first and although it was damp, drizzly, cold and generally unpleasant, I was given a bowl early on to get me involved. But as the game went on I became less and less interested and more and more detached. Standing there at mid-on with not much happening, I was struggling to concentrate on what was going on in the game. It was as though I wasn't really out there at all. Flashes of recent events kept jumping into my head, no matter how hard I tried to keep them locked out. Then, about five minutes before lunch, Jason Pooley, who was captaining the side, called over to me and asked me if I wanted another bowl.

That was the trigger. Suddenly everything hit home – the fight with Jane, her threat that I would never be allowed to see Ellie again, the arrest, the phone calls, the brick, the trial, the lawyers, Lisa … all the images and experiences of the last few days thumped into me like body blows. I was fighting for breath. Jason was standing right in front of me with the ball in his hand; I just stood there, in a state of limbo, thinking, 'What on earth am I doing here, playing a game of cricket?'

'Tuffers,' he repeated. 'Are you all right? Do you want to have a bowl?'

'I, er, I don't know what I want to do, mate,' I replied. 'To be honest, I don't really think I can take any more of this.' And I walked off the field.

Back in the dressing room, I lay on a bench staring into the space between myself and the ceiling, not knowing where I was or what I was doing. The rest of the players trooped off for lunch and after a pause Gatt came to see me. 'Look, Cat,' he said. 'I don't care whether it's a second eleven match or a tenth eleven match, you can't just walk off the field.'

'I'm sorry,' I replied. 'I don't know what is happening.'

'I'll tell you what's happening. You're having problems with your life and you are in trouble, but you are here now doing your job. You have got to get yourself together and out of this dressing room.'

'I'm not doing it,' I protested. 'I can't.'

'You have to,' he insisted.' You have to get today over with. Just get out there on the field and finish the day's play. That is the only way.'

He very nearly had to drag me out of the dressing room, but somehow I managed to get through the rest of the day. At the end of it I got straight in my car and went home. Later that evening I received a phone call from a club official. He was very sympathetic. 'This can't go on,' was the message. 'You're not right. You're obviously very upset. The court case is in a month from now; take the time off, get yourself sorted out, then come back afterwards and we'll start again.' It was very kind of the club to deal with me in this way. Although I thought I could handle everything, the truth was that I couldn't. They recognized that I was in need and I'm grateful to them for that.

The attitude of other parties was not so sympathetic. After Middlesex issued a statement saying I had been released from duty for a few weeks, because I was not 'in the right frame of mind' to give my best on the cricket field, the papers and others jumped at the chance to put the boot in. In the main, they described my break as a suspension, as though the club had taken disciplinary action against me, which was certainly not the case. But the tone was set. Keith Fletcher, quite reasonably, said that as I was not going to be playing county cricket I could not be considered for the three-Test series against New Zealand, but then Ray Illingworth, who had taken over as the new chairman of selectors, said helpfully: 'His demise is another man's opportunity and we'll be having a look at Richard Stemp, Ian Salisbury and Richard Illingworth.' Just what I wanted to hear. One newspaper said that the England bosses had made it clear they wouldn't touch me with a bargepole.

The club suggested that it might be a good idea if I had a couple of chats with the club doctor, which did help me, and then it was recommended that I should go and see Mike Brearley.

During his playing days as captain of Middlesex and England, Brearley was renowned for his intelligence and his powers of motivation. Many people give Brearley the credit for getting the best out of Ian Botham in the 1981 Ashes series, after replacing him as England captain halfway though. Upon his retirement from cricket, Brearley became a full-time psychoanalyst and as such he occasionally helped cricketers who were experiencing a crisis in their game or their life. I had three sessions with him and they helped a lot. He listened to me as I told him everything that had happened and everything I was going through now. He realized that I was in a pretty fragile emotional state and that the last thing I needed was a sermon. His approach was to let me have my say and then deliver a very simple message. 'Be calm, relax and things will sort themselves out,' he told me.

Inevitably, in the lead-up to the trial the papers were full of it. My mates were fine but I found I couldn't live the life I had lived before. Even going into the White Hart, or one of the other pubs in which I had been part of the furniture for a decade or more, became traumatic. A little remark here, or a funny expression there ... Maybe I was a little paranoid, but why was everyone looking at me? I started to spend more and more time down at Lisa's place. Our friendship had developed into a relationship, and with her things just felt right.

I hardly slept a wink the night before the trial, and on the drive down to the magistrates' court at Enfield I was nervous as hell. When we arrived, the press were everywhere, which just made me more anxious. I took my place in the courtroom and then Jane and her family walked in. I wanted to talk to Jane, to try and apologize, just say something, anything that could make things better. But I had been told just to take my place and not to speak until and unless I was spoken to.

I was called up and stood in the dock as they read out the two charges of assault and assault causing actual bodily harm. There was no jury, but as I looked around the courtroom I had the familiar feeling of not really being inside myself at all. This was all happening to someone else, not me. I didn't say anything except to confirm my name. My brief took over, telling the court that I admitted both offences. He put my side of the story, Jane's brief put hers and they had a bit of an argument over various points. They fined me £800, ordered me to pay Jane £250 with £30 costs, and then did me for two driving offences as well – £300 with £30 further costs.

One case down, one to go.

Five days later, on Tuesday 28 June, Jane's father Michael McEvoy appeared in court and pleaded guilty to malicious wounding. He was fined £2,500, ordered to pay me £500 in compensation and £40 costs. His defence lawyer said, 'It was a one-off and is most unlikely to be repeated.'

Outside the court, McEvoy told reporters: 'Justice has not been done. It has to me but not to other people in this case. If I had the opportunity, I would do it again.' As I have said before, I cannot say I blame him.

Nothing was said about me seeing Ellie. I had asked my lawyer about trying to introduce that into the case, but he advised me not even to think about it. He told me that I had to let everything die down, to try to put Ellie completely out of my mind for the time being at least. 'Just put a full stop to all this now and get on with your life,' he said. During the five years between the trial taking place and the time of writing, I had still not been allowed to see Ellie. Time, I can tell you, has not healed this wound.

The next episode in the saga took place a few days later.

The day after the second trial, I was contacted by a guy who had, from time to time, acted on my behalf as an agent. He said he had been approached by the *Sun* newspaper, who had offered £25,000 for a series of articles detailing the whole story from start to finish. I wasn't interested. Already too much distress and sadness had been caused and I just wanted to draw a line under the entire business.

The agent tried to persuade me that, as the newspaper was going to be running a story anyway, I would be silly not to co-operate. At least that way I would have some measure of control over what was written. The way he put it, I could either take the money and give my side of the story, or not take it and let them write what they wanted. I could see the logic, but I wasn't desperately keen. Then other papers started to show interest as well, and I could see the beginnings of another media frenzy. After Lisa and I talked things through, we reluctantly agreed that we should get the story out, over and done with.

It was arranged that I would meet their reporter at the Henlow Grange Health Farm, in Bedfordshire – and if anyone can come up with a more unlikely venue, the carrot juice is on me. The *Sun* booked a room for me there among the jacuzzis, aromatherapy oils and steam baths. And they came mob handed: a couple of reporters with what appeared to be a few minders, just in case. I was duly collected in a hired car and arrived at the place at around four in the afternoon for a six o'clock meeting.

Once in the room I started thinking to myself that I really, really didn't want to do this, and rang Lisa to tell her that I was having very serious second thoughts. By now I was convinced that I didn't want to go ahead with the interviews. 'I'm ashamed,' I told her. 'I don't want to do this for the sake of a few quid. But I've committed myself now and there are a couple of blokes standing guard outside the door. Even if I got past them, I'm stuck here with no car. What the hell am I going to do?'

'Don't do anything,' she said. 'Stay there. I'm coming round.'

When she arrived, the minders looked a little confused by her presence, and as I let her in one of the reporters appeared from the next room as if by magic. 'Everything all right?' he asked.

'No problem,' I said. 'See you at six o'clock.'

Lisa came straight to the point. Did I want to do the articles or not? I did have a choice. If I didn't want to go ahead we could just leave now. I said I wanted to forget the whole thing, but I felt trapped. If we tried to leave now, the minders were bound to try and stop us.

The phone rang. It was six o'clock. Were we ready to meet? Not yet, give us ten minutes. What were we going to do? How could we get away?

Rrriiing. Not quite ready yet. Give us five minutes.

And then Lisa came up with a completely barmy idea. If I didn't want to go through the door, what about the window? Brilliant, I said, we're on the first floor.

'Come out here,' she said, leading me through the French windows on to the balcony. She pointed to some climbing-plant frames connected to the poles that supported the balcony, and said: 'That's how we're getting out.'

So we did, climbing down these rickety structures until we could drop down to the ground. Then, giggling like schoolkids, we ran across the flower beds to her car and fled. On the journey away from Henlow Grange, all I could see was the image of the reporters opening the door to find an empty room. Later I rang to explain that I had changed my mind. They could write what they liked. The deal was off. They were really quite cross.

And so, thank God, for the time being at least it was back to the cricket.

I have to say that at first I was convinced my international career was over. Several of the comments being attributed to Illingworth left me in no doubt that I was at the very bottom of the list. For instance: 'This was a pretty poor performance from Tufnell and we're not prepared to put up with that sort of thing. He may be the best left-arm spinner in the country, but he's got it all to do at the moment. He's got to prove himself to us all over again.' Not much room to read between the lines there.

I felt a bit miffed about Illingworth's attitude. He didn't really know anything about my situation or what had gone on, but he seemed to have made a pretty firm judgement, based purely on what he had read in the newspapers. There was a little more to the story than that, and it would have been nice of him to have rung me up to make some enquiry into the actual truth of what had taken place, instead of jumping on the bandwagon.

After a chat with Athers, though, I felt much more encouraged. He told me to keep my head down, get back into my game and take a few wickets. He told me that I was still in his plans.

So the bad boy returned. After a run-out in the Sunday League match against Durham, I was back in earnest for the Championship match at Derby, among my mates and breathing many huge sighs that the whole sorry business was over at last.

What now?

What now, after the close of play on the first day of the match, was that I was approached in the hotel lobby by a couple of reporters from the *Mail on Sunday*. 'Philip, can we have a word?' it started. Here we went again. Jane had sold her side of the story to the paper.

The possibility had always existed, of course, and the money on offer would have been attractive. I understood that. She had Ellie to look after. But, according to the reporters, what she had come out with was far more damaging to me personally than anything I could ever have imagined. Without going into the gory details, she put the knife in good and proper.

I went into the bar and told some of the players, who were very supportive. I believe they were thinking that I had been adequately punished for my misdemeanour and that that should be the end of the matter. I should now be allowed to try and get my life back on track. When the allegations appeared, the club reacted by dismissing them. They told me to forget the matter. And from then on I concentrated on bowling people out for Middlesex.

I put the thought of playing for England again at the back of my mind. Naturally I'd taken some notice of events in the first Test against South Africa at Lord's, during which the entire nation seemed to be embroiled in the controversy over the England captain's dirty trousers. But being part of the international scene was so far removed from my thinking that when, on my arrival at

Uxbridge for a Sunday League match against Essex on 31 July, John Etheridge of the *Sun* collared me in the car park and asked if he could have a quiet word, my immediate thought was, 'F***ing now what?'

'No, no,' he said. 'I want to have a chat with you about playing for England again.'

'Well, I'm not concerning myself with all that,' I said. 'It would be nice if it happened, but I can't think too far ahead.'

'What do you mean?' he asked. 'Do you mean to say you haven't heard?'

'Heard what?'

'Blimey. Well, I'm not sure I should be the one telling you this, but you're in the squad for the second Test against South Africa at Headingley.'

It hadn't occurred to me to listen to the announcement of the squad on the radio. On the journey to the ground I had been entertained by some rather loud dance music, as it happens. And now this.

The next day there was a lot of stuff in the papers about me being offered a lifeline and so forth. In fact I had been drinking at the last chance saloon so many times that its owners were thinking of using me as a front-man for a new chain of theme pubs. Illingworth said: 'He has been on probation. You could say he has served his time and we welcome him back. We will, of course, be considering him for Australia this winter, so we felt it was better to find out now whether he could do the business on and off the field. The last thing we want is to take him to Australia and then have problems.' Allez-oop.

Jane and her mum had another right go in the papers, for the second time in a month, but that apart, the reaction was fairly favourable.

What has intrigued me ever since, however, is the suggestion that my selection might have been part of a hidden agenda. Not to be too devious in my thinking about this, but two weeks after Illingworth had apparently ruled me out of contention he was killing the fatted calf. I wasn't complaining, but one article in particular set me thinking. Written by Graham Otway in the now-defunct *Today* newspaper, it began: 'If Ray Illingworth wanted to take the heat off Mike Atherton this week he could not have made a shrewder move.'

Quite apart from Athers' dirty fingers, there was the small matter of South Africa winning by 356 and bowling England out in the second innings for 99. In the circumstances, what better way of deflecting attention than by sending for The Cat?

I did all right, as things turned out. I took a few wickets on a flat track and the match was drawn. And although I missed the final Test at The Oval – where Devon Malcolm took his nine for 57 to set up the win and ensure the drawn series – when the squad was announced for the 1994–95 winter Ashes tour, I was included.

A few weeks later, at the Epping register office, Lisa Barr became Lisa Tufnell. A champagne reception at the Ivy was followed by me flying off to Manchester to record *A Question of Sport*.

Er, what happened next?

SIXTEEN

'Nutter'

My marriage to Lisa in September 1994 took place in the face of considerable scepticism. Various friends and colleagues thought I must be crazy to be jumping into such a long-term commitment so soon after the appalling upheavals of the previous few years.

But it has always been the same with me. The more people say I shouldn't do something, the more determined I am to do it. I knew Lisa was the girl I wanted to marry. We had spent a lot of time together that summer and had grown very close. With all that was going on, sometimes it felt to us as though it was Lisa and me against the world.

She hadn't needed to do anything for me, but she had done a great deal. She was very supportive and, when necessary, had enough strength and intelligence to steer me on the correct path. With a tour to Australia coming up, I didn't want to just bugger off and say see you when I get back. I felt a real need to put the relationship on more of a permanent footing. I wanted to let Lisa know how much I appreciated her and that I had fallen in love with her. So I asked her to marry me.

The ceremony over, at last I felt that my life was

progressing somewhere other than down the drain. I understood that leaving Lisa to go on the tour would be very difficult. Only a couple of weeks after getting hitched, I was off for four months down under. But at least certain things were in place, and I felt the storms of 1994 were finally over. Little did I know that what I was experiencing was merely a lull before the next one came along.

I felt slightly uneasy from the first day of the tour. Lisa was still getting a few odd phone calls and she was clearly feeling more and more vulnerable about my being away. I tried to throw myself into the training routines and the early matches, but after I was not selected for the first serious match of the tour, against Western Australia in Perth at the end of October, the phone calls from home became longer and more anxious.

Once again things started to build up inside me. Lisa was suddenly being presented with the fact of what our relationship would be like, rather than the prospect. The long absences are hard enough at the best of times. But now, after what we had both been through, all she could see was a long stretch of being left on her own in an empty house. She knew I had a job to do, that this was what I did for a living, and that overseas tours were part of that life. But it didn't make any difference. She was lonely and – after the threatening phone calls – frightened as well.

Phil DeFreitas had returned to the England scene by this time. Daffy and I went back all the way to our first day on duty for the MCC groundstaff a decade ago and knew each other inside out, so I told him what was happening and he tried to help.

Then one morning, during one of our long telephone conversations, Lisa told me she was having second thoughts about the marriage. She was seriously questioning whether the relationship could continue. It just seemed like such hard work. I tried to comfort her, to tell her that everything would be all right, I tried to reassure her and convince her that in the end, if we could only hold our nerve, being together would be worth everything we had to go through. We spoke for a couple of hours, but the longer we talked the worse things seemed to become.

Afterwards I was in a terrible state. All I wanted was for everything and everyone to be all right. I just wanted to have a nice life, and now the one thing I thought might help me do that – my relationship with Lisa – seemed to be over before it had really started. Everywhere I looked I could see only misery, and I seemed to be the cause of it all. I was unhappy, Jane and Ellie were unhappy, and now Lisa was unhappy. No matter how hard I tried, I just couldn't straighten anything out. I couldn't straighten my own life out. It was becoming a never ending stream of crises. I thought to myself that I was never ever going to be happy again, that nothing could ever be solved. My life was shit. I just wanted to rewind it so that I could start all over again.

Depressed beyond the power of reason and unable to help myself, I had no idea what I was going to do. I didn't want to see anyone. I didn't want to talk to anyone. I certainly didn't want to go down to the ground to pour out the drinks and fetch and carry for the boys. The state I was in, I couldn't face anyone, so I phoned Dave Roberts, told him how I was feeling and took to my bed. And then I started to get really upset. I couldn't sleep and my mind was racing.

I rang Roberts again, this time reaching him during the

lunch break at the ground. I tried to explain just how low I was feeling, but nothing was coming out how I wanted it to. My thoughts and emotions were jumbled up. 'I don't feel very happy with my life. I don't feel very happy with myself,' I told him. 'I'm ashamed for what I've done and now I just can't seem to get a handle on anything. I can't see anything working out for the best. I've still got another three and a half months left of this tour and I can't see an end to it. I can't see how to resolve any of this. All I want to do is curl up in this bed and die.'

Roberts came straight away. He did his best to calm me down and gave me something to help me sleep. Then later, after close of play, Daffy and Graham Thorpe, who was fast becoming one of my most trusted friends, came to the room to see how I was. We had a couple of beers and chatted. I just poured out my heart, about the year and everything that had happened, about not seeing Ellie, about the fight with Jane, about being bashed up, about the pressures that had built up inside me and about the latest situation with Lisa.

Apart from the few sessions with Brearley, my way of coping with everything had been to try and suppress my feelings and my emotions, to bottle them up and to present a front to the outside world that said, 'I can cope.'

But now it all came out in a rush. I started sobbing, huge gutting sobs that I felt welling up from inside my stomach. I was rocking and running into things, completely out of control. Lampshades, cricket coffins, anything I could see was booted or punched or thrown. I didn't have a clue what I was doing, and it must have been very scary for Graham and Phil. They were talking to me, trying to get me to relax, but although I could hear their voices, I couldn't understand what they were saying.

Alec Stewart came in, then Athers, and later Roberts. They all tried to calm me down, but nothing worked. I was physically unable to stop myself crying, stop myself from being upset. Was it a breakdown? What else can I call it?

After a while M.J.K. Smith, the tour manager, came in. He and Roberts said they had sorted something out for me and that I was to go with them. I followed them out of the hotel and into a waiting cab, still not really aware of what was happening. After about five minutes in the taxi, I started to come round. The next thing I knew I was in a room, lying on a bed, holding a pillow and crying. Roberts was there telling me that everything was going to be all right. Then he told me he wanted me to speak to a doctor who would be coming to see me shortly.

By now I was starting to get my bearings. I was aware of a bed, a table, chairs, a lamp on the table. And I was aware of this chap sitting there saying to me: 'Don't worry. We're just going to have a little chat. I'm just going to ask you a few questions and I want to you to answer them truthfully.'

At this I started to come round fast. It was as though I had woken from a terrible nightmare. Hold on a minute, I thought, just what *is* going on? 'Excuse me,' I said to the doctor, 'but I have some questions for you. Where am I? And who the f*** are you?'

'Oh well,' he replied, 'you've just come here and we're having a chat. There's no problem. Now, just relax. I want you to think back as far as you can and tell me about your childhood.'

Then it hit me. This bloke was a psychiatrist. And if he was a psychiatrist, what did that make me? I thought to myself: This has gone on long enough. Why am I letting all these people make me so upset? I know what I am. Deep down I am a good bloke. I'm over here playing cricket for England. I want to be here. This is my life. Why am I getting so upset about things? F*** 'em. F*** everyone. Get a grip of yourself, stop blubbing and act your f***ing age.

'Sorry, mate,' I told him, 'but I think you've got the wrong bloke.' I flung the door open and ran. He ran after me. I can't imagine what the rest of the hospital staff would have thought, watching a psychiatrist chasing one of his patients through the hospital. Eventually I stopped, turned to him and said: 'Listen, doctor. Thanks for all your help. But I think there has been a very big mistake. I'm sorry I let all my problems get on top of me, but I feel fine now. I apologize for having wasted your time. Now I wonder if you could please phone a cab for me? I've got to get back to the hotel.' And with that, I discharged myself. I had been booked into the psychiatric unit for overnight observation; I was there for little more than an hour.

Back at the hotel, I went into the bar and bought myself a bottle of lager and a packet of fags. Then the thought occurred to me that I had better go and let Athers and the rest of the lads know I was all right again. I went upstairs to the floor where all our rooms were, wondering, as I approached the team room, what I was going to say now. I knew the likelihood was that the management would be sitting there discussing what to do with the 'nutcase' Tufnell and were probably already making plans to send for a replacement, so I decided I had better busk it.

I knocked on the door and pushed it open to see M.J.K. Smith, Athers, Roberts and Keith Fletcher sitting round a table doing exactly what I had predicted. I believe Kent's Min Patel had been nominated as my replacement, but had not yet been contacted. With a drink in one hand and a fag in the other, I said: 'All right lads? How's it going?'

Athers went white as a sheet. Roberts blinked. Fletcher nearly fell off his chair. M.J.K. Smith looked as if he was having a near-death experience.

'Athers,' I said, 'can I have a word?'

He stood up.

'I'm terribly sorry, skipper. Time to grow up. Sorry I've let everything get a bit on top of me. It won't happen again. I've been a silly boy and I'm terribly sorry for the inconvenience. I'm now going to go back to my room to get on with my life and get on with the cricket. All right? All the best.' Then I went round, shook everyone there by the hand and, to stunned silence, left the room.

I bumped into Graham next and then, one by one, the rest of the boys. They were a bit wary, but I just told them that the drama was over. The next day I went to the ground, trained with the rest of them, bowled hard in the nets, did the twelfth man duties and felt a huge load had been lifted. I'd had my cry and now I felt better.

There was one final bit of unpleasantness remaining – namely disciplinary action taken against me by the management. In their wisdom, the management decided that they needed to punish me for suffering an emotional collapse.

They waited until the next day, which was awfully good of them, then, after the match had ended, M.J.K. knocked on my door and asked me to go with him to the team room. At first I thought he wanted to check that I was okay and that everything was back on track, but when I walked in, there were Athers and Roberts again. I sat down in front of them and they told me they were fining me £1,000. 'We cannot have conduct like that on a cricket tour,' they told me.

What can I say? I'd been upset, I'd gone through a

terrible experience. But whatever it was that did the trick, I was now fine and ready to get on with the tour. And they decided that the best way of helping me come through the crisis was to take money out of my pocket and treat me like a schoolkid.

'Take it out of my salary,' I told them, and walked out.

The next problem was trying to keep the story quiet from the usual army of press men, radio and television commentators and photographers that accompanied us all over Australia. Immediately after the incident Lisa rang to tell me that she had seen a few reporters and snappers hanging around our house, but they soon disappeared. Clearly someone knew something, but we managed to keep the lid on the story for the whole tour.

Lisa agreed to come out to join me as soon as was practical, and once she got there, things improved very quickly. As for the cricket, that started badly and didn't really improve much at all.

In fact the main feature of the tour was the beginning of the tension between Athers and his chairman of selectors Ray Illingworth. The difficulties had begun even before we left for Australia, when Illingworth forced Atherton's hand over several aspects of selection. I shouldn't complain too much, I suppose, but the make-up of the squad did cause controversy and ill feeling between Atherton and his chairman. Illingworth appeared to be trading on his conviction that he had saved Atherton's career by pre-empting ICC disciplinary action over the dirt in the pocket at Lord's the previous summer. Certainly I think Athers felt from that moment that he was in Illingworth's pocket.

The first point of conflict was the inclusion of Graham Gooch and Mike Gatting. Both had tremendous records, and on merit both probably deserved their places. But their selection confused Atherton's thinking. He had been appointed with a promise that he would be allowed to select younger players, and now Illingworth had simply reversed the strategy. Also, as former England captains – and with Gatting, it became known, Illingworth's choice to replace Atherton should the need arise – their presence seriously undermined his authority.

The other problem was Angus Fraser. Illingworth, it seemed, was not a fan of the big man. God knows why, but ever since he had taken over, his comments had left no one in any doubt that he felt Gus was not what England required. He reckoned that the pitches in Australia would be quick and bouncy – like they were when he last played there in 1971, one presumes – and now, directly against the wishes of his captain Atherton, Illingworth put his foot down. In place of Angus we had Joey Benjamin and Martin McCague. No disrespect to them, but it soon became clear that Gus should have been with us.

Athers didn't admit to it publicly at this stage – how could he? – but from this moment the two men never really saw eye to eye again. What was worse, the politics spread throughout the camp. Most of the lads felt in their hearts that they should be supporting Athers and did so up to a point. But self preservation also came into the equation. After all, Illingworth was the chairman of selectors and the evidence of this squad was that, after Lord's, what he said went. It certainly did among his co-selectors, Fred Titmus and Brian Bolus. Among that group Athers was very much on his own. The press, too, with only a couple of notable exceptions, hung on every word Illy said. This was mainly because he could always be relied upon to come up with an angle or a juicy quote which made their jobs that much easier.

Illingworth and his supporters could not have suffered a more disastrous start to the Test series than what took place in Brisbane. Of Illy's fearsome pace attack Devon Malcolm had chicken-pox, Benjamin was also unwell and McCague broke down. Having won the toss and first use of a belter, Australia racked up 329 for four at the close of the first day. Michael Slater smashed it all over the place for 176 and Mark Waugh went on to complete an exquisite hundred the next day. We made just 167 in our reply, and although I had more success when they batted again, taking four for 79, with the pitch wearing considerably survival was always going to be difficult.

Graham Thorpe and Graeme Hick held the Australians up for a while and avoided the embarrassment of defeat in four days. Then Shane Warne struck. He got both batsmen in successive overs, took six for 27 off 25.2 overs on that final day and finished with eight for 71. It was an extremely impressive performance, although I felt I snatched the vote for the comedy highlight of the contest when, in trying to pad away a ball he bowled outside my leg stump, I got my feet entangled with my bat and ended up falling over backwards, much to the amusement of Ian Healy behind the stumps. 'That's a new approach, Phil,' he said. 'I've never seen anyone try to play Warney with his arse.'

We were finally beaten by 184 runs.

Athers had tried to organize an emergency call for Gus to join us prior to the Test, but when Illingworth got to hear of it he immediately put the block on the move. Then, back home, he followed up with some less than complimentary remarks about the captain, saying he had saved his job at Lord's and had received no thanks for doing so. Now that really was good for team spirit, and when Illingworth arrived in time for the second Test in Melbourne over Christmas, he received a welcome that was, at best, on the tepid side of lukewarm.

In Melbourne we were moosed. On his home ground Warne again weaved his magic, taking nine wickets in the match, including a second-innings hat-trick, as we were bowled out for 92. Daffy, Darren Gough and Devon were his victims and I'm very pleased to say I wasn't. Result: lost by 295 runs and fading fast.

Enter Gough and Angus Fraser, the latter on a white charger.

After Melbourne Illingworth realized he had to back down over Fraser. The evidence of his own eyes, as well as repeated urgings from Athers to let him send for Gus, finally persuaded the chairman to relent in time for the third Test in Sydney. The effect was dramatic. Darren and Devon starred with the bat in our first innings, scoring 80 between them as we took our first-innings total to 309. Then, after the pitch had sweated under the covers and with the sun obscured by clouds, they and Gus tore into the Aussies, reducing them to 65 for eight on their way to 116 all out. From then on, with the pitch drying out, the plan was first to bat ourselves out of their reach and then to go all out for victory with the ball.

At this point Athers did something which demonstrated the ruthless side of his nature. After he and Gooch had given us a good start, Hick and Thorpe carried on the good work. They had put on nearly a hundred for the third wicket and were closing in on the score we wanted to set the Aussies when Hick got stuck in the nineties. Now we were all aware of what a boost to his confidence a hundred

...now? Another Australian umpire has to be placated by an England captain. My thoughts ...atly summed up by the advertising hoarding. Or is that what the umpire is thinking of me?

Ray Illingworth – chairman of selectors, manager, coach, supremo, bottle-washer – presides over the nets prior to the final Test of the 1995 series against the West Indies. He later admitted that I had little chance of being picked, just in case I did well and forced them to consider me for the upcoming tour to South Africa.

I celebrate snaring Adam Parore in the first one-day international against New Zealand in 1997. After taking four for 22 in ten overs here in Christchurch and winning the man-of-the-match award, I was never considered for the one-day team again.

Below: Mike Gatting is about to hit the deck. Hundreds perish in St John's Wood earthquake.

Above: Fielding deep at Christch Watch out for th noodles. They h

Above: I didn't actually. This time the allegations went up in smoke.

Lisa and me tie the knot at Epping y Office in September 1994.

Below: Lisa holds onto Poppy for dear life. Hardly surprising. I might have lost them both.

DOCS PUT CRICKET AC
TUFNELL I
MADHOUS

WARNING: Atherton   DITCHED: Jane and daughter

We managed to keep the story of my emotional collapse in Perth out of the papers, until so let the News of The World *know after we had got home. I'd love to know who that friend*

WHEN THE   **GOING GET**
TOUGH GE
TUFNELL...

PLAY IT COOL – *Darren Gough soaks up the party-style atmosphere*

I'M FAGGED OUT – *Darren takes a drag from a friend's cigarette*

JUDGE DREAD – *Robin Smith doubles to stop it on Gough's guardian*

DAZZA'S A DRAG
ARTIST

The Sun calls for my return to international cricket prior to the fifth Test against West Ind 1995. You can tell that from the photograph on the right.

CAUGHT GIGGLING TUFF
NEAKING PUFF OF POT

England cricketer 'smoked drugs in the loo' at diner

Boss John Barclay, left, with Tufnell before yesterday's win

Posh joint . . . restaurant general manager Tracey Nixon outside Bardellis — the eaterie where Test ace Phil Tufnell is said to have smoked marijuana

Joy . . . hugged Ben yesterday

Oh no she didn't. The pantomime season in full swing in New Zealand in 1997.

SPORT

CRICKET

Tufnell faces ban over claims he efused drug test

JOHN GOODBODY

ews Phil Tufnell
ntly refused to give a
mple for a drugs test
t could have the most
ercussions for the
's spin bowler.
charge is proved,
uld be dropped from
and party to tour the
es in January and be
from cricket for at
whole of the 1998
because refusing to
sample is as serious
g a positive test for a
substance.

. 31, has just fought
Test cricket after a
incidents that have
eared him to the
.
ngland and Wales
nard (ECB) yesterday
d it has received a
om the United King-
rts Council (UKSC),
oducts drug-testing
sports, that Tufnell
to give a specimen
Middlesex's game
sset at Chelmsford
the last fixture of the
ason. When Tufnell
from his holiday
he will face an ECB
ry hearing.
arsh, the ECB chief
said yesterday: "It is
a serious matter

Tufnell: faces ECB inquiry

but it would be quite wrong of
us to pre-empt the result of the
disciplinary hearing. It is only
right to give Phil the opportunity to put his side of the
story."

Point seven of the ECB's
guidelines on drug-testing
says: "It is an offence regarded
as serious as giving a positive
sample. There is no excuse for
failing to comply with the
notice to take drug control
tests and, if you do not take it,
you are liable to be dealt with
as if you have been shown to
have had a prohibited substance in your body."

There are about 130 drug
tests in cricket every year and
the most notorious positive
case was when Ed Giddins,

the Sussex fast bowler, was
found to have taken cocaine.
He was banned from cricket
for 19 months and will be
allowed to return on April 1
next year.

Tufnell's career has been
studded with controversy. In
1994, he was fined £800 by a
North London court for assaulting his former fiancee,
Jane McEvoy, while she was
pregnant. She later claimed
that Tufnell had taken cocaine, which he denied. However, Tufnell was attacked
with a brick by his fiancee's
father and Middlesex had to
give him compassionate leave
while he sorted out his personal life.

He once spent a night in a
mental hospital after repeatedly hitting his head against the
walls of a hotel in Perth, Australia. On the field, he was
fined in 1993 for snatching his
cap from an umpire during
the England tour of India and
also fined for hurling the ball
to the ground against the
Australians. Middlesex have
fined him for making an
obscene gesture to spectators
at Lord's.

The latest incident was in
February this year, when he
was alleged to have smoked
marijuana in the lavatory of a
restaurant in New Zealand, a
claim he denied.

After all the controversy, he
kept trying to get a regular
place in the England team. He
was selected for the first live

Failure to take a drugs test at Chelmsford during the final match of the 1997 season cost me dear.

hittall hits heights

F.R.Kton
reach to end
Derbyshi

You beauty. I mark my return from exile by taking eleven Australian wickets at The Oval in 1997. Our victory persuaded Mike Atherton to delay handing over the captaincy to Alec Stewart by one tour.

The only way to travel. I celebrate with a and a drag.

Glenn McGrath is caught by Graham Thorpe. Australia are all out. Get the beers in, boys

: Do not try this after a curry.

Nothing much happened for me during 98 tour to West Indies. Not for lack of though.

assistant coach John Emburey with Robert Croft and me. We would have loved to have in tandem more often for England as we had done in New Zealand so successfully.

Right: Darren and I had some fun and games in South Africa. Sadly neither of us shone in the field as we would like to have done.

Below: I know my place – it pays to let the captain in the game. Football practice on the Millennium tour to South Africa.

Right: On the end of some heavy punishment from the Zulu during the second Test at Port Elizabeth. I had my revenge against Lance Klusener in the first innings at Durban.

in such circumstances might have been for Hick. And everyone assumed that, even though we had gone a couple of overs beyond schedule, Athers would allow him to get to three figures before declaring.

We were willing Hick on, but also had one eye on the clock. Hick had scored only a couple in three or four overs when Athers stood up and said: 'Right. That's it. I'm pulling them in.' He declared with Hick on 98 not out.

There was a deathly hush in the dressing room. Hick didn't exactly storm in, but he walked in briskly and took his gear off without a word. Nothing was said between him and Athers from then on and, for the rest of the tour, the atmosphere between the two men was prickly. I could see both sides of the coin. Personal triumph can never be put before the needs of the team and there was a match to win. But a few of us were also very sorry for Hick.

Like me, Hick is someone who has never had a comfortable ride. I don't think he ever really felt at home with selectors and captain but, possibly a victim of his own early success, always felt under a lot of pressure to live up to his reputation. Put simply, I believe he always thought he was expected to do more than anyone else. Test hundreds against Australia do not grow on trees. This one might have been the making of him.

When Slater and Mark Taylor completed a double-century opening stand, it seemed as though the pitch was just too good for us to bowl them out. In fact it even looked possible that they might actually score the 449 they needed to win, so we were forced to try and slow things down a tad. But then a smattering of drizzle freshened the pitch up and changed the picture completely. Angus came into his own and nicked out the middle order with four wickets in nine overs. From 208 for none, they were 292 for seven, and there was a glimmer.

We still had time, but the light was fading fast. With Gus and Gough able to bowl only three of the last fifteen overs as darkness started to fall, and the stock cars started revving up for an evening's racing behind the ground, Warne and Tim May kept the rest of us out quite comfortably. Nobody minded when Warne was put down by Devon off Gooch from what we thought was the final ball, but then, with the batsmen almost through the gate and up the pavilion steps, Athers noticed that there was still time for one more over. He got in the ear of the umpires and we all trooped back out again. May blocked four balls and we all went off again, this time for good.

I don't know whether it was frustration at not being able to push for the victory, the realization that we could not now win the Ashes, or vindication for his stance over Fraser, but this was the moment Athers chose to give vent to his feelings, as in, 'No complaint against the ones in place, but younger players and selectors more in touch with the dynamics of the game, please.' Illingworth, having returned home, went bonkers.

In Adelaide we proved how mad this game is by winning the fourth Test with a side that included our five remaining fit batsmen and Chris Lewis, who had been playing sub-district cricket in Melbourne. How many times has it happened that England have been out of a series, dead and buried, and then come jumping back to life? Perhaps we should start each series believing we are already two-nil down.

Very funny business, Adelaide. Before the start of the Test, Gooch announced that he was retiring from international cricket at the end of the tour – and a few of us were none too sure about that. While respecting his right to make the decision, some of the boys thought that by making it public before the start of the Test match, in a series we could still, theoretically at least, draw 2–2, he might just be sending out a message perilously close to premature surrender. With so many injuries disrupting our plans, the announcement was yet another negative when we needed all the positives we could get. Prior to the event we all felt that his retirement was a possibility, but I can recall clearly the instant I knew he was going to do it.

We were playing against Victoria in Bendigo and Gooch got out caught behind to a left-arm seamer named Corbett. No idea of his first name and no disrespect to him, but he was the kind of bowler we had all seen Gooch absolutely smash to kingdom come. Now he just played this little leaden-footed poke at him and that was that. When he got back to the dressing room I saw something in his eye that said: 'I can't do this any more.' He tried to make a joke of it. 'Corbett?' he said. 'F***ing Ronnie Corbett.' But I just felt then that something had gone from him. I was looking at one of the greatest batsmen in the world coming to terms with the fact that it was no longer necessary to be a great bowler to get him out. Sad, really.

If his decision to quit sent out an unfortunate signal, what about the team talk Keith Fletcher delivered to the troops on the eve of the match? To this day I cannot decide whether he was being defeatist or brilliant. 'Come on lads,' he said as we were getting ready to pack up. 'We've got to keep going. We're playing for our pride … you never know, we might even f***ing win!' Clever ploy or raising of the white flag? You are the ref.

But much respect for Gatt here. He'd had a poor tour and it wasn't funny. Well, not all of it. Against Queensland in Toowoomba he made a double-hundred in the first innings, then, in the second over of their reply, dived at a ball which popped over his hands and into his mouth. Resisting the temptation to eat it, he did need several stitches and took no further part. On the way back to the hotel we were assured by Roberts that Gatt would be unable to eat solids, but as I passed his room I noticed several empty pizza boxes stacked against the door.

By the time we reached Adelaide, he must have thought he had played his final innings not only of the tour but also of his Test career. But he went out and grafted a hundred against some highly accomplished bowling. In the circumstances it was a great knock, but the climax to it was one of the most nerve-racking experiences of my career. Gatt sailed through the nineties, but then got stuck on 99. For *thirty-one minutes*. In the end he and everyone else could stand it no longer. He pushed the ball straight at Steve Waugh and ran for his life. Daffy responded as quick as it was possible to do, considering he knew full well there was never a run available and had decided to switch off and wait for the next ball. He would have been run out by half a track with a direct hit, but Waugh missed and Gatt celebrated. Fair play to him. The bowling was exceptional, Craig McDermott took three for 66 in 41 overs and Gatt showed a lot of guts. (Sorry, how could I resist?)

Their response was instructive. Twenty-three-year-old Greg Blewett, approaching a hundred in his debut Test, came running down the track at Angus Fraser and three times threw himself off the ground with the effort of trying to smash him out of the park, before finally succeeding. Slight contrast in attitude and approach to Hick and Gatt. But we stayed in the game, and when the time came for them to chase, we made sure the target was a stiff one – 263 in 67 overs.

When a ploy Gatt and I had been working on in training finally came off, they were 64 for five. It works like this: he fields at short leg, I drag down a long hop outside leg stump, the batsman hammers the ball with all his might at Gatt's foot, it bounces up and lodges in his midriff for the catch. Then came Devon's express delivery to uproot Steve Waugh's off stump before he had scored a run, which was one of the most inspirational sights I have ever seen on a cricket field. We needed to take the last two wickets in just under a session, but Ian Healy's resistance held us up horribly, and we finally broke through to win with just 35 balls to spare.

John Reid, the match referee, celebrated this magnificent match, full of twists, turns and drama, by fining Lewis 30 per cent of his match fee for giving McDermott a send off, reprimanding Athers for the way we played, and fining us 15 per cent for our slow over rate. Considering we had been sledged to death throughout the entire series thus far, this was a very fine decision indeed.

Maybe we had nothing left by the time we got to Perth, but it all ended messily. Despite being the only bloke to stay fit for the entire tour, thus proving the efficiency of my unique fitness regime, I was not selected for the final Test. We knew that our only chance to win would be to grab everything that was going, but out there we couldn't catch a cold. In the first over of the match Gooch dropped Michael Slater off Devon. He went on to get 124 out of 402, and we shelled at least another six in the innings and ten in the match. The funniest, though not the worst, was when Graham Thorpe let one fall in the slips, then booted the ball past cover for the batsmen to take two runs. We shambled from bad to worse and Athers summed up everyone's frustration when he killed a plastic chair with his bat on the way back from his second-innings eight.

The win in Adelaide apart, I hadn't enjoyed the trip. When I started head-butting the walls in Perth early on, it could have been the end of it. The crisis passed, Lisa came out to join me, and the wickets in Brisbane and Melbourne set me up for a successful series. But in Sydney, where I had anticipated taking a few on the normal turning wicket, nothing moved. The only wicket taken by a spinner there was Malcolm being bowled by Warne after he had already slogged him for two sixes. Adelaide had been flat. In Perth we were a tired nonsense.

After the trials, traumas and tribulations of the last few years, at least I was returning to something approximating to normal life. Considering all that had gone before, this was a giant step in the right direction.

But I spent the journey home once again thinking that my Test place was in severe jeopardy.

SEVENTEEN

Leper

Once we returned from Australia in early 1995, the narkiness between Illingworth and Atherton continued. For some reason the bosses at the TCCB conveniently ignored Illingworth's selection policies and decided that the can should be carried instead by the team manager, Keith Fletcher, who was sacked. They then gave Illingworth even more power by making him manager as well as chairman of selectors. No one has ever had more influence over the running of the England cricket team.

He, Brian Bolus and Fred Titmus, his co-selectors for the Australian tour party, had been well miffed with Atherton's comments about younger players and selectors. Had those three remained in charge of selection when we returned, Illingworth would almost certainly have dumped him. But Athers had one very powerful ally already in place – TCCB chairman Dennis Silk – and when the counties took Atherton's advice by replacing Bolus with David Graveney, for the time being his position as captain was safe. As it was, Illingworth did all he could to drag out the reappointment. Subsequently Titmus told various newspapers that he had wanted Atherton out at this stage. By the end of the season, for very different reasons, I was feeling the same thing myself.

It was clear that Athers felt I had let him down on and off the field down under. The episode in Perth had not endeared me to him, especially after my behavioural aberrations in the West Indies the winter before. The story finally made the newspapers in the middle of February. In the *News of the World*, beneath the understated and sensitive headline, DOCS PUT CRICKET ACE TUFNELL IN MADHOUSE, a version of events was presented that, while full of errors, did contain the essential truth that I had been admitted to the psychiatric unit at Perth hospital.

That apart, from the perspective of my bowling in Australia, I had hardly burned my name on to future team sheets so I knew the selectors wouldn't be banging down my door. I was disappointed about that, because West Indies were over for a six-Test series and, the prospect of once again taking my life in my hands against their quicks apart, I really fancied getting among their batters. I knew the form, though. As usual, there was nothing I could do about it except take buckets of wickets.

I didn't know who was more anti-Tufnell at this stage, Illingworth or Atherton; whenever I bumped into either of them on the circuit the atmosphere was cordial but cool. It seemed obvious that the prevailing strategy over our spin attack was that everyone was up for consideration, so long as their surname didn't begin with the letter T. Richard Illingworth was given first go, then, when he broke his finger prior to the fourth Test at Old Trafford, they went for the Lancashire off-spinner Mike Watkinson and another off-spinner, none other than Embers, now aged forty-two. Finally, when the sheer weight of wickets

I had taken in the Championship forced them to include me in the squad for the final Test at The Oval, I had to endure one of the most humiliating experiences of my career.

I've never known anything like it. To put it bluntly, I was treated like some kind of leper. From the moment I arrived at The Oval, I sensed that the other players were very uneasy about me being there. Normally, even after one of my enforced breaks, I would get back into the swing of things very quickly and be made to feel at home. This time I was made to feel as though I was a piece of shit. It was almost as if the word had gone around that close association with me might not go down too well for those seeking to get on the plane for the winter tour to South Africa, which was to be followed by the 1996 World Cup in India, Pakistan and Sri Lanka. One or two of the lads I knew well actually went so far as to spell it out.

I was told: 'Sorry, mate, I don't want to blank you, but one or two of us have been tipped the wink to give you a wide berth. The message is that if you are looking to go on tour you don't want to be seen hanging around Tufnell.' It gave me a terrible, hurt feeling. I was like the kid in the school playground that nobody wants to play with. Granted, this squad of players, inspired by Dominic Cork setting the place alight all summer, had done brilliantly to be 2–2 with one to play. Maybe they did feel that they didn't want to disrupt whatever spirit had been built up within the team – not that I would ever accept that my presence was bad for team spirit.

But if they really didn't want me there, why did they pick me in the first place? Were they really only selecting me to stem the tide of criticism from the people who were saying I should be playing, i.e. virtually every current first-class cricketer, most rational observers and the majority of supporters in the street? Could Atherton and Illingworth really be so petty and so shallow? Had they already decided, as one rumour indicated, that they didn't want me on tour with them, and that if they picked me here and I succeeded it would have been impossible to leave me out? Surely trying to win this Test match was the priority. After all, no England side had won a series against West Indies since 1969 (under Ray Illingworth, as a matter of fact) and selection should have been governed by that thought alone.

In view of the cold-shoulder treatment, it was hardly surprising that I didn't make the final eleven, and soon afterwards I discovered that I had been left out of the touring squad as well. Then, about a month after the announcement, came confirmation that those who had brought me into the squad for that final Test at The Oval had been wasting my time for the sake of political expediency.

Immediately prior to England's departure for South Africa, the *Sun* ran a series of articles they called the Boycott and Illingworth tapes. They had arranged for Geoffrey Boycott, their paid columnist, to meet with Illingworth for head-to-head interviews. Illingworth earned a tidy sum for his time, and by the end of the interviews the *Sun* had got their money's worth.

On Wednesday 18 October, the very day the party left England for South Africa, Illingworth spelled it all out. According to the chairman: 'For the sake of balance, it might have made sense to play an offie and a left-armer, which would have brought Tufnell into the frame. But we've had a lot of problems with Tuffers over the years. If we weren't going to take him on tour, it didn't make sense to play him in England. If he came in and did well we could put ourselves in an invidious position.'

In other words, they couldn't risk picking me at The Oval in case I won them the bloody Test match and in so doing forced them to pick me for the winter tour – where I might have won some more Tests and forced them to keep me in the side.

On the subject of who exactly was behind this brilliant strategy, Illingworth was equally illuminating:

Boycott (on Atherton): 'You have a twenty-six or twenty-seven-year-old Cambridge lad. He has no great knowledge of life or cricket and he's only played a few bloody years in county cricket. That's why I feel a captain like him in selection is buggering things up. Because I can't grasp some of the things and nor can the public. I mean, you talk about Tufnell. Is that the situation – they don't want him?'

Illingworth: 'Yes. I think you and everyone else knows there have been problems with Tufnell on tour, losing his temper and that sort of thing. When I was there in Australia, though, I had no problems with Tuffers.'

Boycott: 'That begs a question, you see.' (You're damn right it does, Geoffrey. Get in there boy.) 'You said when you took over that everyone starts with a clean sheet. I know the cricket grapevine says Tufnell isn't wanted because of his attitude, he's not a good tourist and nobody can handle him. Michael doesn't want him, I know that … Why can't you try to handle Tuffers?'

Illingworth: 'Michael's got to handle him on the field. He's got to play with him.'

So it wasn't Illingworth sticking in the knife – at least not according to Illingworth. And who did that leave? It seemed clear that Atherton was now the enemy and, although not entirely surprised by this, I was disappointed.

Having touched a raw nerve, the *Sun* rang me up for my reaction and I gave it.

'I'm getting a bit sick of all this.' I told their reporter. 'I read that the slate has been wiped clean, but it seems to have been wiped clean for everyone except me! I thought that's the way it was, but now it wouldn't have mattered if I had taken 200 wickets – I still wouldn't have been picked. I've been let down. All I have ever asked is that all the hope is not strangled out of me. But no matter how well I performed, I would not have been in the Test tour squad. I find that extraordinary to say the least.

'It's hard to take because I'm passionate about the game, passionate about playing for my country. I'm fed up being painted as this surly, unruly bloke who is running amok, is bad for the team and bad for morale.'

'England's left-arm spinning role has gone to Richard Illingworth,' the reporter wrote, 'even though Tufnell's record last season was superior. He took 74 wickets at an average of 22.08 with best figures of six for 111. Illingworth managed only 45 wickets at 26.93 with a best of four for 30.'

I went on: 'I accepted I was not in the tour party, but to discover I probably had no chance of being in anyway makes me think I've been picked on.'

I didn't say it at the time, but what really hurt was to discover all of the above from an article in the pages of the *Sun*. If Atherton wanted to play politics by bringing me into the squad just to get people off his back, that was his business. If all the above really were the reasons why he didn't want me in South Africa, if he felt he couldn't trust me, that was his decision. But not once did either Atherton or Illingworth confront me with the truth. Not then and never since.

For a few days I hoped that Athers might ring me from South Africa to explain the position, or even refute what Illingworth had said. Although I appreciated he had enough on his plate trying to run the team out there I knew he would either have read or been informed about the content of the articles and a phone call wouldn't have gone amiss. He uttered not a word, either to me personally or to the papers, in response to what Illingworth had said, and the message contained in his silence was deafening.

I did feel let down by Athers. We had known each other for years and shared good times together. Rejection by someone I considered a friend was very hard to take. It seemed to me that my selection had nothing whatsoever to do with my ability to bowl, but everything to do with the perception of me as being 'the problem'. I was the buck. The buck was being passed between Atherton and Illingworth and back again. Buck 'em.

So I discovered gardening. Lisa and I had a lovely winter together. It was our first opportunity to spend time with each other without me being halfway around the world or nipping off around the country with Middlesex. And after the initial anger and disappointment of being buggered about by Athers and Illingworth had subsided, I got nicely used to it. I kept half an eye on what was going on in South Africa and, I must admit, on how Richard Illingworth was doing, and I was willing them to do well almost despite myself. But I couldn't really get into it. When they moved on for the World Cup, it was obvious that the strife between the captain and chairman was making their relationship untenable. From time to time I would read a piece suggesting that I should have been out there but, by and large, I was well out of the limelight and well out of it all.

Normal married life. Only a few years earlier the very words would have had me running for the pub. But one Sunday that winter I woke up late, looked across at Lisa, we stayed in bed an hour or so longer, got up, read the papers, had Sunday lunch, drove to the gardening centre, came back, watched telly, went for a walk, watched some more telly and went to bed – and when I woke up the next day, I thought what a brilliant day I'd had yesterday.

For the first time I could ever really remember since my mum started to become ill, I was actually feeling a little bit of contentment in my life. In between, I'd had some brilliant times, as well as some pretty dodgy ones. I'd had some fantastic laughs and moments when I was the life and soul of the party. But beneath all the outward signs of cheerfulness had I ever really been happy? I honestly think the answer is no. Anyone looking back and studying my behaviour over the years would probably have come to the same conclusion. The kind of scrapes I got myself into, the rebellion, the obsessive behaviour when it came to the drink or the girls, and the constant feeling I had of being judged all the time, all added up to a picture of someone who was not all that keen on himself.

Throughout my career, the prospect and fact of doing well at cricket for Middlesex and England were the only things with which I could prove to myself and to others that I was not worthless. Now the demons within me seemed to be abating.

As 1995 turned into '96, I also realized that I was soon to be thirty years old. I wondered if what I felt was what is known as growing up. I didn't know whether I would ever play cricket for England again. I suspected I wouldn't. But for the time being at least I was free of worrying about it. It was out of my hands.

EIGHTEEN

Healed

After cricket cranked up again at the start of the 1996 summer season, the all too familiar story unfolded once more. At first the usual suspects were rounded up for the two short series against India and Pakistan, and once again it appeared to be 'pick anyone but Tufnell'.

The disastrous end to the winter tour had led to a new selection committee being formed. After some bizarre politicking, which involved David Graveney being forced to withdraw as a contender for Illingworth's job, Raymond remained as chairman, although his power base was removed when Graveney and Graham Gooch were appointed his co-selectors. A new coach, David Lloyd from Lancashire, was installed to replace Illingworth in that capacity, but the attitude towards yours truly was just the same.

The wind of change blew in three England debutants for the first Test of the summer at Edgbaston, including a new left-arm spinner – Min Patel, who was discarded after the third, with figures of one wicket for 180 runs from 46 overs. Then, against Pakistan, Ian Salisbury returned and Robert Croft, the Glamorgan off-spinner, was given his debut in the final Test at The Oval. But while Pakistan's leg-spinner Mushtaq Ahmed helped them win the series 2–0 by taking seventeen wickets, Salisbury, Croft, Hick and Atherton (yes, Atherton) managed six between them.

And so the rumours began again, and the whispers. The difference was that this time I completely ignored them. I had had just about enough of the seemingly never ending rollercoaster ride of building up hopes, then having them dashed, then building them up again, then having them dashed, living my whole life around what appeared on Ceefax page 340 every other Sunday. They knew my number. They knew where I was. They knew what I could do and they knew what I was like. Winter, spring, summer or fall, all they had to do was call and I'd be there. But if they didn't I wasn't going to lose any more sleep over it. I was too old and life was too short for that now.

In any case, there were other things beside cricket, as Lisa was soon to remind me. Towards the end of August she told me she was pregnant; I was going to be a father again. This time the pregnancy had been planned, and when Lisa told me the news, there was no ambivalence in my emotions. It sounded and felt exactly right.

Relieved of the anxiety of bowling for my Test place, I had another good season for Middlesex, taking 72 Championship wickets in all, and although I bored the pants off everyone at the club all season about how I should be playing for England, most of it was tongue in cheek. So when, at the beginning of September, we travelled up to Old Trafford for a match against Lancashire and Atherton, I honestly just thought of it as another county match. The idea really didn't occur to me that this was the last match the England captain would be playing in before the squads for the winter tour to Zimbabwe and New Zealand were picked.

With exquisite timing, though, I took six wickets in the first innings and seven in the second. It wasn't until Lancashire's second dig that it started to dawn on me that I might be doing more than bowling Middlesex to victory. Just as I was preparing to run in to bowl to Athers, Angus Fraser, a huge mate of his, called out, 'Come on, the best bowler in England.' Athers proceeded to pad up offering no stroke to me and was given out leg before, and as he walked off, I just caught the faintest suggestion of a smile on the face of the England captain.

At the end of the game, Angus was particularly and strangely keen that I should go with him into the Lancashire dressing room for a beer and a chat with their players. This has always been a post-match ritual for some blokes but I rarely did it. My reckoning was that my business was all about hating the opposition batsmen, and while still at the place of work I just liked to keep a little distance. Angus was just so insistent, though. When I got there, after a while Athers came over and engaged me in a quite pointed conversation.

'Well bowled, mate,' he said.

'Hello …' I thought.

'I hear you've been bowling well all season.'

'Yeah, I suppose I have been,' I replied.

'Well, look,' he carried on, 'you know you've been a bit of a silly prat in the past.'

'Yeah? So …'

'So, look. What I am saying is that there is a bit of a chance of you coming on tour this winter. Is everything all right at home?'

'Yeah, fine,' I said.

'Everything all right in your head?'

'Yes,' I said, wondering to myself exactly what he meant by that but managing to stop myself saying anything. A few days later my exile from international cricket was over, eighteen months after it had begun. I'd done my time, it seemed. Or was the real reason once again that they had run out of alternatives?

My approach to the 1996–97 tour to Zimbabwe and New Zealand was totally different to how I had gone about things before. I had given up trying to second guess the selectors and Athers some time before, but I went out thinking that, however the tour panned out, I was not going to give anyone the slightest excuse to criticize me.

I threw myself into the training routine, devised by the sadistic new physio Wayne Morton (a recruit from Leeds rugby league club) and his fiendish fitness co-ordinator Dean Riddle. When I turned up at the training camp in Lanzarote for the pre-tour fitness work, David Lloyd went so far as to describe me as the fittest player in the squad. I'm not a hundred per cent sure this was true, as after one run it took me ten minutes to get enough breath back in my lungs to light up a fag, but I appreciated the thought. I appreciated a lot of what 'Bumble' was about actually. For the first time at this level I felt I was working with a bloke who didn't treat me like a child, someone who didn't see me as a problem all the time, who wasn't interested in pulling me up for petty misdemeanours just to slap me down to show me who was boss, someone who respected my ability, someone who actually quite liked me. It was a real eye opener.

There had been some rucking among the boys about Atherton's insistence that no wives or girlfriends and kids would be allowed on the trip. It was going to be a long tour and no one really enjoyed the prospect. I may have been biased because Lisa was pregnant, but I didn't agree with Athers' proposition that their presence had an adverse effect on team spirit. If team spirit was so fragile as to be adversely affected by their presence, then how strong could that team spirit have been in the first place?

My first night after saying goodbye to Lisa was spent sharing a poky Harare hotel room with John Crawley. After five minutes he got out his guitar and started strumming, and then it hit me – four and a half months of f***ing Wonderwall. It has to be said that some of us struggled with certain aspects of life in Zimbabwe. We didn't mean to be rude or ungracious, but there was a general feeling that our hosts weren't exactly bending over backwards, as we always seemed to do when people come to England.

One or two of the players had been on the road with England without a break for four or five years and now faced the prospect of a winter without any family contact whatsoever. On top of that we felt as a group, and Athers did as captain, that the press boys had come out here more than ready to take the piss should we do poorly against the newest Test-playing nation. All the ingredients came together to make for a mood of grumpiness and suspicion. And the mood didn't improve when we proceeded to lose our first two completed matches, against the Zimbabwe President's XI and Mashonaland, for whom James Kirtley – a twenty-one-year-old Sussex bowler who had taken sixteen wickets in six matches in the 1996 county Championship – took seven in the match.

We won the next two games, but when we followed that by losing the first one-day international in Bulawayo, some of the press reporting became quite nasty. We were painted as being surly, downright rude to our hosts and unwilling to make any effort to get into the place or the people. We were even criticized for not enjoying ourselves more socially. Blimey. I wish some of this lot had been around when I started touring. It was claimed that none of us wanted to go and visit Victoria Falls. Cobblers. We tried a few times, but the weather was too bad for us to get off the ground. Then, when we finally did manage it, we had a great time. The transport was a tad dodgy – the captain of the single-engine aircraft asked us all to sit at the back of the plane when we took off and at the front when we landed, which was a little unnerving – but it was an excellent trip and the falls were truly amazing.

So we reacted to what we felt was some deliberately unhelpful reporting, designed purely to stir things up at home, by declining the press's offer to be entertained at their Christmas panto. Now they got the pin even more, and it was in this atmosphere that we narrowly failed to win the first Test, again in Bulawayo – the infamous murder that never was – and suffered an almighty hammering as a result.

To be fair, we felt we did murder Zimbabwe. We played all the cricket, we were not helped by the rain, and when we set off after a target of 205 in 37 overs, we were cheated out of the win by bowlers sending down blatant leg-side wides that the batsmen couldn't reach but the umpires never called.

As the match reached its climax, with us closing in on the runs, the mood around us in the stand became pretty hairy. On most Test grounds in a tense situation like this, the players are cut off from the public. Here in Bulawayo, because there was no view of the pitch from our dressing room, we were all sitting outside, more or less mixed in with a highly partisan and vociferous crowd. Whereas under normal circumstances, had one of us reacted in the heat of the moment by shouting out 'wide' or worse, no member of the public would have been any the wiser. As it was, anything and everything we were thinking or saying was picked up by the crowd around us. We were out there to win the Test match, and with all the ridicule that had been heaped on us by the papers we were desperate to answer our critics. So, as the wides continued, our sense of frustration and anger grew. And so did the reaction of the crowd. Not to put too fine a point on it, they began goading us – and Bumble was not the only one who gave as good as he got.

That we failed by just one run, when needing three off the final ball of the match, was an outstanding effort considering the Zimbabwean tactics. Yet when Athers and Bumble walked into the press conference afterwards, they felt the atmosphere was highly unsympathetic, not to say openly hostile. When one of the reporters asked Athers if he felt the Zimbabweans had employed legitimate tactics, the two of them engaged in a staring match before Bumble came out with the immortal line: 'We murdered them, flippin' hammered 'em. They know it and we know it.'

His words were only what we all felt to be the case, and I understand that Heath Streak, the main culprit, admitted afterwards that he felt he and his colleagues *had* got away with murder. We felt we had been cheated out of the win by a combination of them bending the rules and the umpires allowing them to get away with it, and now we were being unfairly pilloried for expressing our disappointment.

Back home Sir Ian MacLaurin, the new chairman of the TCCB, and his chief executive, Tim Lamb, were quoted as having a bit of a go at Bumble and the rest of us, which didn't go down terribly well among the boys. In fact, Athers was plainly getting a bit pissed off. His back wasn't in great shape and he was also out of nick. One or two of the papers started suggesting that maybe the time was approaching for him to quit the captaincy. Although they used his back condition as a lever in the story, a few of us couldn't help feeling that some of Illingworth's supporters among the press were sticking the knife in hardest. Was this their pay-back opportunity?

Not surprisingly, MacLaurin and Lamb received a cool welcome when they arrived in Harare for the next Test, but things improved when they changed their tone slightly after being informed of some of our feelings. MacLaurin even went so far as to announce that henceforth the players would have their own rooms on tour, which got a few of the lads back on side immediately.

In the second Test we started badly by conceding a first-innings lead, but once Alec Stewart and Graham Thorpe had responded with a partnership of more than a hundred in the second innings, we were thinking in terms of a declaration – until the rain washed the match away to complete a drawn series. Then we went down in the final two one-day internationals to finish off 3–0 losers.

The reaction to us failing to beat Zimbabwe, the inevitable ravings of politicians and pundits alike, left no one in any doubt as to how vital it was for all our futures that we beat the Kiwis. Athers knew that his head in particular was on the block. He had said publicly that failure to beat New Zealand would have been the signal for him to step down from the captaincy and let someone else have a go. The change in scenery had no beneficial effect at first: he carried on playing as though his bat had a hole in it, and although no one could discern any sign of panic, it was obvious that he was concerned.

In the first Test in Auckland, though, he returned to form in dramatic fashion, making 83 out of 521, in which both Alec Stewart and Graham Thorpe scored hundreds. New Zealand had managed 390 in their first innings and half an hour into the afternoon session on the final day they were just eleven runs ahead, in their second, with only one wicket remaining. How could we fail to win? Ask 'Danny the Duck'.

Danny Morrison, the New Zealand paceman and confirmed No 11, was the proud holder of a world record of 24 Test noughts. This was a distinction he had earned on merit, and he had attempted to commercially exploit his utter hopelessness with the bat by bringing out a range of duck callers named as above. However, he chose this moment to bat for two and threequarter hours, successfully defend 133 balls, and score 14 not out to help Nathan Astle in an unbroken last-wicket stand of 106 to earn the draw. He never looked remotely in trouble.

The pitch was as dead as a dodo during most of that final day, nothing moved off the straight, and Morrison and Astle showed how easy it was to survive. We tried everything. Athers switched the bowling about and I did my best, but not only did we not drop a catch or even create a chance, I can't recall a single ball beating the bat. It was the most painful passage of play I have ever taken part in. As it went on, sales of the duck caller went off the scale and so did the noise they created. There we were, busting a gut to try and get the last wicket and win the Test, and all we could hear were a thousand ducks, quacking in unison.

I recall the moment I knew we weren't going to win. It

was almost surreal. I had bowled a ball at Morrison that got lodged in between his bat and pad. Then it rolled backwards almost in slow motion and missed the off stump by a fag paper. I was so disappointed. That ball was the Test match. I fell backwards to the ground, treating the crowd to my best starfish impression. It was the last ball of the over and I just didn't want to get up. I was lying there on my back, gazing up at this beautiful blue sky with a few wispy clouds and a couple of gulls gliding overhead. The next thing I knew a giant shadow came across the sun. It was Steve Dunne, the umpire, leaning down to hand me my cap and saying: 'Tuffers, I think that's just about it.' I could have lain there forever.

This was getting beyond a joke. Cheated out of a victory in Bulawayo and now this. Talk about Devon Lock.

Inevitably the pressure increased. It was pointed out that we were still without a Test win away from home for two years – since the victory in Barbados in 1995 – and even some of us were wondering if Athers was destined never to win another as captain.

How he proved us wrong! In Wellington, great bowling by Darren Gough and Andy Caddick in the first innings and a hundred by Graham Thorpe set us up for victory by an innings. Then, in Christchurch, Atherton showed just how tough and stubborn he could be. After making 94 in the first dig, he followed with 118 in the second as he, Crawley and Dominic Cork successfully led the chase to make more than 300 for England for only the second time in history. I was not present for his 185 not out in Johannesburg to save the second Test against South Africa on the previous winter tour, but those who were say this gave him more satisfaction, simply because it earned victory and a 2–0 series win. What is more, it got everyone off his case.

Little did I know that a few people were about to get back on mine. For our celebrations the next day were rudely interrupted by a story that had broken back home. 'I CAUGHT TUFF SNEAKING PUFF OF POT' ran the headline in the *Sun* on Wednesday 19 February. Here we go again, I thought.

'A restaurant manageress claimed yesterday that she kicked out cricket ace Phil Tufnell for smoking POT – hours before England's Test triumph in New Zealand. Stunned Janelle Rossiter said the giggling star and a pal sneaked into a loo – which was left thick with marijuana fumes. Waitress Caitlin Cherry said: "Smoke billowed out of the toilets when the door was opened." Middlesex spin-bowler Tufnell, thirty, and two pals – one of them a woman – also ordered three bottles of wine. They were eventually asked to leave posh Bardellis restaurant in Christchurch.'

As I told one of the reporters when quizzed over the allegations, 'The next thing you know they will be saying I wear stockings and suspenders under my flannels.'

I was in Bardellis that night and I did share a couple of bottles of wine with some mates. The fact is that I was on my way back to the hotel when a couple of the Barmy Army I had come to know beckoned me over. I hadn't intended to stay, but one bottle of wine wouldn't hurt and, though one led to another, even the staff at the restaurant made it quite clear that I was not drunk at any time. As for smoking in the toilets – not me matey. Thrown out? I paid for the wine with a credit card. How I managed to sign for it with one arm pinned behind my back I'm not quite sure. It is quite possible somebody had enjoyed a puff or two that evening in that restaurant, but I hadn't. I may be daft, but can anyone really be so gullible as to believe that I would do such a thing in a public place on the eve of the final day of an important Test match, especially after all the warnings I had received regarding my future career? On second thoughts, don't answer that.

John Barclay, the tour manager – very old-Etonian, former captain of Sussex and a top bloke – called me in and I told him all that I knew. Then the very next day information came to light that I believe vindicated me completely. *The Times* ran the following story from a correspondent in New Zealand, the delightfully named Pattrick Smellie: 'The England cricketer Philip Tufnell, who was accused by waitresses of smoking cannabis in Christchurch on the eve of England's Test victory, may have been the victim of a publicity stunt, it emerged yesterday. Bardellis, the restaurant at the centre of the allegations, fell under suspicion when posters saying "Phil Tufnell must agree that Bardellis really is Christchurch's Best Joint" were spotted in the city centre.

'A Wellington bar, Cafe Brava, gained similar publicity late last year when its staff spoke to the media about several late-night incidents involving the Deputy Prime Minister-to-be, Winston Peters.

'Staff at Bardellis would not comment on the incident, which happened before the third Test victory against New Zealand. In a separate development, Christchurch media sources said that Caitlin Cherry, the waitress who made the story public, is studying broadcast journalism at a local college. Ms Cherry is thought to have tipped off local media before informing Bardellis management.'

I would have said that the story took a load off my mind, but there was no load to take. Everyone knew I was an easy target and someone had made a very hamfisted attempt at generating a bit of publicity. What I resented was that had the real story not emerged, some people would have been left with only the allegation, and that was not pretty. Whether entirely fair or not, it was plain that I was on my very last final warning, and these people were messing with my career and my life. Thank goodness the management this time acted on common sense, not rumour. For the first time in any disciplinary matter I have ever been involved in, the management supported me rather than threw the book at me. It was a very far cry from what had happened in Perth. Then again, by the time the allegations appeared in the paper we had just won the series. Does it really all come back to that in the end? I suspect so.

I left New Zealand satisfied that I had achieved all that I had set out to do. Apart from the Bardellis farce, there was no hint of what they used to call a stain on my character. I had even played in a one-day international – in Christchurch a couple of days after the Test – taking four for 22 from my full allotment and earning the man of the match award as we achieved the first of only two victories in the five-match series.

But from a cricketing point of view, the real progress had been made in my spinning partnership with Croft. When we set off for Zimbabwe, I had the feeling that, instead of being along for the ride and to bowl when the seamers needed a breather, Croft and I were regarded as central to the strategy. As it turned out we bowled together in four of the five Tests that winter, taking 42 wickets between us. Both of us enjoyed bowling with the other. We had something going, supported each other, created pressure well for each other and took wickets together. We were looking forward to resuming and developing the partnership against Mark Taylor's Australians.

Dream on.

NINETEEN

Poppy

I returned home to a heavily plump Lisa, the bump we knew as Poppy growing within her and now splendidly visible. They were both fine, I had done okay on tour, things were going well. Too well? You betcha.

I had been home two weeks and was already in pre-season training with Middlesex when, on the morning of 18 March, Lisa went off to keep her appointment with our local GP for a routine check-up. Now seven months pregnant, Lisa was enjoying the bloom, filled with strength, health and energy. So well was she feeling, in fact, that she very nearly opted for a spot more shut-eye. What she didn't know was that had she stayed at home, the probability is that neither she nor Poppy would be alive today. It sounds strange to say so now, melodramatic even, but the plain fact is that I could have lost them both, and very nearly did.

I had never heard of pre-eclampsia, a toxic condition of pregnancy that leads to rocketing high blood pressure, seizures, kidney failure and death. Nor, so far as I know, had Lisa. But almost as soon as the doctor saw her, he recognized the classic symptoms. Lisa was rushed to

Harold Wood Hospital, not far from our home in Loughton, and I was sent for immediately. I didn't know all the details until I reached the hospital, but the news and the scene that I found when I arrived were devastating.

Lisa had already been told by the medical staff that she had to have the baby straight away by an emergency Caesarean section – no ifs, buts or maybes. Then they told her that although they could save her, the best odds they could give the baby were fifty-fifty. In order to proceed they needed Lisa's consent, but by the time I got to her, she was in a terrified state. In her fear and panic she was refusing point blank to sign the consent forms. She kept saying: 'I'm not going to sign, because if I sign I will be killing my baby. I know the baby is not ready to be born.'

There were three bags of saline solution going into her hands, a catheter had been inserted because her kidneys were failing, and they had injected her with steroids to open the baby's lungs. She was petrified, but she still refused to sign. Able to think only of the baby, she just wasn't able to make any rational judgement. Consequently her condition deteriorated rapidly, her blood pressure was now dangerously high and her life was in serious jeopardy. She was at the point where a decision had to be made immediately.

No one can guess how they are going to react in this kind of situation. Thank God most of us never have to find out. Your emotions just go off the scale. First of all you try to be rational and calm about what is going on, then you go into denial, trying to convince yourself that it isn't happening. There must be a mistake, I thought; Lisa and the baby were doing so well. But although we were both being ripped to pieces by what was happening, when confronted by the awful reality of making the choice, it was clear that saving Lisa had to be the priority. She kept saying no, but I pleaded with her: 'Please, darling. The doctor has told me that you are on the way out here. You have to do this.'

By the time she finally agreed, she was too weak for a general anaesthetic to be administered. I wanted to stay with her while the operation was performed, but was asked to leave. Five minutes later, with me pacing up and down the corridors and chainsmoking, Poppy was delivered. Lisa told me later that she was whispering to herself that she was a mum, but when the doctors told her that she had a daughter she just couldn't bring herself to hold her. She was scared of getting too close in case Poppy didn't make it. Although the most violent part of the trauma was past, Poppy's fight was only just beginning.

As Lisa was taken away to recover from the operation, I was led to the infant intensive care unit to see our baby girl. It was such a sad sight. There, in the middle of the room, in total silence apart from the beeping of the monitors and machines, was our daughter, breathing with a respirator and all wired up. She was a tiny little thing, no bigger than my hand, and seeing her lying there so helpless and vulnerable, I broke down. I couldn't touch her. The closest I could get to her was stroking her leg through the incubator and telling her I loved her.

The staff were brilliant. They made a bed for me next to Lisa, and I spent the next two days rushing between the two of them while Lisa recovered slowly but surely. When I went home to get some things, the house was so lonely. For the next five days Poppy was on a life-support machine, showing little or no response. Her lungs and bladder were not functioning, she developed jaundice and was given ultra-violet treatment, and she lost weight.

dropping to three pounds. Things looked very bad. Lisa and I were both in an awful state. I didn't eat, didn't shave, didn't care about anything else. Lisa was suffering torture seeing other mums with their babies, feeding them, looking after them, nursing them, while she couldn't even touch Poppy.

Yet somehow Poppy clung on. After ten days she was moved from intensive care to the high dependency unit. Still we were warned not to build our hopes up too high. After a fortnight Lisa was advized to go home, as there was nothing she could do at the hospital and being there just caused her distress. When we got home, though, the atmosphere in the house was unreal. We were there, but our baby wasn't. She wasn't there in the morning, she wasn't there at night, and the nursery we had prepared as a warm and happy place was cold and empty. Day after day we would visit Poppy at the hospital, and gradually there were little signs that she was improving. But the process was harrowingly slow. The day we were finally able to bring Poppy home, six weeks after she had been born, was one of the happiest of my life. We were both completely overwhelmed with the joy of bringing her into the house and being a family at last.

I have to say that the experience had a profound effect on me. For so long my life had been all about me, my problems, my battles with authority, my worries, me. But going through this with Poppy and Lisa made me forget about all that. At one point I was convinced I would be returning home on my own, neither a husband nor a father, that instead of bringing both my girls back home safe and sound, I would be without either. It was the worst feeling of my life and it taught me to take nothing for granted.

TWENTY

Hero to Zero

The events surrounding Poppy's birth had shown me that there were far worse things in life than being left out of a cricket side.

It goes without saying that I was frustrated to be twelfth man five times out of the first five Tests of the 1997 Ashes series, particularly after Croft and I had got something going in Zimbabwe and New Zealand, but it didn't strike me as the end of the world. I was made to feel very much part of a squad effort, and although I could have done without all that travelling up and down the motorways only to be told no Cat today, thanks, at least there were sound cricketing reasons behind the decisions.

As all Test countries have been for the most of the nineties, we were keen to negate the threat of Shane Warne. There were two schools of thought as to how best to achieve this. One involved sending a wheelbarrow full of pepperoni pizza to his room every night, and the other was to make the pitches as unfriendly to spin as was acceptable within the bounds of good taste. When things went right, as they did at Edgbaston in the first Test, it was bingo and the Ashes were coming home. When they didn't, as at Lord's in the second, Glenn McGrath was able to take eight for 38 in the first innings to bowl us out for 77. By the time we reached the sixth Test at The Oval, the Aussies had won at Old Trafford, Leeds and Trent Bridge, and not only had Warne proved he can turn the ball on any surface, but their seam and swing bowlers had tucked in as well.

Although Croft had played in all five matches until then, he had struggled to make an impact, and had also recently been involved in a televized exchange of handbags with Essex's Mark Ilott in the NatWest semi-final at Chelmsford. Despite being included in the fourteen-man squad, he was told not to bother turning up to The Oval, so I rolled up more or less knowing I would be playing. With the Ashes gone, most of the speculation concerned the future of Athers as captain. Apparently he had pretty much made up his mind he would be jacking it in, whatever happened here. By the end of the match, however, all thoughts of resignation had been put on hold.

The first clue that this pitch might be to my liking came during the second session of play. We were batting, having won the toss, and already I could see the odd ball from Warne just gripping the surface, which perked me up no end. Adam Hollioake's memorable dismissal, when he shouldered arms only to be bowled middle stump for nought by Warne's googly, also proved there was turn available. Incidentally, I enjoyed Adam's reaction when he came back to the dressing room and suffered the indignity of watching countless replays of his dismissal. 'Well,' he said, 'it's just possible I might have made a small misjudgement there.'

Our total of 180 was nothing like enough and appeared to set the seal on Atherton's decision to go, but I was quietly confident that I might have a part to play. And then I had one of those days when everything went right. I cannot remember bowling a bad ball. Sometimes when you come across a pitch which is turning, there can be a tendency to rush the ball through, to put too much effort into the bowling, and you end up bowling too fast. This time, though, I slipped into a good rhythm early on and never lost it. The ball-on-the-string was fully operational, I found a nice natural pace and all the variations landed in the right places. I had a good loop and good pace, with the ball just curving in, bouncing and turning. More or less bloody perfect, and had it not been for Warne slogging me about a bit at the end, I would certainly have bagged my Test best.

I was a bit unfortunate not to get him straight away, as it happens. When he came in I wanted the fielder at square leg, Peter Martin, to move to his right a few yards. Athers wanted him placed dead square. We disagreed but he insisted, and then early on Warne swept me uppishly, straight to where Martin would have been standing. As it was he did brilliantly to get near it, but the chance went down and Warne made 30 to heave them to 220, a lead of 40. Still, mustn't grumble. On the ground where I had enjoyed so much Test success in the past and with the crowd really behind us and me, I finished the first innings with my best Test bowling in England, seven for 66. No wicket in particular gave me more satisfaction than the others, although it is always nice to get Mark Waugh out before he can do you damage. I really got into building the pressure on each batsman. Every one of them presented a new challenge and a new task, and I had a lot of fun.

For all my personal success and that of Andy Caddick, who took the other three wickets, it soon became apparent that our achievements would be in vain. Only Graham Thorpe, Mark Ramprakash and Mark Butcher made double figures as we were bowled out for 163 by the middle of the third day, leaving Australia with a paltry 124 for victory.

I don't know whether Athers had finished his resignation article for the next day's edition of the *Sunday Telegraph*, but there must have been some hasty rewrites that afternoon. To be fair, we thought we might just have had a sniff. Although the pitch was by no means unplayable their seam bowlers had made the ball go through the top and there was a bit of indifferent bounce. No one could have predicted the outcome of the most amazing day's cricket I have ever been involved in.

Devon Malcolm struck a crucial blow early to have Matthew Elliott leg before at five for one, and they never really got over it. Caddick bowled really well, steaming down from the Vauxhall End, and I just kept plugging away. We had a little luck along the way, but we took all our catches and at the fall of each wicket the noise from the crowd increased a notch or two. Under pressure the Aussies just seemed to go in the brain collectively. With all the tension out there, Athers did brilliantly to keep the lid on it and prevent any of us from losing the plot. We jollied ourselves along, but even though we were nicking them out at regular intervals, the total required was so small that I don't think any of us seriously believed we were going to win until Caddick got Michael Kasprowicz out at 99 for nine. With 20 runs needed and McGrath at the crease it suddenly dawned on us that, all bullshit and bravado aside, we might actually win the match.

And then we did. I looped one up around McGrath's middle stump that he tried to whip to leg side against the spin. The ball held its line, hit the leading edge and spooned up behind me and to my left, where I turned and saw Thorpe at mid-off begin running towards it. I swear the rest of the event happened in super slow-motion. 'Cccaaatchhhiiittt!' I cried out. As soon as the ball nestled in his hands, the action speeded up again and we were running around the field like dervishes.

There are two lasting images I have of that moment and the aftermath. The first is of me standing there with my arms raised, shouting at the top of my voice and not being able to hear myself for the noise of the crowd, and the second, a little later, is captured in a photograph of me sitting flaked out in a chair, supping from a huge bottle of champagne and gripping a fag as though it was my last.

The fact is that very soon after coming off the field I realized I was totally knackered, mentally and physically. We had been concentrating so hard out there, and to be the bowler in the middle of the climax was a completely draining experience. I had left my soul out there on the field; all that was left was the husk. My eleven for 93 was my Test best and earned me the man of the match award, but all I could think of was that I was looking forward to a long bath and an even longer kip. How times change!

The series was over, and after a while all speculation over Athers ceased. He had seen enough in our victory and enjoyed it enough to be persuaded to carry on for the winter tour to the West Indies. My season, though, still had one rather nasty sting in the tail – or two to be precise.

The day before our final Championship match of the season, against Essex at Chelmsford, I had been doing some gardening at home when a sharp, hot pain suddenly stabbed the side of my face. Realizing I had been stung by some insect or other, I ran into the house to put some cream on the affected area, and noticed in the bathroom mirror that my eye had already started closing. Later that day, when a reporter arrived from the *Daily Telegraph* to interview me and present me with the Barclaycard/Daily Telegraph Champion of British Sport award for August, she thought I had been punched in the face. Later she wrote: 'Beneath a baby blue flannel he was nursing a swollen, reddened, totally blind eye, the sort of injury that comes from being a very bad boxer, a very brave batsman or a very naughty schoolboy.'

Whatever it was that got its stinger into me, I was plainly allergic to what it had deposited and felt so rough that I very nearly pulled out of the match. Looking back I wish I had done.

However, I woke up feeling slightly better and decided to make myself available. I managed to find some medication for the swelling and the pain but, as the morning wore on, the combination of the medicine and the pain that was now returning made me feel worse and worse. I barely noticed the strangers wandering around the players' balcony at Chelmsford when I got there, but was informed that they were Sports Council drugs testers who were there to carry out a routine test. The way it works is that they pull out two names at random from the batting order and ask the subjects to fill a bottle.

We fielded first and I began feeling really rough. At lunch Paul Weekes, the other Middlesex player required to take the test, duly produced but, try as I might, I failed. I gave up and carried on with the match, intending to have another go later on. As the day wore on my condition deteriorated severely, so I was mightily relieved when we managed to bowl Essex out an hour before the close as this considerably increased my chances of being able to get home early to try and recover. In the change between innings I asked our captain, Mark Ramprakash, if I could leave and, seeing how bad I was, he agreed. I left in something of a rush, and it was not until much later that evening that I realized I hadn't given the testers what they had come for.

I heard no more about the matter for a couple of days – and then the balloon went up. According to the story that appeared in the papers, it was claimed that I had refused to take a drugs test. Bearing in mind the allegations that had appeared in New Zealand earlier in the year, this was all I needed. There were even suggestions that I would lose my place in the tour party. I was on holiday when the club contacted me and explained that I was to be brought before the disciplinary committee of the England and Wales Cricket Board for a full hearing.

What now?

When I arrived at Lord's on 24 October, I did not like the look on the faces of the people sitting before me in judgement. Ramps and another club committee member were there to speak on my behalf, but it was obvious from the questioning of the panel that one or two of them had decided in advance that I was guilty of trying to get away with something. It was clear that my reputation had preceded me as far as they were concerned. In the circumstances I felt that the best course of action was to say sorry and take what was coming. Nothing would be gained by stringing things out; best to get the whole thing over and done with.

I was shocked by the severity of the sentence imposed on me. The committee accepted my explanation, but, because I had been technically guilty of refusing to take a drugs test, they hit me hard. According to their statement:

'The Panel, having heard all the evidence, was not satisfied that Philip Tufnell had deliberately acted in a way calculated to avoid taking the drugs test ... The cricketer accepted the seriousness of failing to complete the test. The Panel wishes to underline the necessity for players to conform to the Anti-Doping Regulations to the letter, so as to maintain the integrity of the drugs testing procedures, and to eliminate from the game those who use prohibited substances.

'Accordingly, the Panel viewed Philip Tufnell's admitted failure as a most serious breach of regulations and imposed in total the following penalties ...

'1. That Philip Tufnell be suspended from playing in all cricket under the jurisdiction of ECB until 1 April 1999, such penalty itself to be suspended:
   a) provided that the player undertakes a DCT (Doping Control Test) in 1997 at a time of the Board's choosing;
   b) provided that the player undertakes a DCT in 1998 at a time of the Board's choosing; and/or
   c) that he does not provide a positive DCT sample at any time during the period of suspension.
2. That he be fined the sum of £1,000 and pay the sum of £250 towards the costs.'

It was one hell of a shock to the system, and I took a bit of time to get my head around it all. When they first read out the penalty, I was so flabbergasted at hearing the words 'suspended from playing all cricket ... until 1 April 1999' that I didn't take in the rest. All I could think of was missing the tour to West Indies, the whole of the next year's cricket and the winter tour after that. To all intents and purposes they were telling me my career was over.

Once it became clear that the suspension was itself suspended, my panic subsided, and when I finally calmed down enough to consider what had happened, I came to see the episode as another useful reminder of how precarious this existence and my career in particular were. Against the Australians at The Oval I was the man of the match, the 'Champion of British Sport', A Number One, King of the Hill. Now I was sitting there in front of a disciplinary committee empowered to finish my Test career, with my cap in my hand and my arse on the line.

No wonder that when the scuba-diving and other associated Lanzarote training regimes had been completed on the eve of our departure to the Caribbean, the good Lord MacLaurin uttered these immortal words. 'Good luck, Michael,' he said to Athers. 'Good luck, Angus. Ah, Tufnell. You will *try* not to get into any trouble won't you?'

Not a squeak all tour, as it happens. Maybe that was the problem. Maybe I was just too well behaved.

Forget Kingston, for a start. A month beforehand, when we saw the desert on which the Test was due to be played, it was quite obvious to anyone with eyes that there was no way on earth a game of Grandmother's Footsteps could be played on that surface, let alone a Test match with a hard ball and very fast bowlers.

Just before I left for the trip I decided to make a will for the first time. The bloke filling out the details said: 'Tell me, Phil. You're making a will because you think Curtly and Courtney are going to kill you, right?' I told him to shut up and get on with making the will. But how those words came back to me that day at Sabina Park as wickets fell, our batters got battered and I searched the dressing room for any and every piece of protective equipment I could lay my hands on. Fortunately for me, I was spared having to make the ultimate sacrifice when the first Test was abandoned after 10.1 overs.

I tried. I really tried. I gave my bowling everything on that tour. The little difficulty in my relationship with Athers was long forgotten and I felt I owed him something for giving me another crack. I genuinely believe that, had we enjoyed an even break when it came to the umpiring decisions, we would have won the second Test in Trinidad. But as that last-day countdown unfolded, it just seemed we could do nothing to get past Carl Hooper and David Williams. Did I bowl over the wicket too much at Hooper? Maybe. Did I bowl at the correct end? Maybe not. But the priorities were set out clearly and the plan adhered to rigidly. Should I have bucked it, though? Should I have said, 'Let's stop playing Hooper and start playing the match?'

The night before the final day I had a horrible feeling, and when Gus dropped that caught-and-bowled chance in the first over, it got worse. Countless shouts for leg before and close-in catches went unrewarded. Was it just a case of someone else's day? In the end I was expected to do the job I am paid to do – and I expected to do it myself. Was I tentative? Did I lack aggression when it really mattered? And if so, why? The bottom line was that, however many chances we felt were denied us, I just didn't create enough pressure to bowl out a side in their second innings as I had done so many times before for Middlesex and occasionally for England. I really should have done.

Revenge was sweet for us in the third Test at the same ground as the roles were reversed. This time we were successful in a harrowing, nerve-jangling run-chase, rain and all. The taste in my mouth was still not pure honey, though. For all the laughs and lagers that followed a result with which we earned parity in the series, and despite all the slaps on the back from their visiting Lordships, I just couldn't get the feeling out of my system that I wasn't doing enough. I was bowling tight, but I couldn't get anyone out. On top of that, the umpires seemed to have been of the opinion that a new rule had been introduced outlawing the upholding of lbw appeals in favour of spin bowlers. Once, in the second of the two Tests in Trinidad, I let it get the better of me. For the seven hundredth time, it seemed, Shivnarine Chanderpaul had padded away a delivery that I would have bet my Bensons was going to hit middle stump. As I turned to appeal, I noticed that the umpire was looking down at his ball-counter, shaking it as though it had got stuck. I didn't even bother to appeal, but I did ask him, 'Aren't you even going to look?' 'No,' he said, 'I'd be guessing.' 'Yeah,' I said, 'but at least you might guess right.'

In Georgetown, Croft and I were paired up for the first time since the final Test in New Zealand and it worked pretty well, mainly for Robert. The pitch started dry and crumbled, so winning the toss and batting first was crucial, and the look on Athers' face when he lost it told its own story. Inevitably, I fear, we fell 2–1 behind with two to play.

Then came the fourth Test in Barbados, where so much was at stake for us as a team, Athers as captain, and all of us as Test cricketers that it was almost painful. Only too well aware how vital this match was, we started hopelessly as, taking first use of a blameless pitch, we were 55 for four by lunch on the first day, with Thorpe retired hurt as well. But from then on, apart from a brief period, we totally dominated the game. Thorpe returned after treatment and with Mark Ramprakash put on 205 for the sixth wicket – a record for England against West Indies – both scoring hundreds as we rattled up 403. When we bowled we let them get off to a flyer, with Philo Wallace and Clayton Lambert moosing the ball everywhere, but they were eventually pegged back to 262 all out. We then pressed on for a declaration, doing so at 223 for three and leaving them 109 overs to make 375. Our push for victory was all set up when rain did for our chances and ensured we could not now win the series.

The rain had a deeper effect on two of us in particular. As for myself, I felt cheated that what I believed was my real chance to make an impact on the series was drowned by the rain. They would have gone for the runs and kept on going, which I was convinced would open doors for me. The night before, I had imagined nicking out the wickets as we had done both at The Oval and on the same ground four years earlier, with the Barmy Army and the thousands of English visitors driving us on to victory.

As for Athers, before the start of the match we all had an inkling that if we didn't win here and a series victory was beyond us, he would do what he first thought of doing at Trent Bridge in the summer. And with the rain came the realization that enough was enough. There is only so much any man can take of the pressure of leading what had been a pretty unsuccessful team. Even though certain things appeared to have been put in place to help the development of future teams, it was what was happening here and now that concerned him.

The champs today/chumps tomorrow nature of our performances would have worn down the most stoical and stubborn of men. After Trent Bridge we were a bunch of losers. After The Oval we were world beaters. After the second Test in Trinidad we were useless. After the third Test in Trinidad we were giants. The only consistent thing about our performances was that you never knew from one match to the next whether we were going to be brilliant or god-awful. What really did Athers in the brain was that no matter how he tried to rationalize things, he just couldn't understand or explain why, let alone do anything about it.

The final Test in Antigua was a case in point. Granted the luck went against us again in terms of having to bat on a wet pitch and we folded for 127. But although they absolutely marmalized us in their innings of 500 for seven, a tremendous rearguard action meant that twenty minutes after tea on the final day, at 295 for four we must have been safe. What happened? A run out separated Thorpe and Nasser Hussain, who had both been batting brilliantly, and before you could say pack of cards we collapsed and were down and out, 3–1 losers.

Watching Athers go and offer himself up to the press afterwards was sad. We all felt for him, and tears were shed. Every time he had set himself again after another defeat, he must have believed that this was the time things would be different. But they never really were. How many times can you pick yourself up?

TWENTY-ONE

What Then?

And what happened to me? Another couple of years doing the old hokey-cokey, as a matter of fact.

In chronological order...OUT, first of all, for the rest of 1998 and, if you believed some of the things that were being said and written at the time, on a one-way trip to the knacker's yard. It didn't quite end up that way, but I was surplus to requirements for the duration of the captaincy of Athers' replacement, Alec Stewart.

I couldn't really argue at first. I knew that, although I had tried my nuts off in the Caribbean, as far as taking wickets was concerned I just should have got more people out. Whatever the circumstances, I felt that I hadn't done myself justice, it did piss me off and I was resigned to a spell on the bench.

Alec wanted to try some other options and good luck to him as well, because against South Africa, somehow and contrary to all the predictions of the experts, he led England to their first victory in a proper Test series for eleven years. Had the spinners chosen ahead of me enjoyed a smattering of success during the summer of 1998, that may very well have been it. Whereas a pace attack of Angus Fraser, Dominic Cork and Darren Gough took 59 wickets between them, the spinners accounted for precisely 58 fewer. The combined figures produced by Robert Croft (87 overs; 20 maidens; 211 runs; 0 wickets), Ashley Giles (36-7-106-1), Ian Salisbury (25-3-106-0) and Mark Ramprakash (5-0-17-0) read as follows: Overs:153; Maidens:30; Runs:440; Wickets:1; Average: 440. Then Salisbury took one for 86 in the first innings of the single Test against Sri Lanka at The Oval, which, after making 445 first up, we managed to lose by the not inconsiderable margin of ten wickets.

Although my ambition and my desire to get back were as strong as ever, I purposely tried to put all thoughts concerning a recall out of my mind. From the outset, my attitude was that if it happened, it happened and brilliant, but that the issue was out of my hands.

Then as the story of the summer unfolded, things changed. Little whispers here, knowing looks there, the usual stuff. As the time approached for the selection of the squad for the 1998/99 tour to Australia and speculation mounted, my name was mentioned with growing frequency and, of course, the inevitable happens; you start to believe what you read. Pretty soon the old wobbly feelings come into play. Well, maybe, you never know...stranger things...might have a bit of a squeak...sure, come to think of it, must have a half-decent chance...yeah, why not? Who else are they going to pick?...yup, that's it, must be on the plane...

After having thought myself back into the frame for the Ashes series (almost against my better judgement), when the squad was announced and I wasn't in, the disappointment was huge. I didn't have to wait long for an explanation. The names of those picked were accompanied by some very familiar sounding references to 'character' and 'commitment' and 'the right sort of player to compete with the Australians' and it did not take a genius to crack the code.

Put bluntly, the message was that Tufnell wasn't going anywhere because of lack of character, lack of commitment and because he was the wrong sort of player to take on the Aussies. By the time the newspapers had completed the usual analysis, the consensus appeared to be that once again I was out of favour for reasons other than ability. The same applied to Andy Caddick, who had had his problems with the management in West Indies in 1998 as well.

Some people have very short memories, considering the last time we bowled in tandem at them in the final Test of the 1997 Ashes series – barely twelve months previously – I took eleven and Caddy eight of the nineteen wickets to fall as we won by 19 runs. Had we been the wrong sort then?

As for the selectors' attempts to justify the picking of Croft and Peter Such on the tactical grounds that the two off-spinners would be bowling into the rough created by Alan Mullally's footmarks, most of the pundits weren't buying it. Why did they need two of them when they were only ever going to play one at a time?

I hadn't taken much notice of the rumours that any chance I had of going to Australia was removed the moment Graham Gooch was appointed tour manager alongside Alec. Sure, I had had my problems with Gooch and Alec's dad Mickey on a previous tour down under — but that was eight years and several lifetimes before. Sure this was the new Team England — driving army jeeps around the woods wearing blindfolds, all for one and one for all and all that jazz — and I can understand that they didn't want anyone who might kick against the pricks, if you'll pardon the expression. But why were they so certain that I would?

The suggestion hurt me deeply. I'd been through all of this before, countless times, but I really felt that by now I had shown I had matured enough for that kind of accusation to be a thing of the past. I also thought that the people running the Test side believed so as well. I was wrong.

For someone to make a judgement that so-and-so is a better bowler and therefore should be picked ahead of you is fine. That happens and we are all big enough to take it. But for people in authority to imply that you are not going to be considered for selection because you are an 'iffy' character is just unpleasant. During the two days immediately after the announcement I was the schoolyard leper again. I wanted to stick up for myself, privately if not publicly, because I felt if I stayed silent that might be taken as an acceptance of their point of view. And the fact was that I didn't accept it. But I couldn't think of whom to talk to, or what to say.

For a brief period I just felt incredibly low, powerless to respond to what I felt was misrepresentation of my character. Next I got cross. Sod you, then, if that's the way you feel. Find yourself another boy and see if I care. And then I stopped feeling sorry for myself and decided to confront the issue head-on.

Whether I should have done, I don't know, but I rang David Graveney, the chairman of selectors, to see if I could get some answers from the horse's mouth. I asked him one simple question: 'Can you honestly tell me that I am not going to Australia purely on the grounds of cricketing ability?'

Graveney answered my question with a question of his own. 'Apart from the cricket', he asked, 'do you think that you did all you could have done in West Indies?'

'Yes' I replied instantly.

'Well, then, you have nothing to worry about.'

I didn't really know quite what to make of the conversation, except that something must have happened in West Indies to upset the management. I racked my brains. I picked over the trip, day-by-day, match-by-match, after-work rum-punch by rum-punch. Nothing. It even crossed my mind, just for a second, that they might have got the pin about the scribblings in my first burst into print, the tour diary *Postcards from the Beach*. Nah.

Try as I might, I just couldn't come up with anything that would explain Graveney's comment.

As I have said, I had no problem with Alec picking whoever he wanted. He was the captain. It was his neck on the block and he had to pick the players he believed would do a job for him. If the truth of the matter was that he didn't pick me because of usual old rubbish about attitude and approach, that he didn't think I cared enough or wanted to play for my country enough, that's his opinion and he's perfectly entitled to it. I've no argument with his right to make the choice he thought was best for England. I just happen to believe he was wrong.

That belief made the winter sabbatical that much more bearable.

And then IN............
Usual story, really. As many have testified in the past, if they leave you behind or drop you and then the team doesn't win, you don't half become a good player in your absence. I must have bowled bloody well that winter

273

during my own five-Test series in The White Hart, The King Of Bohemia, The Rose & Crown, The Six Bells and The Three Horseshoes, because from the moment England's defeat in the Test series was confirmed, it seemed almost to be taken as read that I would be back for the summer series against New Zealand.

An awful lot happened in between and although it is difficult to gauge exactly how much of it helped my own cause, none of the events did me any great harm.

Although England had had a chance in Sydney to come home with what would have been a tremendous 2-2 draw to set alongside the 2-1 win against South Africa, Australia's win made the final score in the series an unflattering 3-1. They started the one-day tournament impressively, but from the moment Alec brushed shoulders with Roshan Mohanama that infamous night in Adelaide when the match against Sri Lanka boiled over following umpire Ross Emerson's decision to call Murali for chucking, things began to go pear-shaped for the skipper and his team.

The tournament in Sharjah turned into a nightmare; Alec was perceived to be running the players' case in a pay dispute with the Board and on the field we were given a shoeing. On the eve of the World Cup Bumble announced he was quitting as coach after the competition, and when England were booted out at the qualifying stage — somewhat embarrassingly the day before the official tournament song was launched — Alec's time was up as well.

As I have said my return had been touted long before Nasser Hussain took over the job from Al. But I have to admit that the elevation in status of someone I always considered to be one of my closest mates in the game might have helped give the bandwagon a final push.

There hadn't been any chats or phone calls prior to the selection of the squad for the first of four Tests against New Zealand at Edgbaston, just a very strong general feeling that the new captain was going to do things slightly differently and that he was somewhat more open to the so-called problem players than those in power during Alec's regime seemed to have been.

For many years Nass had been bracketed along with Tufnell and Ramprakash as one of the hothead nutter rebels himself. Stories about bat-throwing, dressing room trashing and the like were never far from any conversation about any one of us and it is fair to say that we have all had our moments. But he had first-hand knowledge of what it is like when people are not prepared to look beyond your reputation and, as a result, was more than usually prepared to give guys like us the benefit of the doubt.

When it came to the business of cricket I never for a moment felt I was going to be given special treatment because of my friendship with the new captain. But I did feel he knew me well enough to understand the truth of what I am on the field.

Me being me, though, there had to be one last ludicrous cock-up in the tale.

In the days prior to the announcement of the squad the whispers had turned into shouts. Everywhere I went people treated me as though we were sharing a secret about what happened on someone's stag night. But I never said a word. I'd seen what fate could do when roused by temptation, thank you very much. I also decided that, should the call come, I was going to keep my nut well down. There is a school of sports writing that feeds on controversy – 'he said that about you, what do you think about him' etc. — and those who practise it have a way of setting their own agenda. Clearly I was miffed about being left out of the Ashes tour and the papers had written so much about the 'character' angle that it was by now accepted as the reason why, so surely, if I did get back I would have a few words to say to my critics, doubters, those who left me out in the first place.

Well, no, actually. Surely not, in fact.

Instead I had made up my mind, if selected, to keep my mouth zipped, turn up for the game and just play. I did not want to say or do anything that could then be held against me further down the line. In fact I just did not want to say anything, publicly, at all.

And then it happened. On Sunday 27 June, around 9.30am about an hour and a half before the squad was to be announced, the phone rang at home. On the other end was Brian Murgatroyd, the Board's media relations manager.

Nice bloke, Murgers. I had got to know him during the tour to the Caribbean and he trod the line between being one of the management and one of the lads pretty well. Mind you he had the plates to do so. He was ringing first to let me know that I was in the squad and congratulations, and secondly, to get some quotes. Oo-er, I thought. Here we go again.

Now, trust me on this, but I just got the wrong end of the stick, I'm afraid. When Murgers said he wanted some speil I got a little bit confused. The fact is that all he was after was a couple of lines to put out in the general press release that then goes on Ceefax and gets read out on the radio and all the papers use the next day. Job done. This is a time-honoured device designed to ensure that the press guys get the quotes they need without having to bother the players and as a rule it works okay...but I just didn't quite grasp that, I'm afraid.

I explained to Murgers that I didn't really want to say anything, that I felt it would be best all round if I just kept my own counsel and that, if it was all the same to him, I wanted to keep a low profile. I relaxed sure in the knowledge that the management would be proud of my softly-softly approach. But five minutes later David Graveney rang back and gave me one of the biggest bollockings of my career.

'Hello Philip,' he began. *Philip?*, I thought to myself. *He never calls me Philip. What have I done now?*

'What the hell do you think you're up to?' he asked, rather too loudly for comfort. 'Stop arsing about,' he said. 'You've got to give Murgers something. Blimey, you've only just got back in the squad and you're upsetting people.' Just in case I hadn't grasped the point, he went on to suggest that if I carried on like this my Test comeback was going to be one of the shortest in history.

Doh.

I phoned Murgers back, sorted things out and the quotes were duly put out. Ironically, when I scoured the papers the following day I noticed not a single word of them had been used.

It was, however, brilliant to be back, turning up at Edgbaston and feeling part of the England team again.

A lot of people who don't know me or Alec or Nasser expected a touch of friction between us, but there was none. Alec was top class, I have to say. I'm sure he was disappointed to have lost the captaincy but whatever he felt he never showed it. He was, from the first moment, totally supportive of Nasser. As for our relationship, I found him to be just the same bloke I had been knocking around with on England tours for the best part of a decade.

Nasser, also, was just as I thought he would be, excellent on a one-to-one basis and genuinely interested in the thoughts and concerns of his players. We were all positive and determined to do well.

The Kiwis won the toss and made the mistake of batting under overcast skies. I bowled alright, took 3 for 22 from seventeen overs. We got them out for 226 and we were cooking. And the next thing I remember it was close of play, we were 40 for 7 or something, and I was sitting in the showers with my head in my hands thinking 'what is happening?'

Well, from then until the end of the bloody series, just about everything that could go wrong did. We actually managed to win at Edgbaston. Caddick and Tudor got us to126 all out. Then, fired up by Nasser, we bowled them out for 107 (Caddick 5-32) and then, with us requiring a sphincterish 208 on a dodgy pitch, Tudor went in as nightwatchman and played one of the most exquisite innings I've ever seen. There he was, in his first home Test whipping, hooking, clipping, then walking down the pitch to the Kiwi quicks and smashing the ball back over their heads.

I don't want to take anything away from New Zealand who competed excellently throughout the series, but I think you can trace the start of our ride down the slippery slope to the moment Nasser broke his finger fielding in the second Test at Lord's. We had batted badly again in the first innings, probably making the wrong decision to take first use, but until Nasser was injured we still felt confident that we would be competitive. Without his batting in the second innings we were poor again and lost heavily. I provided the comedy moment of the match, departing to a catch by wicket-keeper Nathan Astle off Dion Nash having confirmed with Nathan that he had taken it cleanly, only to be informed that I had to go back because the third umpire couldn't tell from the telly whether the ball had carried or not. But the laughter was starting to sound hollow. The natives were getting restless.

Nasser's absence felt like a big enough blow at the time. In hindsight it looks even worse because, although Gooch and Gatting were operating as temporary coaches, the fact that the new man, Duncan Fletcher of Glamorgan, wasn't due to start until the winter tour to South Africa meant there was a little bit of a vacuum at the top.

And the stakes were being raised day by day. Sensing the way the series was going, one or two of the papers began helpfully pointing out that if New Zealand went on to win, England's ranking in world cricket, according to the magazine *Wisden Cricket Monthly's* unofficial championship table, would be rock bottom. We were, according to them, effectively competing with current bottom-ranked New Zealand for the title of the world's worst Test team.

This is just the kind of confidence booster you need when you are struggling to build a new team. When Nasser and the selectors decided to bring back experienced players like Atherton, Hick and Peter Such for the third Test at Old Trafford and, batting first under temporary skipper Mark Butcher, we were bowled out for 199 there, up went the balloon.

The powers-that-be stepped in, Gooch and Gatt were sacked and coded instructions were passed down the line which, roughly translated, read: 'Pick some new players to get everyone off our backs.' To be honest, I felt sorry for

Gatt and Gooch. We were 1-1 against New Zealand going into a match we desperately needed to win. No disrespect to Aftab Habib, but who would you have picked in the circumstances, him or Hick, a bloke with 100 first-class hundreds to his name? The only crime they committed as far as I could see was trying to apply the basic cricket logic of trying to win one match at a time.

The Oval? Blimey. What was that all about?

The first I heard about the allegation that I had sworn at and abused two young spectators on the first day of the final Test was when I read about it in the *London Evening Standard* on the second day. What can I say? It didn't happen. I never swore at anyone, let alone a couple of children asking for autographs. Grav came up to me and asked me what it was all about and I told him honestly that I just didn't know. There are times when autograph hunters are in the wrong place at the wrong time. When you are busting a gut trying to stay in a game, or trying to come up with a strategy against a particular batsman, your concentration is so cocoon-like that sometimes the sights and sounds of someone thrusting a piece of paper and a pen towards you can simply go unnoticed. A muttered 'not now, mate' can sometimes be taken the wrong way and that's too bad. No offence is meant and generally none taken. But as for this specific incident, the thought of me telling two young lads to 'F**k off' in front of all those spectators is just bonkers.

Normally I would just have let the matter wash over me, but I was not in the happiest of moods at the time. None of us was. The pressure was intense because of the prospect of the consequence of defeat and that put everyone on edge. Also there was a funny atmosphere among the crowd, something I had never before experienced in a home Test. It was almost as though they were expecting us to lose which wasn't great for confidence in the dressing room.

So when Channel Four came to me on the Saturday morning for a comment I went further than perhaps I should have done. Someone asked me if I had anything to say to the two boys whose dad had made the allegation to the *Standard* in the first place. 'Yes, I said. The bogey man will come and get you if you tell lies.' Own goal? Probably, but I didn't half feel better after banging it in the net.

And we lost, of course. We shouldn't have done. We should have won. Behind in the first innings with Ed Giddins leading the attack on his debut, we fought back brilliantly to have them in massive trouble in their second dig. Even after Chris Cairns bashed 80 to drag them to 162 we still should have been able to bat well enough to score the 246 we needed to win the match and the series. But we collapsed and at the end of it listened to the boos ringing around the ground.

It is impossible to describe how much that hurt, really. As an England cricketer you accept you are going to get it in the neck from time to time. People who pay to come and watch are entitled to express their dissatisfaction. Graham Thorpe announced during the match that he wouldn't be available for the tour to South Africa. In the moment of hearing the reaction of the crowd after we had tried our nuts off, one or two more might have been thinking along similar lines. Who needs it?

When Nasser tried to stick up for the players by saying he was proud of them, one of the papers turned round and called him 'Nasser Insane' and the happy picture was complete when a couple of them had a go at me for allegedly getting drunk and disorderly that night in a nearby pub.

The truth of the matter was that, as the closest pub to our hotel, The Chelsea Ram was the place where the players went after work for a pint or two to unwind. That evening I was in there earlier than usual, because the match had finished early, had something to eat and settled back to drown my sorrows with one or two of the other players. We had a session sufficiently fitting to how pissed off we felt with what had happened, no more, no less and just the same as countless previous similar occasions.

The difference this time was that we were unofficially the worst team in the world. For the angry media it was like a red rag to a herd of bulls. We were easy targets and for the usual reasons I was the easiest.

From a personal perspective I had been reasonably pleased with my comeback season. Caddy and me, the two bowlers considered not the right sort for the Ashes trip the previous winter, took 34 wickets between us and finished the top two wicket takers for England. Although I kept reading that I was being outbowled by Daniel Vettori, the Kiwi's left-arm spinner, my figures of 14 wickets @ 22.64 compared favourably with his ten @ 24.9 particularly as I ended up on the losing side.

But funny things happen when England lose a Test series at home to New Zealand, the last home Test series of the century at that. And the boos said it all.

TWENTY-TWO

What Now?

That's it then, is it? I have to say that when the news reached me on 1 March 2000 that I was not one of the twelve players to be contracted to the ECB for the coming summer, the thought did cross my mind.

I wasn't really expecting a central contract, to be honest. I felt I had bowled well on the winter tour to South Africa but once again the number in the wickets column didn't exactly jump off the page. I didn't play in the first Test in Johannesburg — more's the pity, as I would have loved to have smacked Allan Donald and Shaun Pollock around on that featherbed. I did okay at Port Elizabeth and felt I might just have given the South Africans some food for thought. The pitch in Durban flattened into a road in their second innings, we were rolled in Cape Town and I missed out on the one-day Test in Centurion — although I like to think I played my part by winding Hansie Cronje up into making the offer of a last day run chase. 'Tell Hansie I won't take anything more than 250 off 70 overs' was Nasser's message from the pitch to the dressing room, unaware of the fact that we had just negotiated 249 off 76. All part of the service of being a member of the tour management committee, of course.

There were a few 'what ifs?' My former Middlesex team-mate Jacques Kallis forced the umpires to test out the technology after Chris Adams caught him off me in Port Elizabeth and he got away with it. What if? And what if the ball I sent down in Durban that had Gary Kirsten plumb leg before, had not been one of the handful of no-balls I have been called for in fourteen years of first-class cricket.

Before I went, the consensus of opinion was that we were going to lose 5-0 and that, because of the seamer-friendly conditions I should take a few good books with me. Well, we did rather better than that and so did I. And if I had just been able to climb through those cracks of opportunity when they fleetingly appeared, what then?

I wasn't ready for the some of the harsher criticism that came my way. One of the papers described as 'nauseating' the claim that I had ever been a match-winner, which I felt was trifle unfair considering I have never once said any such thing myself.

Overall, it was one of the happiest tours I have been on. We'd heard a lot about the fact that Johannesburg was supposed to be one of the most violent cities on the planet and we were warned, by one Afrikaaner I met in a bar somewhere, to be 'totally vigilant at all times'.

By all accounts the centre of the city is a no-go area at night, when drivers are given carte blanche by police to run red lights as long as nothing is coming. Stuck out at our five-star luxury prison housed in the old world charm of the shopping centre at Sandton City, all that seemed some way away, but many of the locals we spoke to were apprehensive about the future.

A few bombs went off in Capetown in between our visits there, one next to the Villamoura restaurant on Camps Bay where me and many of the boys had eaten, and that made us think twice about bringing out the wives and kids. In East London, much to his and the South African Board's embarrassment, one of the security guards assigned to us managed to get himself mugged, apparently after leaving his gun back at the hotel, but overall the atmosphere was pretty relaxed. Not taking any chances, however, the management of Holiday Inns hotels left this card in each of the rooms we stayed at around the country:

Traveller Safety Tips:

1. Don't answer the door in a hotel room without verifying who it is. If a person claims to be an employee, contact the front desk and ask if someone from their staff is supposed to have access to your room and for what purpose. (*No problem. I'm sure the crazed assassin will hang on while I make the call.*)

2. When returning to your hotel late in the evening, use the main entrance. Be observant and look around before entering parking lots.

3. Close the door securely whenever you are in your room and use all of the locking devices provided.

4. Don't needlessly display guest room keys or key cards in public or carelessly leave them on restaurant tables, at the swimming pool, or other places where they can be easily stolen. (*Idiot*).

5. Do not draw attention to yourself by displaying large amounts of cash, expensive jewellery, cameras etc. (*Chance would be a fine thing.*)

6. Don't invite strangers to your room.

7. Place all valuables in the room or safety deposit box.

8. Do not leave valuable in your vehicle.

9. Check to see that any sliding glass doors or windows, and any connecting room doors are locked.

10. If you see any suspicious activity, please report your observations to the management.

11. When using taxis use only clearly marked taxis or those called by the hotel staff.

12. Do not walk alone on streets, particularly after dark. (*and presumably not while displaying large amounts of cash, expensive jewellery, cameras etc. nor needlessly displaying your room key, or carelessly leaving it a restaurant table or any other place where a person, claiming to be an employee but behaving suspiciously, might enter through a sliding glass window.*)

As for our cricket, the relationship between Fletcher and Hussain grew as time passed and I came to appreciate the thoughtful style of our new coach. Instead of banging on at you about 'do this, do that' etc., Duncan's approach was all about helping you to do better the things you do well.

And I appreciated the change. Discipline was not quite so parade-ground oriented than it had been in the past. Wearing the wrong shirt was no longer seen as evidence that you couldn't give a monkey's about playing for your country and the whole squad benefited from the fact that we were treated as adults doing our job of work rather than the lower 4th form on a school excursion.

And I think the team-spirit such an approach engendered really helped. In the past we might have folded against Donald and Pollock even more spectacularly than we did at the Wanderers and we might also have then disappeared without trace. But we didn't. We competed and the decision to try some younger players was partially vindicated by some forward strides in the process. As for the discards, I was sorry for Ramps that he wasn't picked originally, couldn't really see what he had done to be dropped and am absolutely sure he'll make someone pay on the pitch for his omission.

The work was hard in South Africa, and as things stood at the time, if I had to pick two sides I would back myself to take wickets against, they would be Zimbabwe and West Indies, England Test opponents in 2000. But the truth of the matter is that I did my best and when the selectors sat down to draw up their list of an elite squad, I was not on it.

Anticipating a disappointment doesn't make it any easier to take however and, in the immediate aftermath of the announcement that the single spinner's contract was to go to the young Lancashire leg-spinner Chris Schofield rather than the ageing maverick Tufnell, I have to admit I did feel like jacking it in. The feeling soon passed. I'm a professional cricketer. That's my job. And if I have learnt one thing over the years it is that what is certain and unquestionable one day is complete cobblers the next. I have absolutely nothing against Chris and I wish nothing but the best for him in his future career. If he is the one who makes a difference in the years to come, I'll be standing on my sitting room sofa punching the air with everyone else. But I won't give up because I think I can still do a job. Should anything happen to make England change their plans, they know my number.

I have enjoyed a tremendous career, taking 120 Test wickets and five wickets in an innings five times, and come across some good people who saw me through the torment that was going on inside me from time to time. I've played with and against some truly great players: batsmen like Viv Richards, Sachin Tendulkar, Mark and Steve Waugh, Allan Border, Martin Crowe and Brian Lara; bowlers like Curtly Ambrose, Courtney Walsh, Glenn McGrath, Shane Warne, Wasim Akram, and the greatest of all cricketers, Ian Botham, and I thank my lucky stars that I have done. I didn't choose cricket as a career, it chose me and in so many ways I am extremely fortunate that it did. And while in the past I might have caused even my strongest supporters to shield their eyes and cover their ears, on the field I have always given every ounce of what is in me to give.

One thing I have never been able to work out though is this: the accusation most often levelled at me is that I'm a bad tourist. If that is so why is it that of my forty one Tests, thirty have been played abroad and only eleven in England? Oh well, ours is not to reason why. All I have ever asked of captains, selectors and regimes is that they should judge me for what I can do with a ball in my hand.

Stability has not been my strongest suit. Until recently, when I was living life in the pit my mood oscillated between high optimism and deep depression. Sometimes I was unreachable, untouchable. On occasions I really felt that I was losing control of my life. I don't have any easy answers for how and who I was. It would be all too convenient for me to tell you that all the problems I have had in my life date back from the moment my mother became ill. But not only would that be an insult to her memory, it would simply not be the truth.

I've learnt so much in so many ways from my adventurers and my scrapes. When I look back now there are some episodes which I would rather forget, but recalling them and reliving them has also been therapeutic. I have looked a long way into the darkness inside me and some of the views have not been picturesque. But if I can use the experiences not only to help myself but also to quietly steer someone else away from the cliff edge in years to come then I will. In fact I must.

Plainly I have changed in the past couple of years. The paranoia and the self-obsession have gone, as has the feeling that the figures in authority were to be distrusted simply because they were figures in authority. I'm calmer, more relaxed and more self-confident and the people I have to thank know who they are.

Whatever it has amounted to, I have had a life. I've been fortunate enough to have done an awful lot of things others can only dream of; I've stood out there in the middle of The Oval, and taken a wicket to win an Ashes Test against all the odds and felt, if only for an instant, what it feels like to do something so right. As I said right at the start, an awful lot of things have just sort of happened to me as well, and I can vouch for the fact that when you are staring a brick in the face the sum total of your experiences does flash in front of you.

And my reputation has preceded me in more ways than one. On my return from South Africa I was contacted by a magazine who were interested in setting up an article with me in which they wanted me to explain the many and various tricks I had up my sleeve. Four different types of delivery, they wanted, and I suddenly realised I only had one — as Basil Fawlty would say, 'done, of course, in the four extremely different ways'.

They duly turned up and took their pictures. I did my best; orthodox, arm-ball, errr…slider…errr…chinaman.

Really. I've never bowled a chinaman in my life. And I wouldn't recognise a slider if it jumped up and bit me on the arse.

Looking back my natural feline curiosity has got the better of me at times and I fully appreciate that one or two of my nine lives might already have been used up. But the last thing I want to do at my age is be understood. Many people may have many theories and opinions. They're welcome to them. But the day I think I know what the future holds is the day I will start to really worry.

I'm not perfect, far from it. Perhaps my biggest problem has been that sometimes I thought I knew more than I actually did and wouldn't be told otherwise. I've done some good things and I've been complete rubbish, in cricket and in life. But whatever I have been, I have always been myself.

As far as I'm concerned, the big question still is: what now?

Career Statistics

MILESTONES

29.4.66	Born in Barnet
4.6.86	First-class debut v Worcestershire (Worcester)
7.8.87	Took five wickets in an innings for the first time: v Kent (Canterbury)
19.6.88	Sunday League debut v Northamptonshire (Luton)
22.6.88	NatWest Trophy debut v Hertfordshire (Lord's), taking 3–29 and winning the man of the match award
1.8.89	100th first-class wicket: G J Parsons (Leicestershire) at Lord's
1989	50 wickets in England/1: 55 wickets @ 28.43
24.4.90	Benson & Hedges Cup debut v Minor Counties (Lord's)
7.12.90	International debut v New Zealand (Perth) in limited-overs international – first wicket: C Z Harris
26.12.90	Test debut v Australia (Melbourne) – but did not take wicket in either innings
1990	50 wickets in England/2: 74 wickets @ 35.60
5.1.91	First Test wicket: G R J Matthews (Australia) at Sydney (third Test, first innings)
8.1.91	200th first-class wicket: D C Boon (Australia) at Sydney (third Test, second innings)
10.8.91	Took 6–25 in his first Test match in England v West Indies at The Oval (fifth Test)
11.9.91	300th first-class wicket: I A Greig (Surrey) at Lord's
1991	50 wickets in England/3: 88 wickets @ 25.21

1991	Took 108 first-class wickets in the year @ 25.39
15.5.93	400th first-class wicket: M A Crawley (Nottinghamshire) at Lord's
18.6.93	50th Test wicket: M E Waugh (Australia) at Lord's (second Test)
1993	50 wickets in England/4: 64 wickets @ 23.89
10.9.94	500th first-class wicket: A J Wright (Gloucestershire) at Lord's
11.9.95	600th first-class wicket: W J Cronje (Leicestershire) at Uxbridge
1995	50 wickets in England/5: 74 wickets @ 22.08
1996	50 wickets in England/6: 78 wickets @ 21.94
16.1.97	700th first-class wicket: P J Wiseman (NZ Selection XI) at Palmerston North
14.3.98	100th Test wicket: C E L Ambrose (West Indies) at Bridgetown (fifth Test)
29.6.98	800th first-class wicket: D R Law (Essex) at Southgate

FIRST-CLASS CAREER

$ denotes including Test matches   * signifies not out

	M	I	NO	HS	Runs	Av	100	50
1986	6	7	1	9	32	5.33	–	–
1987	9	8	4	12 *	21	5.25	–	–
1988	11	12	4	20	44	5.50	–	–
1989	14	11	3	12	54	6.75	–	–
1990	23	22	9	37	283	21.76	–	–
$1990–91 A/NZ	8	10	7	8	13	4.33	–	–
$1991	22	24	6	34	210	11.66	–	–
1991–92 NZ	5	4	3	6 *	10	10.00	–	–
$1992	16	15	8	12	55	7.85	–	–
$1992–93 I/SL	7	8	5	22 *	38	12.66	–	–
$1993	18	18	6	30 *	128	10.66	–	–
$1993–94 WI	4	5	3	5 *	6	3.00	–	–
$1994	9	6	1	5	14	2.80	–	–
$1994–95 A	9	13	7	4 *	12	2.00	–	–
1995	17	15	7	23 *	65	8.12	–	–
1996	18	26	10	67 *	290	18.12	–	1
$1996–97 Z/NZ	9	10	5	19 *	69	13.80	–	–
$1997	17	21	6	21	101	6.73	–	–
$1997–98 WI	9	9	3	6	11	1.83	–	–
1998	17	22	6	24	155	9.68	–	–
$1999	16	21	4	48	198	11.64	–	–
$1999-00	5	6	3	7 *	16	5.33	–	–
TOTALS	**269**	**293**	**111**	**67 ***	**1825**	**10.02**	**–**	**1**

Ct	Overs	Runs	W	Av	5wI	10wM	BB	S/R
1	148	479	5	95.80	–	–	2–47	177.60
5	335.2	984	33	29.81	1	–	6–60	60.96
5	433.2	1058	25	42.32	–	–	4–88	104.00
9	602.1	1564	55	28.43	3	–	5–60	65.69
8	1036.5	2635	74	35.60	2	–	6–79	84.06
6	318	887	26	34.11	2	–	5–61	73.38
9	903.4	2219	88	25.21	7	1	7–116	61.61
3	290.3	590	28	21.07	2	1	7–47	62.25
3	596.2	1559	43	36.25	2	–	5–83	82.30
1	227.5	746	14	53.28	–	–	4–95	97.64
7	688.5	1529	64	23.89	3	–	8–29	64.57
3	212.3	554	10	55.40	–	–	4–87	127.50
5	463.5	1107	39	28.38	1	–	6–35	71.35
6	384.2	1018	27	37.70	1	–	5–71	85.40
5	678.1	1634	74	22.08	5	1	6–111	54.98
7	839.1	1712	78	21.94	9	1	7–49	64.55
6	356.3	785	29	27.06	2	–	5–58	73.75
4	561.5	1205	55	21.90	3	1	7–66	61.29
1	333.5	706	22	32.09	1	–	5–42	91.04
2	632	1602	39	41.07	–	–	4–24	97.23
3	577.3	1223	48	25.47	2	–	5–61	72.18
–	258.4	619	11	56.27	–	–	4–124	141.09
99	10879.1	26415	887	29.78	43	5	8–29	73.59

FIRST-CLASS SUMMARY

	M	I	NO	HS	Runs	Av	100	50
England in England	11	16	6	6	20	2.00	–	–
Middlesex	201	211	69	67 *	1618	11.39	–	1
MCC	1	1	0	12	12	12.00	–	–
UK/Home	213	228	75	67 *	1650	10.78	–	1
England Overseas	56	65	36	22 *	175	6.03	–	–
TOTALS	269	293	111	67 *	1825	10.02	–	1

Highest Scores & Best Bowling

England	22*	v India (Madras) 15.2.1993
	7–47	v New Zealand (Christchurch) 22.1.1992
Middlesex	67*	v Worcestershire (Lord's) 17.8.1996
	8–29	v Glamorgan (Cardiff) 5.7.1993
MCC	12	v Worcestershire (Lord's) 18.4.1990
	Did not bowl	
England	22*	ENGLAND v INDIA (Madras) 15.2.1993
Overseas	7–47	ENGLAND v NEW ZEALAND (Christchurch) 22.1.1992

Ct	Overs	Runs	W	Av	5wI	10wM	BB	S/R
4	475	122	47	25.95	3	1	7–66	60.63
69	8015	19277	673	28.64	32	3	8–29	71.45
0	7	13	0	–				
73	8497	20510	720	28.48	35	4	8–29	70.80
26	2382.1	5905	167	35.35	8	1	7–47	85.58
99	10879.1	26415	887	29.78	43	5	8–29	73.59

TEST MATCH SUMMARY

		M	I	NO	HS	Runs	Av	100	50
1990–91	Aus	4	6	4	8	13	6.50	–	–
1991	Aus	1	1	0	2	2	2.00	–	–
1991	SL	1	1	0	0	0	–	–	–
1991–92	NZ	3	3	3	6 *	8	–	–	–
1992	Pak	1	2	1	0 *	0	–	–	–
1992–93	Ind	2	4	3	22 *	28	28.00	–	–
1993	Aus	2	4	2	2 *	3	1.50	–	–
1993–94	WI	2	2	1	0 *	0	–	–	–
1994	SA	1	–						
1994–95	Aus	4	7	3	4 *	6	1.50	–	–
1996–97	Zim	2	2	1	9	11	11.00	–	–
1996–97	NZ	3	3	2	19 *	38	38.00	–	–
1997	Aus	1	2	0	1	1	0.50	–	–
1997–98	WI	6	8	3	6	11	2.20	–	–
1999	NZ	4	6	3	6	14	4.66	–	–
1999–00	SA	3	4	2	7 *	9	4.50	–	–
TOTALS		41	57	28	22 *	146	5.03	–	–
In England		11	16	6	6	20	2.00	–	–
Overseas		30	41	22	22 *	126	6.63	–	–
v Australia		12	20	9	8	25	2.27	–	–
v Sri Lanka		2	3	0	1	2	0.66	–	–
v New Zealand		10	12	8	19 *	60	15.00	–	–
v Pakistan		1	2	1	0 *	0	–	–	–
v India		2	4	3	22 *	28	28.00	–	–
v West Indies		8	10	4	6	11	1.83	–	–
v South Africa		4	4	2	7 *	9	4.50	–	–
v Zimbabwe		2	2	1	9	11	11.00	–	–
TOTALS		41	57	28	22 *	146	5.03	–	–

Ct	Overs	Runs	W	Av	5wI	10wM	BB	S/R
1	140	345	9	38.33	1	–	5–61	93.33
0	60.3	175	7	25.00	1	–	6–25	51.85
1	41.3	117	5	23.40	1	–	5–94	49.80
1	186.1	367	16	22.93	1	1	7–47	69.81
1	34	87	1	87.00	–	–	1–87	204.00
0	80.3	274	4	68.50	–	–	4–142	120.75
1	104	319	5	63.80	–	–	2–78	124.80
2	113	291	4	72.75	–	–	3–100	169.50
1	55	112	4	28.00	–	–	2–31	82.50
2	207.4	442	10	44.20	–	–	4–79	124.60
1	82.5	192	7	27.42	–	–	4–61	71.00
0	132	242	7	34.57	–	–	3–53	113.14
0	47.4	93	11	8.45	1	1	7–66	26.00
1	212.4	439	7	62.71	–	–	2–43	182.28
–	132.2	317	14	22.64	–	–	3–22	56.71
–	171.4	433	6	72.16	–	–	4–124	171.66
12	1842.1	4387	120	36.55	5	2	7–47	92.10
4	475	1220	47	25.95	3	1	7–66	60.63
8	1367.1	3167	73	43.38	2	1	7–47	112.36
4	559.5	1374	42	32.71	3	1	7–66	79.97
1	82.1	259	8	32.37	1	–	5–94	61.62
1	450.2	926	37	25.02	1	1	7–47	73.02
1	34	87	1	87.00	–	–	1–87	204.00
0	80.3	274	4	68.50	–	–	4–142	120.75
3	325.4	730	11	66.36	–	–	3–100	177.63
1	226.4	545	10	54.50	–	–	4–124	136.00
1	82.5	192	7	27.42	–	–	4–61	71.00
12	1842.1	4387	120	36.55	5	2	7–47	92.10

ENGLAND OVERSEAS

		M	I	NO	HS	Runs	Av	100	50
1990–91	Aus	8	10	7	8	13	4.33	–	–
1991–92	NZ	5	4	3	6 *	10	10.00	–	–
1992–93	Ind/SL	7	8	5	22 *	38	12.66	–	–
1993–94	WI	4	5	3	5 *	6	3.00	–	–
1994–95	Aus	9	13	7	4 *	12	2.00	–	–
1996–97	Zim	4	5	2	10	29	9.66	–	–
1996–97	NZ	5	5	3	19 *	40	20.00	–	–
1997–98	WI	9	9	3	6	11	1.83	–	–
1999–00	Aus	5	6	3	7 *	16	5.33	–	–
TOTALS		56	65	36	22 *	175	6.03	–	–

CHAMPIONSHIP

	M	I	NO	HS	Runs	Av	100	50
1986	6	7	1	9	32	5.33	–	–
1987	8	8	4	12 *	21	5.25	–	–
1988	9	10	2	20	41	5.12	–	–
1989	13	11	3	12	54	6.75	–	–
1990	20	20	9	37	235	21.36	–	–
1991	17	18	4	31 *	120	8.57	–	–
1992	14	13	7	12	55	9.16	–	–
1993	15	13	4	30 *	113	12.55	–	–
1994	8	6	1	5	14	2.80	–	–
1995	16	14	6	23 *	65	8.12	–	–
1996	16	26	10	67 *	290	18.12	–	1
1997	14	18	5	21	89	6.84	–	–
1998	16	21	6	19	131	8.73	–	–
1999	12	15	1	48	184	13.14	–	–
TOTALS	184	200	63	67 *	1444	10.54	–	1

Highest Score & Best Bowling

67*　v Worcestershire (Lord's) 17.8.1996

8–29　v Glamorgan (Cardiff) 5.7.1993

Ct	Overs	Runs	W	Av	5wI	10wM	BB	S/R
6	318	887	26	34.11	2	–	5–61	73.38
3	290.3	590	28	21.07	2	1	7–47	62.25
1	227.5	746	14	53.28	–	–	4–95	97.64
3	212.3	554	10	55.40	–	–	4–87	127.50
6	384.2	1018	27	37.70	1	–	5–71	85.40
5	157.3	407	14	29.07	1	–	6–78	67.50
1	199	378	15	25.20	1	–	5–58	79.60
1	333.5	706	22	32.09	1	–	5–42	91.04
–	258.4	619	11	56.27	–	–	4–124	141.09
26	2382.1	5905	167	35.35	8	1	7–47	85.58

Ct	Overs	Runs	W	Av	5wI	10wM	BB	S/R
1	148	479	5	95.80	–	–	2–47	177.60
5	316.2	939	31	30.29	1	–	6–60	61.22
4	349.2	876	19	46.10	–	–	4–88	110.31
9	562.1	1482	51	29.05	3	–	5–60	66.13
7	948.5	2389	65	36.75	2	–	6–79	87.58
7	733.4	1818	70	25.97	5	1	7–116	62.88
2	517.2	1366	41	33.31	2	–	5–83	75.70
6	583.5	1210	59	20.50	3	–	8–29	59.37
4	408.5	995	35	28.42	1	–	6–35	70.08
5	638.1	1523	68	22.39	4	1	5–74	56.30
7	780.4	1568	72	21.77	5	1	7–49	65.05
2	474.1	1000	41	24.39	2	–	5–61	69.39
2	608	1512	36	42.00	–	–	4–24	101.33
3	445.1	906	34	26.64	2	–	5–61	78.55
64	7514.3	18063	627	28.80	30	3	8–29	71.90

SUNDAY LEAGUE

	M	I	NO	HS	Runs	Av	100	50
1988	2	–						
1989	2	1	1	13 *	13	–	–	–
1990	2	1	1	0 *	0	–	–	–
1991	1	–						
1992	1	1	1	1 *	1	–	–	–
1993	6	–						
1994	10	2	0	2	2	1.00	–	–
1995	6	4	2	5	7	3.50	–	–
1996	1	–						
1997	2	1	0	7	7	7.00	–	–
1998	3	2	1	5 *	5	5.00	–	–
1999	1	1	1	1 *	1	–	–	–
TOTALS	36	13	7	13 *	36	6.00	–	–

Highest Score & Best Bowling

13*   v Glamorgan (Merthyr Tydfil) 11.6.1989

5–28   v Leicestershire (Lord's) 8.8.1993

NATWEST TROPHY

	M	I	NO	HS	Runs	Av	100	50
1988	1	–						
1989	1	–						
1990	1	–						
1991	1	1	0	8	8	8.00	–	–
1994	1	–						
1995	1	–						
1996	2	–						
TOTALS	8	1	0	8	8	8.00	–	–

Highest Score & Best Bowling

8   v Somerset (Taunton) 12.7.1991

3–29   v Hertfordshire (Lord's) 22.6.1988

Ct	Overs	Runs	W	Av	4wI	BB	RPO
0	14	62	1	62.00	–	1–32	4.42
0	10	44	1	44.00	–	1–44	4.40
0	15	85	1	85.00	–	1–40	5.66
0	8	28	3	9.33	–	3–28	3.50
0	–						
1	50	203	15	13.53	3	5–28	4.06
2	71	319	12	26.58	–	3–28	4.49
0	43	192	7	27.42	–	3–43	4.46
0	5	28	0	–	–	–	5.60
0	16	103	1	103.00	–	1–56	6.43
1	22	99	3	33.00	–	2–39	4.50
1	4	29	1	29.00	–	1–29	7.25
5	258	1192	45	26.48	3	5–28	4.62

Ct	Overs	Runs	W	Av	4wI	BB	RPO
0	12	29	3	9.66	–	3–29	2.41
1	12	50	1	50.00	–	1–50	4.16
0	12	22	2	11.00	–	2–22	1.83
0	12	29	1	29.00	–	1–29	2.41
1	11	71	1	71.00	–	1–71	6.45
0	12	56	0	–	–	–	4.66
1	24	66	2	33.00	–	2–22	2.75
3	95	323	10	32.30	–	3–29	3.40

BENSON & HEDGES CUP

	M	I	NO	HS	Runs	Av	100	50
1990	2	1	1	7 *	7	–	–	–
1991	4	3	1	18	19	9.50	–	–
1992	1	1	1	15 *	15	–	–	–
1994	1	–						
1995	2	–						
1996	3	1	1	3 *	3	–	–	–
1997	2	2	0	10	12	6.00	–	–
TOTALS	15	8	4	18	56	14.00	–	–

Highest Score & Best Bowling

18   v Warwickshire (Edgbaston) 6.5.1991

3–32 v Northamptonshire (Lord's) 26.4.1994

Ct	Overs	Runs	W	Av	5wI	BB	RPO
0	18	78	1	78.00	–	1–42	4.33
1	39	187	4	46.75	–	3–50	4.79
0	10	65	0	–	–	–	6.50
0	11	32	3	10.66	–	3–32	2.90
0	18	67	1	67.00	–	1–28	3.72
1	22.5	90	4	22.50	–	2–31	3.94
0	16	72	2	36.00	–	1–35	4.50
2	134.5	591	15	39.40	–	3–32	4.38

FIVE WICKETS IN AN INNINGS

+ denotes second innings. CAPITALS denote in a Test Match

		For	Against	Venue	Season
1	+6–60	Middlesex	Kent	Canterbury	1987
2	+5–78	Middlesex	Derbyshire	Lord's	1989
3	+5–68	Middlesex	Leicestershire	Lord's	1989
4	+5–60	Middlesex	Northants	Lord's	1989
5	+5–57	Middlesex	Northants	Luton	1990
6	6–79	Middlesex	Hampshire	Bournemouth	1990
7	+5–61	ENGLAND	AUSTRALIA (T2)	SYDNEY	1990–91
8	5–108	England XI	Queensland	Carrara	1990–91
9	6–34	Middlesex	Gloucs	Bristol	1991
10	+6–82	Middlesex	Leicestershire	Uxbridge	1991
11	7–116	Middlesex	Hampshire	Lord's	1991
12	6–25	ENGLAND	WEST INDIES (T5)	OVAL	1991
13	+5–94	ENGLAND	SRI LANKA	LORD'S	1991
14	+5–30	Middlesex	Notts	Trent Bridge	1991
15	+5–17	Middlesex	Surrey	Lord's	1991
16	+5–66	England XI	NZ Emerging Players	Hamilton	1991–92
17	+7–47	ENGLAND	NEW ZEALAND (T1)	CHRISTCHURCH	1991–92
18	5–83	Middlesex	Durham	Lord's	1992
19	+5–130	Middlesex	Surrey	Oval	1992
20	5–77	Middlesex	Notts	Lord's	1993
21	+5–47	Middlesex	Sussex	Lord's	1993
22	+8–29	Middlesex	Glamorgan	Cardiff	1993
23	+6–35	Middlesex	Gloucs	Lord's	1994
24	+5–71	England XI	Queensland	Toowoomba	1994–95
25	6–11	Middlesex	West Indians	Lord's	1995
26	5–74	Middlesex	Notts	Lord's	1995

		For	Against	Venue	Season
27	+5–76	Middlesex	Kent	Lord's	1995
28	5–102	Middlesex	Leicestershire	Uxbridge	1995
29	+5–100	Middlesex	Leicestershire	Uxbridge	1995
30	+5–56	Middlesex	Cambridge University	Cambridge	1996
31	5–72	Middlesex	Derbyshire	Derby	1996
32	+5–71	Middlesex	Warwickshire	Lord's	1996
33	5–56	Middlesex	Surrey	Oval	1996
34	6–74	Middlesex	Lancashire	Old Trafford	1996
35	+7–49	Middlesex	Lancashire	Old Trafford	1996
36	5–78	England XI	Mashonaland	Harare	1996–97
37	+5–58	England XI	NZ Selection XI	Palmerston North	1996–97
38	5–90	Middlesex	Lancashire	Uxbridge	1997
39	7–66	ENGLAND	AUSTRALIA (T6)	OVAL	1997
40	5–61	Middlesex	Notts	Lord's	1997
41	+5–42	England XI	Guyana	Everest Club, Georgetown	1997–98
42	+5–61	Middlesex	Gloucestershire	Bristol	1999
43	5–107	Middlesex	Worcestershire	Worcester	1999

TEN WICKETS IN A MATCH

		For	Against	Venue	Season
1	11–228	Middlesex	Hampshire	Lord's	1991
2	11–147	ENGLAND	NEW ZEALAND (T1)	CHRISTCHURCH	1991–92
3	10–202	Middlesex	Leicestershire	Uxbridge	1995
4	11–123	Middlesex	Lancashire	Old Trafford	1996
5	11–93	ENGLAND	AUSTRALIA (T6)	OVAL	1997

PAIR

1998 Middlesex v Warwickshire (Lord's)

INTERNATIONAL LIMITED-OVERS SUMMARY

	M	I	NO	HS	Runs	Av	100	50
1990–91 B&H WSC	7	3	2	5 *	7	7.00	–	–
1990–91 NZ	2	2	2	3 *	3	–	–	–
1991–92 NZ	2	–					–	–
1991–92 World Cup	4	2	2	3 *	3	–	–	–
1993–94 WI	3	2	2	2 *	2	–	–	–
1994–95 Zim	1	1	1	0 *	0	–	–	–
1996–97 NZ	1	–					–	–
TOTALS	20	10	9	5 *	15	15.00	–	–
v New Zealand	8	3	2	3 *	5	5.00	–	–
v Australia	5	2	2	5 *	5	–	–	–
v India	1	1	1	3 *	3	–	–	–
v West Indies	4	2	2	2 *	2	–	–	–
v Zimbabwe	2	2	2	0 *	0	–	–	–
TOTALS	20	10	9	5 *	15	15.00	–	–

Highest Score & Best Bowling

5*   v Australia (Melbourne) 10.1.1991

4–22 v New Zealand (Christchurch) 20.2.1997

Ct	Overs	Runs	W	Av	4wI	BB	RPO
2	63	256	6	42.66	–	3–40	4.06
1	20	91	3	30.33	–	2–45	4.55
0	18	48	0	–	–	–	2.66
0	28	133	3	44.33	–	2–36	4.75
0	21	106	3	35.33	–	2–52	5.04
0	10	42	0	–	–	–	4.20
1	10	22	4	5.50	1	4–22	2.20
4	170	698	19	36.73	1	4–22	4.10
2	78	262	9	29.11	1	4–22	3.35
2	42	207	5	41.40	–	3–40	4.92
0	4	25	0	–	–	–	6.25
0	26	126	3	42.00	–	2–52	4.84
0	20	78	2	39.00	–	2–36	3.90
4	170	698	19	36.73	1	4–22	4.10

DOMESTIC LIMITED-OVERS SUMMARY

	M	I	NO	HS	Runs	Av	100	50
Sunday League	37	13	7	13*	36	6.00	–	–
NatWest Trophy	8	1	0	8	8	8.00	–	–
Benson & Hedges Cup	15	8	4	18	56	14.00	–	–
TOTALS	60	22	11	18	100	9.09	–	–

Highest Scores & Best Bowling

Sunday League	13*	v Glamorgan (Merthyr Tydfil) 11.6.1989
	5–28	v Leicestershire (Lord's) 8.8.1993
NatWest Trophy	8	v Somerset (Taunton) 12.7.1991
	3–29	v Hertfordshire (Lord's) 22.6.1988
Benson & Hedges Cup	18	v Warwickshire (Edgbaston) 6.5.1991
	3–32	v Northamptonshire (Lord's) 26.4.1994

Four Wickets in an Innings

These were all in the Sunday League, and in consecutive matches

4–44 v Gloucestershire (Moreton–in–Marsh) 11.7.1993

4–50 v Hampshire (Lord's) 25.7.1993

5–28 v Leicestershire (Lord's) 8.8.1993

COMPARATIVE BOWLERS' RECORDS IN TEST MATCHES

	M	I	NO	HS	Runs	Av	100	50
R D B Croft	15	24	6	37*	268	14.88	–	–
I D K Salisbury	12	22	2	50	284	14.20	–	1
R K Illingworth	9	14	7	28	128	18.25	–	–
P C R Tufnell	41	57	28	22*	146	5.03	–	–

Ct	Overs	Runs	W	Av	4wI	BB	RPO
5	258	1192	45	26.48	3	5–28	4.62
3	95	323	10	32.30	–	3–29	3.40
2	134.5	591	15	39.40	–	3–32	4.38
10	487.5	2106	70	30.08	3	5–28	4.31

Ct	Overs	Runs	W	Av	5wI	10wM	BB	S/R
8	579.5	1254	36	34.83	1	–	5–95	96.63
3	346.2	1346	19	70.84	–	–	4–163	109.05
5	247.3	615	19	32.36	–	–	4–95	78.15
12	1842.1	4387	120	36.55	5	2	7–47	92.10

Index